RECKLESS YEARS

A DIARY OF
LOVE AND MADNESS

HEATHER CHAPLIN

SIMON & SCHUSTER

New York London Toronto Sydney New Delhi

Simon & Schuster
1230 Avenue of the Americas
New York, NY 10020

First Simon & Schuster hardcover edition July 2017

SIMON & SCHUSTER and colophon are registered trademarks
of Simon & Schuster, Inc.

For information about special discounts for bulk purchases,
please contact Simon & Schuster Special Sales at 1-866-506-1949
or business@simonandschuster.com.

The Simon & Schuster Speakers Bureau can bring authors to
your live event. For more information or to book an event
contact the Simon & Schuster Speakers Bureau at 1-866-248-3049
or visit our website at www.simonspeakers.com.

Interior design by Lewelin Polanco

Manufactured in the United States of America

10 9 8 7 6 5 4 3 2 1

Library of Congress Cataloging-in-Publication Data
Names: Chaplin, Heather, 1971- author.
Title: Reckless years : a diary of love and madness / Heather Chaplin.
Description: New York : Simon & Schuster, 2017.
Identifiers: LCCN 2016039309| ISBN 9781501134999 (hardback)
ISBN 9781501135002 (paperback)
Subjects: LCSH: Chaplin, Heather, 1971—Marriage. | Chaplin, Heather,
    1971—Divorce. | Divorced women—United States—Biography. |
    Journalists—United States—Biography. | Chaplin, Heather, 1971- author. |
    BISAC: BIOGRAPHY & AUTOBIOGRAPHY / Personal Memoirs. |
FAMILY & RELATIONSHIPS / Love & Romance. | PSYCHOLOGY /
Mental Health.
Classification: LCC CT275.C4725 A3 2017 | DDC 070.92 [B]—dc23
LC record available at https://lccn.loc.gov/2016039309

ISBN 978-1-5011-3499-9
ISBN 978-1-5011-3501-9 (ebook)

AUTHOR'S NOTE

This book is based on notebooks I kept between April 2006 and July 2008. At the time, my writing was copious, covering not only my emotions but also conversations, descriptions of places, what was happening in the lives of those around me, and bits of random observation. For periods when my notes were thinner, I pieced together hundreds of email exchanges—I recall chasing down the date of an event to a time stamp on a photo someone had posted on flickr. I also consulted the memories, diaries, and datebooks of friends not only to confirm facts but also to try and get a sense of other people's perspectives.

When I first started writing, my only rule was I had to be completely honest. I meant this in two ways. I had to be honest in the sense that I was going to put it all out there—I wasn't going to make myself or anyone else look better than their actual behavior indicated. I also meant honest in the journalistic sense of sticking to the facts. My rule was that if something I thought I remembered wasn't in my notes, and I couldn't confirm it elsewhere, I didn't get to use it.

Yet as time went on—it took me about six years working in the summers and Januarys to finish this book—I began to conceive of truth in a different way. I started the project convinced that I alone knew the reality of those years, but as I got farther away from the events, I began to see just what a slippery business truth is, how totally unavoidable the subjective is. I began to see that there is truth beyond mere accuracy.

Everything in this book is true, in the sense that it is an honest account of my experiences. But I did not in the end stick to the second part of my initial rule. In the interest of publishing this, I cut back on the number of characters and gave their lines to those who remained (not the main figures, but some of the friends). Also, I moved dates around to serve the narrative and to protect people who wanted to remain anonymous. A few conversations actually took place after the time period of the story. And, toward the end of the book in particular when my notes were thinner, I relied on memory to reconstruct conversations and events—as long as I felt I could justify my choices by what I found in emails and talks with those involved. Last, as I faced the book's publication, I changed almost everyone's name and altered many identifying details.

PROLOGUE

Wednesday, July 27, 2016

On April 3, 2006, at 1:33 p.m., I started taking notes. I don't know what to tell you except it was my attempt to stave off going mad. Although I didn't fully know it yet, I was recording an extraordinary period in my life—a time of freedom and exaltation such as I'd never known, as well as darkness that threatened to bury me.

It's been ten years since I started writing in those Moleskines, and now I'm scared. Sometimes I lie in bed, sick with anxiety at what I'm revealing, sick that I'm causing pain to real people in my life. I say to myself, you have no right to do this. But in the morning, the need to proceed is stronger.

I don't know why I wrote everything down. You could say it was a compulsion, although I'm not crazy about that word. It seems to imply something unhealthy, while I would say keeping those notebooks and then turning them into this book saved me.

BOOK ONE
LEAVING

Monday, April 3, 2006
1:33 p.m.

What to do now, I don't know. You see, I no longer love my husband.

It's one of those New York spring afternoons when, as if overnight, the slush is gone and the blustery wind has ceased. Hyacinths, daffodils, and crocuses splash the ground with color, and the magnolia trees are just beginning to unfurl their fleshy blossoms. It's one of those days when you simply have to be outside. But I'm not outside. I'm inside, my dog, Sakura, sitting like a sphinx on the floor at my feet. I'm on my couch in the back of our apartment, watching the spring day through my windows, smoking a spliff, listening to Coldplay (don't even start with me about the Coldplay), and trying to figure out how I'm going to get out of this situation.

I had that dream again last night—the one where my father and Josh are chasing me. I can feel their breath on my neck, and I'm trying to scream, but no sound comes out. Bluegrass music plays. Then we're all in the air, flying, cruising over an enormous crater in the earth, and I realize something terrible is happening beneath me. And then I'm falling, plummeting downward 100 miles an hour toward the terror, and trying, desperately, to cry out, *please, someone, save me*—but no one does.

I used to have this exact dream except instead of trying to get me, Josh was trying to help me. Sometimes when we fight, Josh still shouts at me about this dream.

How did this happen? How can it be that one day you're so in love with a person that just being near him is like bathing in golden light, and then the next thing you know, you're fantasizing he gets in a car accident or contracts a disease that doesn't require any nursing and kills him quickly?

I've always believed that the really great writers are generous to their characters. But I warn you: I don't feel generous toward Josh. I'll have to throw myself on your mercy and say, forgive me, I've lived with the man for thirteen years. I have no generosity left.

At this moment, as I write this, my husband is sitting on the couch at the other end of our apartment watching the Golf Channel and sucking on a can of Coke. Sometimes I think Josh tries to stay as still as possible, hoping against hope that one day life will, at last, just leave him the fuck alone. What he doesn't know is that I too may leave him alone.

Or maybe he does. He's a crafty bastard beneath that gentle stoner demeanor.

I don't know why I'm putting all this down on paper. I'm writing God knows what for God knows whom. I feel somehow that if I don't write everything down, I will simply come flying apart. The center cannot hold! But maybe, just maybe, if I document every single thing I see, hear, and feel, I can keep it together, spinning a web of words around myself that will keep me from breaking apart from the inside out.

I've been doing this since I was a kid, really, writing everything down, even tracing words on my forefinger with my thumb like a tic—trying to make sense, I suppose, through the calming logic of language, of a world that is simply too chaotic and too mad to make sense of.

For the record, I was born in Baltimore, Maryland, in Sinai Hospital, not one mile from the Preakness racetrack. My mother was a German-Jewish immigrant from South Africa. She grew up in a prefabricated house in New Haven, Connecticut, with her mother, sister, and grandparents. She never knew why the older generation spoke German—Holocaust, what Holocaust?—and she never knew why they left South Africa for America without her father. (He had a child with another woman.) She knew she never saw her father again and that she couldn't move the left side of her body very well because of a childhood bout with encephalitis. From pictures, I know that my mother was slim and lovely with violet eyes, black eyelashes, and an impossibly small waist, like a young Elizabeth Taylor.

Anyway, the reason she ended up in the postindustrial, recession-ridden nightmare that was Baltimore in the 1970s with two small children and a quite possibly psychotic anarchist of a husband had something to do with bluegrass music and a strong desire at nineteen to escape that house in New Haven. Still, marrying my father was not her best move. Neither was having children, really. Can you imagine? It's 1965, you marry some asshole you meet at a Country Gentlemen concert, you move to Baltimore, of all places, you have two kids, and then—bam! The sexual revolution hits. The women's movement! Oh wait, I didn't have to get married? I didn't have to procreate?

My father was gone before I was one, and she hit the Baltimore nightlife with a vengeance. Baltimore was still a thriving seaport in those days, and she seemed far more interested in Greek sailors and disco dancing than keeping house and raising children. In the afternoons, my brother, Seth, and I used to play we were in Vietnam as we fought our way through the fruit flies that infested our kitchen. At night we heard laughter and stumbling on the stairs and ran into men who didn't speak English in the bathroom. What can I say? It was the seventies. My mother had a life she wanted to live. And who can blame her, really? Well, me for many years, until I got older and fucked up my own life.

My father, I'll give you the basics. He grew up in a tiny apartment in the Bronx, his father a Russian-Jewish immigrant. My grandfather—Zaidie, we called him—was the kind of guy who when you telephoned said, "Oh, it's you, how come you never call?" And when you asked him what he was doing, said, "Oh, just sitting here in the dark." Photographs of that side of my family show people with faces so dark and stormy it's as if they're perpetually standing in shadows.

My dad hit Bronx Science at ten and Johns Hopkins at fifteen.

Graduated: never. He was a first-generation computer programmer who didn't believe in the twenty-four-hour day, a smuggler for the Sandinistas, and a professional mandolin player. He thought 1968 was the high-water mark of human civilization, and he was waiting for the day when humans shared a single consciousness and boundaries of all kinds disappeared. When I was a kid, I said that sounded terrifying, but he said that was just because I had petty bourgeois values. He took my brother and me to New York with him and left us under blankets in the back of his van in the middle of the night while he dropped off computers for the Nicaraguans. He took us to Florida for vacation and drove 100 miles an hour the whole way because we were running late—me sitting in the passenger seat, afraid to close my eyes, sure that if I did, even for a minute, I would be killed.

I officially cut off contact with my father fifteen years ago. I've seen him once since. I was arrested covering an International Monetary Fund protest in DC, and, while hog-tied in a police gymnasium, I heard my name called out and found that someone—someone with the exact name of my father—had bailed me out. Who knew, but he'd been in DC protesting the International Monetary Fund. I hadn't seen him in all those years, and there he was waiting for me outside the jail, proud as if I'd provided him with a grandchild. No words of reproach for the years of silence. No apologies. No requests for apologies. It was like he didn't remember that I'd cut off contact. Or why. Just, "In times like these, Heather, getting arrested is a badge of honor." I was so stunned by his physical presence, I forgot that I'd sworn never to let him near me again. I actually got in his van with him. And then he nearly killed me by falling asleep while driving us back to the Washington Monument.

Why am I telling you all this? I don't even know who you are. You're the person I've been writing to all my life, I suppose—you're someone who cares about me, whose attention I have a right to claim. In other words, you're nobody at all. And perhaps that's what feels so good about this. I can write anything here, because it isn't for anyone. I can say whatever I want and suffer no consequences.

Yes, this is my life right now—a lovely day of streaming spring light and blossoming spring flowers. And me sitting here on my little couch, mouthing the words I've tried so long to avoid. I no longer love my husband. I don't want to be his wife.

Wednesday, April 5, 2006

Me and Josh, just now, in the kitchen:

"I talked to Abe this morning," Josh says, beating a rhythm on the countertop with his hands. "He's pumped about the movie." And he moves as if to give me a high five.

Abe is a director friend of ours in LA.

"We're going to be riiiiich!" Josh says.

Josh thinks he's writing a movie based on the book he thinks he cowrote with me. Considering that Josh's contribution to the book was basically to sit around smoking pot and playing video games; considering the fact that Josh seems unable to leave the house except to buy a can of Coke every morning; and considering the fact that he has yet to write a word of said movie, I find the notion that he's now going to become a Hollywood mogul amusing at best. At worst, I think I'd be justified in stabbing him through the heart with a steak knife.

"Aha," I say.

I roll my eyes—I can't help it; it's involuntary when he talks.

I was looking for something to eat in the fridge, something that was neither rotten nor in need of cooking. I haven't been home for a month and the fridge is empty except for condiments.

"What's the matter?" Josh says. "Aren't you excited?"

I have two options here. One, lie—which I have decided to stop doing. Or two, say no, I'm not excited, you've hardly done anything you said you were going to do for the last ten years so why would I waste the emotional energy now? I choose a third option: silence.

This of course makes him ask me again. "Aren't you excited?"

And then the inevitable: "What's the matter? Are you okay? Are you okay? What's the matter?"

Oh dear God, I'm so sick of being asked that. No, I'm not okay, I'm married to you, I think. But I don't say it. I can't muster up the energy to be that snotty. He's looming over me too, which drives me crazy. I'm only five feet—five one on a good day—and when he gets really close like that, all six foot three of him, I feel as if he were blotting out the sun. I can't stand to look at him. He's a pasty imitation of the man I married.

Later

Josh and I met at a funeral. Good sign, I know. I was twenty years old. I walked into that room full of mourners the night before the service. My friend called out his name. Josh turned toward me as if in slow motion. I remember his height; the black hair brushed back from his face; a cigarette clenched between his teeth; those wild green eyes. He was wearing jeans, a horizontally striped T-shirt, red suede Pumas, and a brown suede jacket. You know how when you think back to the time you first met the people you end up loving, and they somehow seem bigger or brighter or somehow set apart from the scene? Well, that's how it was with Josh. He turned toward me and the rest of the room faded into a blur.

The service was for my childhood friend Gabriel, murdered while trying to park his car in Los Angeles. Josh and Gabriel were cousins and best friends. Josh was in the car with Gabriel when he got shot. He tried to stop the bleeding with his hands on the way to the hospital, watched him die before they even arrived.

I know every detail of what happened that night, because Josh told me, back in our courtship days, when participating in Josh's pain was like looking up into a starry night. How proud I was to be his confidant. His tragedy set off fireworks in my chest. As Josh used to say, Faulkner had nothing on his family. There was his uncle, Gabriel's father, killed in a car accident in a town called

Truth or Consequences; his mean drunk of a father; and his mother, who got diagnosed with terminal cancer six months after Gabriel got shot. I met Josh and I looked into his eyes and I saw something I'd never seen before. I thought I saw a soul who knew the things I knew. I thought Josh was a Byronic hero, dark and sulky and full of anguish. I took his pain the way some women get their mother-in-law's jewelry.

Is it worth mentioning how handsome Josh was at twenty-four? How amazed I was that someone so handsome could want me? Six three. Wide shoulders, long muscled arms, a narrow stomach and waist. His eyes were dark green and such an unusual, long shape that they almost seemed to touch the sides of his face. His eyelashes and hair were black, his lips full and red, and his cheekbones chiseled. He'd grown up a surfer in Huntington Beach—behind the Orange Curtain, he used to say, where neo-Nazis painted swastikas on his parking space in high school and his friends' moms made cocktails from gallon bottles of vodka in the afternoons.

A bunch of us refugees from the Gabriel tragedy were all living in the same apartment building in San Francisco. I assumed Josh was an idiot because he was a surfer from Southern California and because everyone else said he was a genius. But then, one day, Josh and I started talking and it was as if my brain were a bottle of champagne that had just been uncorked. Pop. Pop. Pop. I thought, holy shit, he *is* a genius. The man had a degree in molecular biology, had been writing screenplays with Gabriel before the murder, read philosophy in his spare time, played every instrument imaginable, and wrote poetry that actually wasn't terrible. Once he and I started talking, we just never stopped. We roamed the streets of San Francisco together late at night when everyone else was asleep. We drank from jugs of Gallo wine on the swing sets at the top of Nob Hill. And when finally he admitted it was me he loved and not his mealymouthed girlfriend left over from college, we kissed on every street corner that city had, under the rain, under the stars, in winds and through sleet.

Josh couldn't sit still in those days. He was always yelling at the rest of us to get off our asses and come out and do something. Anything. It was as if there were a fire burning in him that wouldn't let him rest. You could see it crackling in his green eyes, sense it when he tore at his guitar until the sweat poured down his neck. But I was always watching, so I'd see sometimes when his head fell into his hands, or when he looked up unexpectedly and his face was suddenly ravaged, years older than his twenty-five-year-old self. When he left a room it was like he took all color with him. I thought he was brave and noble. I thought I could save him.

Sunday, April 9, 2006

I had a little birthday party today. Tomorrow I will be thirty-five. I've been gone so long it was the first time I've seen my friends in months. Josh said he'd take care of getting the brunch stuff, but then, when the minutes kept clicking by and still he was mining ore in Star Wars Galaxies, I leashed up Sakura, who was sitting by the front door giving us the evil eye, and went myself. The plastic bag handles of everything I hauled back sunk into the flesh of my hands, leaving angry red indents.

I've told you what Josh was like when I first met him. Should I tell you what he's like now? Let's just say that the brilliant fire, which raged so brightly in him at twenty-five, has burned itself down to a fine, chalky dust. His very presence, as far as I'm concerned, is an affront to how much I used to love him. The man who couldn't sit still now can't move. The man whose intelligence kept me mesmerized now spends his days playing Star Wars Galaxies and watching third-rate movies on pay-per-view. When I look at him I see a corpse pulled from a river. I see deathly white skin and pot-glazed eyes. I see passion that has turned into uncontrolled rage and grief into depression so deep it's like watching someone drown.

(I warned you I felt no generosity toward the man.)

Josh says something happened to me when I started taking antidepressants; he said I lost the ability to empathize. I remember watching him when he said this, or screamed this, because he was screaming at the time, his finger an inch from my nose, and I didn't say anything out loud, but in my head, I was saying, no, I haven't lost the ability to empathize; I just no longer want to be in a co-dependent death race with you to the bottom of the ocean.

I never know what's going to be the flip that sends Josh spewing insults and shouting at me. When he gets like that, though, my heart pounds so heavily I always dimly wonder if I'm about to have a heart attack. Was there a middle? I loved him at our wedding. I think I did. That was in the middle. The man could be incredibly charismatic. Funny. Insightful. Josh at his best was *the* best. I remember thinking at our wedding, please let this be the version of Josh I get to spend the rest of my life with.

Anyway, I was so sad at my birthday party I could barely hold my head up. I felt I wasn't even there; I was just drifting through. Josh was telling people he was going to LA to make a movie based on "our" book. I doubt anyone in that room believed him any more than I did. After everyone left, I went and sat out on the back steps that lead down to our garden—or rather, the plot of land that belongs to Josh and me that could one day be a garden but today, on this day, is just a plot of land with weeds growing up higher than the fence that surrounds it and covered in dog shit, because, although he says he does, Josh obviously doesn't walk Sakura while I'm gone.

The first summer after we moved into this place, I went into the "garden" and discovered the construction people had buried all their leftover materials back there. Every day I dug up bricks, bags of cement, old Coke cans, cinder blocks, you name it; it was there and I dug it out. It took me two summers to dig everything up. Eventually I had a pile that stretched from one end to the other and came up to my waist. We had to threaten to sue the developer to come haul it away. Then I finally got it smooth. I brought in new soil and laid down a thin sprinkling of grass seeds. Soon, tiny little heads of grass began poking their way through the dirt. I didn't think I'd ever seen anything so lovely. I was already picturing foxgloves and lilies, hydrangeas and lavender, sweet-smelling thyme.

When I had to leave on my first trip to Dallas, I gave Josh simple instructions. Water it every morning and don't let Sakura back there. When I returned, all the grass was dead, the soil was dry as sand, and the ground was littered with dog shit. This happened three more times before I gave up.

I think our "garden" may be the most depressing thing I've ever seen in my life.

Later

Josh comes into the back of the house.

He sits down next to me and puts an arm around my shoulders. I try to pretend my shoulders aren't my shoulders so I won't have to feel his body touching mine.

"Did you have a good time today?" he asks.

"Yes," I say.

"It's nice to have you back."

"Thanks."

"You're not really that glad to be back, are you?"

"Of course I am."

"Well, it's hard to compete with the St. Regis." And then to Sakura, sitting beside us, "But we'll try, won't we?"

Sakura just sits there looking regal and ignoring us. Sakura is a white Shiba Inu with triangular ears, a curled tail, and coal-black eyes with white eyelashes. I'm pretty sure he was a pharaoh in his last life. He doesn't have much time for Josh or me.

"I wasn't at the St. Regis," I say.

Josh sighs.

"Okay," he says. "I'll be in the front if you need me."

I don't say anything as he gets up to leave, but my heart hurts. Josh's rage I've learned to handle. The doing nothing, I'm used to. But Josh trying, now, when it's too late, this feels like it could kill me. But I must not pity him. If I pity him, I won't be able to leave. And if I don't leave, I won't survive.

Later

I was at the St. Regis, but that was last summer when I was in Aspen. Now I'm just back from Dallas, where I stay at the Hotel Crescent Court, which has an enormous marble lobby with enormous, ever-changing orchid arrangements and a rectangular swimming pool on the roof. I've been ghostwriting a book for a billionaire. Did I want to ghostwrite a book for a billionaire? No. But we were desperate for money. The advance for the book had seemed so big at the time—but it was only supposed to take one year, and instead it had taken three. The line of credit on our mortgage was maxed out (eighty-five thousand dollars), as were our credit cards (forty-two thousand dollars). We owed my mother seventy thousand dollars from one of her credit cards. It never even came up that Josh should get a job—because that would have been to admit that he hadn't actually worked on the book and wasn't actually a house husband, which would have been to invite a rage so great and bitter that the last time I'd done it, he'd spit on me and told me to go fuck myself. His spit had landed right in the middle of my chest.

Much to my surprise, the billionaire and I hit it off right away. He flew me out to Dallas to talk, and when I got stranded because of a snowstorm in New York, he put me up at the Four Seasons and told me to do a little shopping and get a massage. At Christmastime he sent me a thank-you card and a check for ten thousand dollars. I thought, ok, now this is someone I can do business with.

I finished our book and then I went straight to work on his. That's why I've been living in hotels for so much of the last year. I've just gone wherever my billionaire went. "We're a two-Learjet family," he'd say with a chuckle as we walked across the tarmac to his private plane. Inside it was all creamy-white leather and gold fixtures. The seat-belt buckles were gold. The cup holders were gold. The toilet fixtures were gold. He even had his own stewardess, who prepared his favorite meals and served them to him on fine china with gold silverware. A private stewardess, I thought. Now that's wealth.

I lived in Aspen most of last summer and I was strangely happy there. I realized that when Josh wasn't there, I could *breathe*. I was working superhard, and I'd sprint out of my hotel room when I needed a break and ride my bike as fast as I could along the roaring Fork River with the biggest, most intensely bright blue sky I'd ever seen above my head. I started hiking in the mornings, charging up rocky paths, across alpine meadows filled with wildflowers, to the top of mountains where the air was so thin it hardly seemed like air at all.

I also had a butler who brought me coffee in the morning. But now I'm digressing.

Josh came to visit me out there. I didn't want him to, but he'd say, "Do you miss me?" and I'd say, "Of course I do," even though I didn't at all. I could tell my billionaire pegged him for a loser the minute I introduced them. No, I wanted to say, this isn't the man I married. The man I married could have taken you on. This stammering geek shifting nervously from foot to foot is some imposter who showed up at the airport with Josh Reed's driver's license. I don't like him any more than you do.

I told my billionaire, in the strictest of confidence, that Josh had Asperger's. I don't know why I said this. I just couldn't bear the shame of the association without an excuse.

Josh's visit was a nightmare. He'd promised he'd leave me alone in my room to work, but then when he asked if he could stay with me, I didn't have the nerve to say no. He was making a website for "our" book and I was trying to be encouraging that at least he was doing something. But then he started crying and making little choking sounds of rage in his throat because the background color wasn't coming out right. I said, "*Please*, Josh, I *have* to do this work." And the next thing I know he was yelling at me for being unsupportive. "*You fucking cunt . . .*" His finger an inch from my nose.

I don't know if you've ever spent a lot of time in hotels, but after a while you start to feel discombobulated, as if maybe you aren't really who you thought you were. Your identity becomes thin and wavery, easily swayed by people you meet in the lobby, by the values of people you wouldn't normally associate with, by ideas you would never entertain anywhere else. In a good hotel, on an expense account, real life never intrudes. Everything is magically taken care of as if the thing to be taken care of—the unmade bed, the dirty dishes—had never been there in the first place. It's weird and isolating. You do the thing you're there to do and otherwise it's just swimming in space, watching your identity flare up and flicker out. It was like being on another planet—and since I was on another planet, I could think things I wasn't usually allowed to think. I said things in the quiet of that room that I'd never have been able to say in any facet of my regular life. I imagined what life would be like without Josh—coming home to an empty apartment, grocery shopping only for me, watching TV alone, going through life without a wedding ring to tell the world that I was loved.

I remember when Josh and I first went to couples therapy. On day one, I said to the therapist, "Josh and I are an organism that has gotten sick." And the therapist looked at me and said, "No two people are a single organism. You are two individuals." I thought, what?? If we were two individuals, then one individual could leave the other individual. This had never occurred to me.

All through writing the book my friend Eleanor had said, "Don't engage the question. Finish the book, then figure out the relationship." Eleanor and I have been friends since we were five, when our school principal told our parents to introduce us. I don't think either of us had any friends; I certainly didn't. Until about a year ago, Eleanor lived around the corner from me in Park Slope and those were the salad days. But Eleanor hated New York, and now she lives in Washington, DC, where she's a reporter for NPR. (Eleanor is a Stein. Becoming successful was not an option but an obligation. Am I jealous? Let's just say it's complicated.) She says the thing about living in DC is that every day she gets to feel thin and well dressed, to which I say, yeah, but you have to live in DC, to which she says, yeah, but you don't know what you're talking about. She's marrying someone she met at the Environmental Defense Fund in two months. Anyway, Eleanor is very sensible and I always take her advice, so I listened when she said the thing about the book. But once I got to Dallas the book was finished.

"What if I had an affair?" I said to her one day from my hotel room.

"Don't you think it would be better to tell Josh how you're feeling?" she said.

No, I thought. Instead, I fantasized constantly that he would get killed. Quickly. No nursing.

It all sounds very calm and cool when I write it out now. Maybe you even think it's funny. But trust me, it wasn't. I spent a lot of time in the fetal position, bawling my head off, alternately cold and hot with fear. You have to understand, I used to put my hand over Josh's heart at night while he was sleeping to make sure it didn't stop beating. Even as I've grown to despise my husband, I still curl up behind him in bed and press my face against his back and pray he won't abandon me.

Monday, April 10, 2006

Mike calls from Los Angeles. I don't think he even knows it's my birthday.

"Mike, what do we do?"

"We go cold turkey," he says.

Oh, Mike, I say your name over and over in my mind!!

"I don't know how to do that," I whimper.

"Well, we don't live in the same city, so, you know, it'll kind of naturally pass."

Oh, Mike, how can you???

He gets off the phone so fast, I don't have time to say a single thing I'd imagined saying.

The story of Mike Talese really starts with Benjamin Green or, rather, Cecilia Green—it's funny isn't it, when you try to untangle what led you to the people you know? Cecilia is married to my brother—they've been together since their days in a Cajun band at Columbia so I've known the Greens since I was a teenager. Cecilia's brother Ben and me, we got to be pretty tight. Although that was before Josh forbade me to see him, and yes, to my shame, I let myself be forbidden.

Ben is a literary agent, and one day he called and said he knew an editor who wanted a book about digital culture—something about the Internet and virtual worlds and what people were going to be like in the future. Now, if you knew me, you'd know this was not exactly up my alley. I once bought a new VCR because I thought the old VCR was broken when really it was just unplugged. But I'd thought about the way Josh, the most brilliant man I knew, had recently started locking himself in his room to play video games. And I'd thought about my brother and me as kids, when our father didn't have a house but just lived at his work—how we'd sleep on blankets under his desk and play Zork all day while mainframes whirred around us. (This was back before I was old enough to refuse to see my father.) Ben's book idea had filled me with a kind of queasy longing to understand something I couldn't even name and I'd said yes.

Which brings us back to Mike. Mike is the editor of a tech magazine, so he knew lots of people I was trying to meet for my book. Perhaps I should mention that he's also extremely cute, with black hair and hazel eyes. With all the conferences I've gone to while writing this book, I've seen Mike more in the last few years than most of my closest friends.

Now, don't get the wrong idea about me. I haven't touched Mike Talese more than a hand on the shoulder. If you knew me, you'd know I'm hardly the type to sleep around. But, oh God, he's all I think about. I feel like he's the only pleasure I've had in my life for as long as I can remember.

This is Mike explaining how we met: "So there's Heather," he'll say, in his thick Boston accent. "And she's grilling Rich Vogel. I

mean *grilling*." Here he always pauses, looks at me, and then tries
to imitate me, which means he pulls himself up tall and puts on an
air of taking himself very seriously. "So you're saying it took four
hundred people to build this virtual world? But what does it say
about our world that people will pay to live in yours? And I don't
understand, how many servers do you have?"

At this point, he's usually gotten a laugh and looks at me, which
is my cue to shake my head as if I disapprove of his mimicking me.
As if.

It's funny, I can't tell you anything specific I like about Mike.
All I know is how electrified I feel when he's near me. Sitting side
by side in all those press rooms over the years, feeling his thigh
against mine. Whispering in corners. Swatting at each other. Oh
lord, when did we start swatting?

About three weeks ago, I saw Mike at a conference in San Jose.
And something changed. We were coming back from a party together late one night and ran into this twenty-three-year-old writer
from Austin in the lobby. It took us ten minutes to ditch him, and
when we got into the elevator, just the two of us, I said, giggling
inanely, as if I were uttering some witticism, "Oh *great*, now *everyone*
will think we're having an affair."

Mike was in the front corner by the elevator buttons. He an-
swered without turning around to look at me, cool as a cucumber.
"We are having an affair," he said. Time slowed down around me
and I sputtered something high-pitched and stupid like, "Oh my
God! No we're not!" And Mike said, "It's a platonic affair. Like
Lost in Translation." And I thought, he's not so stupid after all.

I barely slept that night. All I could think about was kissing
him. How his lips would feel on mine, what his breath would taste
like. I kept imagining him putting his arm around me and saying,
"I'm crazy about you, Heather. Everything is going to be okay."

And then the next day, I'd been around the corner from the
San Jose conference center at a crappy little Indian place having
lunch with a dreadlocked futurist and a blogger who used to travel
around the country in hot pants as the official PlayStation girl when

my phone rang. It was Mike, calling because he was abandoning the conference to go back to LA.

I said, "What, you're leaving without saying good-bye to me?" My heart sinking and pounding at the same time.

And he said, "I'm calling you now, aren't I?" Sounding gruff. Unlike himself. And then, "You know, I don't really like this."

I barely dared breathe.

"What do you mean?" I whispered.

"When you act the way you've been acting, all flirty, all in my space."

"But, Mike . . ."

"And you know what, I know what's going on. If I were younger, I would totally do it. It would be easy in a way."

"Mike . . ."

"And you know what else?" Sounding heated now. Angry at me. "Something is *really* wrong with your marriage. I don't care what you say. Your heart is just sitting out there waiting for someone to take it. And you know what, I'm not going to do it. It's not going to be me."

And then, I don't know if it was the reception, or he hung up on me, or what, but he was gone. And it didn't matter, because I wouldn't have known what to say anyway. And for some reason, standing on that street in San Jose, outside that crappy Indian restaurant, it had just felt like the end. My heart just finally collapsed. All the hairline fractures from my marriage gave, and the whole thing shattered. Just like that. Not because of anything particular my husband did but because of being told off by a man I don't even really know.

Tuesday, April 11, 2006

Rain is hitting the windows at the back of the apartment as if someone were throwing bucketfuls of water against them. It gives my sitting room a ghostly, beneath-the-sea kind of light. Who cares,

I think. I'm sitting in the dark at 3 p.m., smoking pot and doing nothing. So sue me. Josh is in the front of the house doing whatever it is he does all day. I wonder what he thinks I'm doing. I never do nothing, but I've barely moved from this spot since I got home. All I do is sit here, writing this story for God knows who, Sakura watching me from his position on the window ledge with his imperious black eyes. I would call him over to come sit next to me, but I don't know that he'd come. Sakura has never fully accepted the dog-master paradigm.

How do I articulate the feeling I have that my heart is dead? That there is no life in the cavern of my chest?

The ivy that covers the windows is shaking in the wind; the trees in the yards that surround our yard wave their branches wildly. One day, I think, my yard too will have something in it to blow about when it storms. I went out there this morning to clean it up, but I got so angry and demoralized I just turned around and walked back in.

When I was a little kid our next-door neighbor gave me a pansy from her garden. I thought it was the most beautiful thing I'd ever seen. I was sure a fairy lived inside it. My mother helped me plant it in the backyard, and every day I would go outside and watch for the fairy to come out. None ever did, but every day I would kiss the pansy on its purple-and-yellow face anyway. I wish I had some pansies to kiss now.

Later

Finally get off the couch and go over to Mac and Katy's, who live a neighborhood over in Windsor Terrace. I've known Mac my whole life. Our mothers were pregnant with us at the same time, and our older brothers were in a toddler group together. Mac's older brother was Gabriel. Who got murdered. Are you keeping up? I remember when Mac and Gabriel's mother ran off to an ashram, abandoning them to their father, who they barely knew. When I was having "problems" in college, Mac came. He lay beside me while I was having nightmares that made me too scared to close my eyes. When his brother was murdered I moved in with him. And so it goes.

When I walk in Katy says, "You looked so sad at your birthday party." And I feel sadness like a living thing pulling me down. *He doesn't even see I'm dying here.* That's the refrain running through my mind, and it's hard not to drop my forehead onto the Formica kitchen table. Josh loves me—I have no doubt he would die for me if given the choice. But if no one warned him, I could die slowly before his eyes and he wouldn't even notice. Who knew love could be so useless?

Mac is out, and I find myself grabbing Katy by the arm. I've never really talked to her about the disaster of my marriage but I find myself suddenly unable to stop. "I know how much he's suffered," I say. "I told him, just be the best version of yourself you can be. When he said not being able to surf had wrecked his life, I told him I'd make the money and he could travel to every surf spot in the world. When he said he wanted to be a musician, I said great! He bought himself a professional-quality recording studio, but he never made music anywhere except our living room."

There's a pause and Katy says, "You want a whiskey?"

No doubt because of that enormous Irish-Catholic family of hers, Katy has great respect for whiskey as part of the healing process.

We sip.

"When the publishers asked me to do radio publicity for the book and not him, he said I was a fucking cunt for doing it."

"He called you a cunt?"

"He insisted on doing all the readings when we were on the book tour even though he'd barely done any of the writing. In our hotel rooms at night he threw furniture because not enough people had come. Katy . . ." My heart is pounding. It comes out as barely a whisper. "What if I leave him and he doesn't make it?"

Since Dallas, I've been practicing in my mind what to do if I leave and Josh kills himself. That was part of our story, how I had saved Josh from suicide back after Gabriel got shot and then his mother got diagnosed with terminal cancer. I imagine the phone call. "Hello, Ms. Chaplin . . ." I imagine how I would be tormented for the rest of my life with questions of culpability. How he would haunt me in my dreams the way Gabriel haunts him.

When I was a kid, I lived in terror that my father was going to commit suicide. I used to have nightmares about it. I once mentioned this to a shrink and was surprised that she seemed surprised. "Why did you think that?" the shrink asked. "Does he threaten it?" No, I'd said. I hadn't known how to explain. Did other girls not think the same thing about their fathers?

When Katy asks me what I mean, I don't say any of this. I say, "Josh hasn't had a job in eight years. What will he do?"

Katy says what feels like maybe the nicest thing anyone has said to me in a long time.

"Everything is not about Josh," she says. "You have a right to live too."

I think, I do?

Right when I'm leaving, Katy slips a pair of keys into my hand.

"You know, for while we're in California," she says. "Just in case you need a break."

I drop the keys into my purse.

Later

It's still raining. I wish it were time to go to sleep. Mike, I say in my imagination, what are you doing here? We're on a beach in Mexico. Neither of us knew the other would be there. I'm wearing a bikini and my legs look long and lean from all that biking in Dallas. (Otherwise, I would never put myself in a bikini in this recurring fantasy.) I see fear on your face, Mike. It hits us: we're alone in a foreign country, unchaperoned. In my imagination I cut to twilight. We're on the beach, coconut cups in hand. We're staring at each other. The sun goes down in a glory of pastels and bright fuchsias. You take my hand.

Despite the intensities of my longings for Mike Talese, I don't think I actually want to have sex with him. I just want to kiss him and have him hold me. Christ, what am I, twelve? Do other people remain entirely clothed in their sexual fantasies? My friend Summer says you can do whatever you want in your fantasy life as long as you keep it clean in real life. So why even in my imagination do I remain chaste? Sometimes I think something is really wrong with me, that I'm not like other women.

Here's a memory that haunts me.

It's San Francisco, 1995.

The setting is a Mission-neighborhood coffee shop—all used couches with sagging cushions and threadbare coverings; a mural on the wall of Che Guevara; another of round, Diego Rivera–style peasants picking coffee beans. *Bleach* is playing over the speakers, and Josh is pleading with me.

"Please," he says. "If I don't do this now, I never will. I'll never learn to stand on my own."

He's wearing a dark green V-neck sweater. A piece of his black hair falls over his eyes. I think, he is the handsomest man I've ever seen. I think, how did it happen that he became mine?

I'm trying to convince him that we ought to move in together. I'm twenty-four. He's twenty-seven.

"Why do men always think they can't simultaneously be in a relationship and grow?" I say. "I don't see why it's mutually exclusive. I don't see why you assume that living with me will somehow rob you of your independence."

"Heath, this is my last chance," Josh says. There is pleading in his eyes. But I am merciless. I don't say, forgive me, I'm so in love with you I'll die if you don't want to live with me. Instead, I say: "I don't buy it. Two people together make each person stronger."

Oh God, I didn't know I was manipulating him. I didn't know back then what I know now, which is that I can be brutal in the pursuit of what I want, or what I think I want.

A month and a half later and we're moving into a little place on Divisadero at California Street. With the U-Haul double-parked outside and a carful of friends on their way to help us unpack, Josh pulls me toward him in the corner of the empty living room. He hoists me up against the wall like I weigh nothing at all. He pulls my skirt off, puts his hand inside my underwear and a finger right inside me. The first time Josh ever kissed me, he'd done that—and for months afterward the thought of that moment, of his finger inside me, had left me panting with desire. But now, in our new apartment, I'm dry. His finger might as well be sheathed in a plastic glove like the gynecologist's. Ouch, I think, I hate you. This has been happening to me lately, these involuntary flashes of hatred at the very moment we should be most loving.

"I love you so much, Heather," Josh whispers in my ear. He's pushing against me, beginning to undo his belt. I think of a rutting dog. My head bangs against the wall behind me.

Sometimes in these moments I think about Josh's old girlfriend as my private aphrodisiac—well, not her exactly, but how I stole him away from her, how I was victorious. This makes me feel passionate.

At the beginning with Josh, when we first got together, it was like nothing I'd ever experienced. I was like, oh, *this* is what everyone has been going on about all these years. Once, when Josh went back to his old girlfriend, I actually thought that not being able to have sex with him again would drive me mad. In fact, it did drive me a little mad. I remember I had the sense that my body was made of doors. My desire for Josh had caused one door to pop open and then they were just flying open willy-nilly until the air of the outside world was breezing right through me. I had the sense that there were no boundaries, that I was just open space that anything or anyone could have access to. That's when I first had the dream, my father chasing me, bluegrass music playing.

Josh is moaning as he thrusts himself inside me. He whispers: "I want to anoint this place with how much I love you." I'm just thinking, ouch, ouch, ouch. Fucking ouch. But I don't say anything.

When he finishes, we sink to the floor. His body is covered in that thin sheet of passion sweat. I'm as cool and dry as if I'd been having a glass of iced tea. He kisses me on my neck and on my face and then lays his head against my chest. I'm curled up on his lap. I always love him again after he comes. It's only while we're having sex that I feel overtly hostile.

"This is our place," I whisper. "This is where we're going to live."

I listen to his breathing and think that I love him so much I want to weep.

"You're my whole life, Heather," he says, "my whole world. You're everything to me."

At the time, my heart soared. Now of course I know how utterly, ruinously claustrophobic it is to be someone's whole world.

I stopped having sex with Josh not long after we moved into that apartment. He'd reach over to touch me and I'd start crying. And when he complained about it, I was outraged. I pulled the old college feminism bullshit about it all being up to the woman and threw it in his face as though he were a dirty old man trying to cop a feel. But the thing is, once he'd admitted that he loved me, once we were a couple, his touch felt like a betrayal, and my passion for him disappeared as if it had never been.

Oh God, I wish I'd been nicer about it. I wish I'd had the nerve to discuss it instead of just pretending it wasn't happening. When we first went into couples therapy, this business about sex was the first thing Josh brought up, and I was shocked. I hadn't even known he was angry about it. How could I not have known?

It was in that apartment on Divisadero that the dream changed, that Josh became my antagonist instead of my protector. When I told him, he shouted, "You refuse to deal with your issues! You've destroyed this relationship! You've destroyed me!" And I wept.

Thursday, April 13, 2006

I can hear Summer's food processor whirring over the phone.

"What are you making?" I say.

"Mashed potatoes but without the potatoes," she says. I think, uh-oh. Summer is another childhood friend. She used to live in Williamsburg, but then one day she came home and Ricky Martin was filming a music video in her hallway, and she said, okay, time to go. She moved to Los Angeles last year and has since become a raw foodist. This worries me because Summer has a way of doing things that seem completely crazy and then a few years later all the rest of us are doing what she's doing as if it were the most normal thing in the world.

I'm thinking, God, I hope I don't become a raw foodist, while Summer is saying, "Honestly, Heath, it breaks my heart for both of you."

Summer insists on being frustratingly compassionate toward Josh. Don't get me wrong, I know all about compassion. I go to yoga every day and it's the only good thing in my life right now. (And yes, it was Summer who made me try it after much sniggering and eye rolling on my part.) But at this moment, I don't want to hear it. Eleanor, on the other hand, hates Josh. She doesn't say so explicitly, but she does, deep down in her bones. I can tell, and it thrills me.

I change the subject. "Did you get the scarf I sent you?"

"I did," Summer says. "It's beautiful."

"Lavender to go with your blond hair," I say.

Sakura comes trotting up. Glares at me, like, who are you to make all this noise and why aren't you serving me steak on a golden plate?

Since I've been making all this money with the billionaire, I buy a little something for Summer whenever I get something for myself. See, these are my people here—Summer, Eleanor, Mac, and Katy. I have another Level 1 friend too. Faith—we were the kids in the after-school program who'd still be there at five, hoping our parents remembered to pick us up. But I never hear from her since she moved back to Baltimore to have kids. I have lots of Level 2 friends also, but I'm not going to throw them all at you, or we'll find ourselves in a Dickens novel here. Eleanor says I have a gift for relationships. That it's what I do best. Although apparently, this gift does not apply to romantic relationships.

Wednesday, May 10, 2006

Josh is in LA. He went to discuss his movie with our director friend. I think this is the first time I have ever had the house to myself. It's heavenly.

Friday, May 12, 2006

Eleanor is not as happy at Vera Wang's as I am. It's all white latticework, white satin couches, and thick white carpeting, more like fur than carpeting. We're surrounded by satin, lace, tulle, taffeta, embroidery, and little bits of this and that sparkling everywhere. I'm so excited I'm nearly hyperventilating, but Eleanor is staring at the floor, thinking (I believe) how suicide would be preferable to this. But she is a Stein and Steins have big weddings. I've known this family since I was five, and I know Eleanor really had no say in the matter.

"Come on," I say. "Try on some duchess satin for your old friend Heather."

In the dressing room, which is quite a bit larger than my apartment, even though my apartment is pretty big, we're nearly buried in crystal beads and seed pearls and yards of ruffled taffeta petticoats. I am trying not to die of jealousy thinking how her folks' place on Martha's Vineyard has been spruced up for the big day with extra plantings and new gravel on the driveway, of the carts of champagne and lobsters ordered. I'm thinking, as I have since I was five, why wasn't I born a Stein? I would have been such a good Stein. Why does Eleanor get to be a Stein and not me?

Then, before I even have time to ponder, Eleanor has dropped to the floor, all the silk and tulle of her gown billowing up around her. She busts into tears. Eleanor is two months pregnant. Besides her fiancé and her mother, I'm the only one who knows.

"It's the hormones crying," I say.

And then, when she doesn't respond, "The walk down the aisle is one minute. The ceremony, twenty. Then you're at the party. Then, bam, three hours later, the whole thing is a distant memory."

"I want to *be* married. I don't want to *get* married," Eleanor cries.

"You've got it backward," I say. "Getting married is awesome. It's the being married that sucks."

Eleanor looks up. She scooches over in all her silk and tulle. Puts an arm around me.

"Hey, who would I least like to meet at the end of a dark alley?"

"Me," I sigh.

"That's right," she says. And then, "At least we have each other."

"At least we have each other," I say.

Saturday, May 13, 2006

Josh came back today, and something seemed different. He looked kind of handsome. Less puffy. And his eyes actually seemed to have some life in them. God, it's worse when I look at him and he's actually there.

"Everything is going to change for me, babe," he said. "Something's clicked. I feel completely different. Better than I have in a long time. This movie is going to happen. Just watch. I'm going to take care of *everything*."

I don't think I even bothered to answer. I've heard it so many times, the only satisfying response I can imagine would involve shattering his face with my fist.

Monday, May 15, 2006

Scene: our living room, around 3 p.m., yesterday.

I'm paying our bills at the dining room table. It's an eighteenth-century Quebecois worktable, picked up at an antiques shop while we were in the Berkshires at a friend's wedding and still thought it was appropriate to buy expensive antique furniture on a whim. The chairs I bought in a fit of trying to make the whole place perfect all at once, back when we first got here in November 2001. They're from ABC. They have wide woven seats and painted green backs with chips and nicks in them to make them seem old.

I'm hating these pretentious chairs (which I picked out) as I'm paying the bills and remembering the invitation we sent out to both our families for Thanksgiving that first year—even though we'd just moved in and didn't have any furniture. We'd thrown away our old furniture because Josh didn't think any of it was good enough for our new digs, although I suspected he also didn't want to be bothered moving it. I was trying to show off to everybody by saying, look at me, I can get a six-figure book deal, buy a loft, and host a fabulous Thanksgiving two weeks after moving in.

What an idiot I am.

All we had was an enormous television that Josh had insisted on buying. There'd been nothing in the place except that TV surrounded by video game consoles and a folding camp chair set up in front of it. I remember coming home one evening with a couple of friends. And there was Josh, his mouth hanging slightly open, alone in the darkness, not a single light on, tethered like some enormous, obscene baby to the TV by the cord of a video game controller. Yes, hello, friends, this is my life—a huge loft we can't afford, no furniture, and a husband who just wants to sit in the dark playing video games.

Josh had wanted this loft so badly it had been like a fever. He'd told the real estate agent that we could easily afford it, even though we couldn't, and when I brought this up to him, he'd shouted, "Don't you trust me? Why don't you ever listen to what I have to say? Does it ever occur to you that maybe I know something?"

No, I'd thought, no I don't trust you. I just watched you puff yourself up in your own eyes as you inflated by one hundred thousand dollars what we'd agreed to spend. Is the kind of person who needs to impress a real estate agent trustworthy?

But that was inside. On the outside, I cried. I hate being berated. I always want to be forgiven, allowed back inside the fold.

"Of course I trust you. Of course." Weeping, copiously.

We were supposed to move in on September 12, but then September 11 happened, and we were stuck down in Baltimore at my mother's house, where we'd been spending a few days. September 11 is Josh's birthday. Maybe that was part of it. Maybe he was retraumatized the way people with posttraumatic stress disorder can be. I don't know. But he flipped that day. I remember standing on a street corner in Baltimore while he screamed at me so loudly that people in their cars turned to look at us. I'd bought a frozen Pepperidge Farm cake for his birthday because we were all so disoriented and horrified by what had happened in the morning that we'd canceled our plans to go out to dinner. Josh had agreed to this. But then there we were on that street corner—and I'd ruined his birthday. And this would never have happened if his mother were still alive. And I was a terrible wife and a terrible friend. "A fucking frozen Pepperidge Farm cake!" he kept shouting. I just remember looking at him and thinking, are you crazy? Terrorists just blew up the World Trade Center.

You could say that was the end of the middle.

By the time we moved into our new place, Josh was already furious with me about our book. Every time I showed him something I had written, his face would get tight with anger and he'd say, "What is this? This isn't what we talked about." He said, "If I were writing this with Gabriel, we'd be done already." He said, "I dropped out of graduate school to write this book with you and now it's a disaster. We're never going to finish. We're totally fucked."

It's true I'd asked Josh to work on the book with me. I'd been growing increasingly anxious that he was no longer going to class, even though he'd spent two years working to get into that fancy philosophy-of-mind graduate program. I thought asking him to cowrite the book was like throwing him a life preserver. But I didn't say that to Josh. Instead I said, "I need you to help me with this. I can't do it by myself."

Christ on a crutch, what bad decisions we make.

Anyway, we sent out that invite for Thanksgiving. We were

going to show everyone what big shots we were. After I bought the dining room and living room furniture, Josh decided we needed bookshelves before the guests arrived. And he was going to build them himself. But he didn't start until the day before—and mind you, the wall on which he was building them is about ten feet high and ten feet across. At first he was meticulous, finding every stud, putting brackets in, checking the level as each new piece of wood went up. But as day turned into night, he grew increasingly sloppy, not putting brackets at the ends of the shelves and eyeballing levels. I begged him to just leave them unfinished. But Josh had been telling stories all day of what a lousy builder his father was and how these shelves were going to put him in his place. Josh said he'd put in those last brackets after Thanksgiving but that he had to finish the whole wall in time for his father to see. He wanted to dazzle his father with his success—a book deal! (no matter he wasn't actually writing it), perfect furniture! (no matter that his wife had picked it out and paid for it on credit), a beautiful loft! (no matter that we couldn't afford it), and a beautifully conceived set of book shelves that didn't actually have the support they needed to hold up our books.

Sitting there paying the bills, I was thinking about that Thanksgiving and looking at our still unfinished bookshelves, sloping down perilously on the ends, and wondering, as I always do when I'm paying our bills, what exactly happens to all the money I'm earning. This was the first time I'd been home and paying the bills in months and months, so I'd decided to actually go through the charges instead of just writing a check for the total amount as I usually did. I found more than two thousand dollars' worth of electronic deductions from our credit cards—for online services, music equipment, computer parts. We were still paying monthly fees to a hosting company for the website Josh had built for the book and then abandoned a month later.

I felt it all rise into my throat, a rage that all my hours of work, of zigzagging around the country to earn all that money and bring in speaking fees, was being thrown down the toilet by an imbecile who couldn't even be nice to me while he did it.

Josh did not get mad when I asked him about the charges, as I was expecting. Instead he got kind of nervous and hangdog. I could tell he was trying to be "different" as he'd promised after getting back from LA. He apologized and said he hadn't realized he'd spent so much.

I got up from the dining room table and found that I was laughing. Josh stood where he was, over in the kitchen, watching me. His brows were knitted together. I turned to the windows that face out over Eleventh Street, put my hand on the glass, and just kept laughing.

"What?" Josh said.

All I could do was shake my head. It was so clear, so obvious— so ridiculously, absurdly obvious. For a moment I really thought Josh would just say, "You know what. Why don't I just pack my stuff and go." But when I looked over at him, he looked irritated. And he said, "What? Why are you laughing?"

"Josh . . ." I said. Could he really not know?

He intensified his gaze on me, shrugged his shoulders as if in bewilderment.

"Stop saying my name. What? What is it? Speak."

I think his ability to be simultaneously aggressive and oblivious kept me to my purpose.

I sat down on one of the bamboo chairs that line the front wall. My heart had begun thumping. I could feel it in all my muscles. I am not good at confrontations. I never have been. It's like my brain, which works just fine in other stressful situations, shuts down.

I said it quickly, before I could have time to think and get too scared.

"I want a separation."

I could barely hear my own words because of the pounding of my heart. I thought for a second I might pass out. I wished for a second I could take it back, shove the words right down my own throat in some desperate attempt to avoid whatever was going to happen next. Which was—what? I didn't know, but I knew it was going to be terrible.

"What?" Josh said.

Keep breathing. Keep breathing. It's going to be okay.

"Did you just say what I think you just said?"

There's nothing he can do or say that can hurt you. Breathe in. Breathe out.

Suddenly he was right above me, his face contorted with fury.

"You couldn't wait, could you?" he shouted. "Just when everything was about to change for me. Just when I was getting it together. But no, you couldn't wait. You couldn't wait for just a few months until I made it."

You are delusional, I thought. But I said nothing. I closed my eyes so I didn't have to see his face. I didn't want to go away to that place where all I want is forgiveness, where I find myself groveling.

"Look at me! Look at me!" he shouted. "Open your eyes!"

I looked at him, right in the eye. I tried to will him to understand what I seemed unable to communicate verbally. *Don't you see I'm dying here?* But I was afraid to open my mouth, because if I opened my mouth I would start apologizing. It took all the will I had not to do this—I didn't have anything left over to speak.

"Oh, that's right. Do the victim thing," he shouted. "Poor overwrought Heather. I know this one. It's a good one. Really. But actually, no, save it. Actually, go fuck yourself."

That was my cue to get up and leave the room. I'd told myself that the minute he started insulting me, I would leave. But Josh didn't want to let me leave. He blocked me at the mouth of the hallway, all 230 pounds of him, moving from side to side so I couldn't pass. And then the cursing started.

"You fucking bitch. You're a fucking bitch, you know that? You're a cunt. You're a dirty sniveling cunt. I fucking hate you, you fucking cunt."

I stood still, waiting for him to let me pass. This is what I'd been practicing for. I'd told Eleanor I was developing a policy of nonviolent resistance—beat me, curse me, do what you will. I won't fight back but neither will I back down. I'd seen *Gandhi* on TV while in Dallas and been struck by the scene of all the Indians lining up to get beaten by English soldiers. I'd wondered what they did with their selves during that moment—not with their bodies, which they were willingly handing over to be violated, but with their *selves*. I thought, they must have taken themselves somewhere far away from the situation, to a different place entirely. And this is what I tried to do. I could hear, but I stopped listening. I could watch his face contort, but if I believed enough that I was doing the right thing, I didn't have to let the sight penetrate beyond the outermost senses. It was just what he was doing. It had nothing to do with me. I kept taking long, even breaths, listening to the sound of the air coming in and out. I was in the room, but I was nowhere near it.

Finally Josh stepped to the side with a snort and a big show of letting me pass. Then he followed me down the long hallway, whispering in my ear and pounding on the wall with his fist. "Fucking bitch. Fucking cunt. Cunt. Cunt. Cunt."

Breathe in. Breathe out.

I went to my closet in the back of the house and pulled out my biggest bag. I tossed in underpants, socks, yoga clothes, and a book. I had a toiletry bag with supplies to last several days, which I'd already taken to carrying with me. I dropped that in.

"Oh, you're leaving," Josh hissed. "Perfect. That's right. Run off. You fucking bitch."

I made it to the front door and got it open before Josh slammed it shut again with the palm of his hand. Now he was really hulking over me. He was all I could see or smell. I was afraid, except I wasn't afraid because I thought, even if he breaks all my bones and I end up in the hospital, I will have done the right thing. They say the primary tool dictators have over their people is fear. If Josh was my oppressor, I was going to deny him his most powerful weapon. Nonviolent resistance. No fear. Just keep breathing.

He took hold of my bag and tried to pull it from me. I yanked it back from him. I don't know what he was saying but he was screaming and spit was flying in my face. He had nearly pulled the bag away from me when suddenly I dropped back into the situation. I was in the middle of it. This was happening. I was leaving my husband. Suddenly we were both screaming, and wrestling too. I was yelling at him right back in his face. Shouting at him to go fuck himself right back. I was twisting and turning, trying to get away from him. He slacked for a second, startled, I think, by my sudden turning on him, and I pushed him in the chest with all my might. I threw the door open and ran out and down the stairs. There were so many voices in my head. My brain was shouting, no, no, no, go back! My heart felt like it was splitting in two. Some part of me was praying, oh please, dear God, take me out of this, please, please. But that other part, the new part, was hovering above it all, just watching, waiting, saying, okay, open the door. That's right. You got it. Left foot. Right foot. Keep walking. Good job. Anything you do, don't look back. Just keep moving. There you go. Don't look back. Don't look back.

I went straight to Mac and Katy's apartment. Let myself in with the keys Katy had given me. I don't remember anything at all from the walk. When I got to the apartment, I lay down on the rug in the living room and hung on to its edges. I wailed. I've never heard myself make such noises. I thought, I sound like someone at a funeral. I thought of the sounds Gabriel's grandmother had made at his funeral. I cried for who the man I married had become. I cried at my own weakness in staying so long. And I cried for the will it took not to run back. The sheer act of not letting anything he'd said penetrate left me prostrate. In my mind I erected a wall between him and me and I refused to let him in. I held on to the edges of that rug as if for dear life.

Friday, May 19, 2006

Scene: our bedroom. Josh is lying down on the bed. I am sitting on the edge. It's the first time I've been home since leaving.

"Heather, please, please!" Josh is sobbing, more than I've ever seen him. He's clutching my arm. Everything is foggy. I feel like

I can't see clearly. "Please don't go, please don't leave me. I won't make it if you leave me." He pulls back. Looks right at me. "Don't you see—I'm sorry, I'm not trying to make you feel bad, I know it's not your responsibility—but if you go, the jig is up. That's it for me." More sobbing. And now I'm sobbing too, and thinking, please don't kill yourself. Please don't kill yourself. I say, "Josh, look at me. Look at me. Don't you know we have to do this? Are you happy? Can you tell me you're happy?" But of course he can't, and this makes us cry all the harder. We cling to each other.

Monday, May 22, 2006

Josh is leaning not just his head but his entire torso out the front window. I'm walking away, up Eleventh Street, thinking, so much for "talking."

"You're a fucking rat!" he's shouting. "I knew it! I knew I should never have trusted you!"

Cunt! Cunt! Cunt! Like a chorus following me up the street. I'm thinking, yeah, the rat survives when the ship goes down, motherfucker. And then, is this really happening to me?

Thursday, June 15, 2006

It's been almost a month since I told Josh I want a separation. I've been eating a lot of Oreos dipped in vodka. Every day I get stoned and drunk and talk to Eleanor and Summer on my cell phone, and then I trudge back to my house to "talk" with Josh. But Eleanor's wedding is tomorrow, and before driving up to Martha's Vineyard, I go to Philadelphia to see my brother, who is on tour with a very famous Rock Star.

I rarely see Seth, even though he and Cecilia live in Greenpoint. The truth is I feel uncomfortable around him—primarily because the sight of him makes me feel as if there were a swelling in my chest, as if I have so much love for him and so little idea how to express it that it's actually constricting my breathing. He's my older brother, and if you have an older brother, maybe you know the feeling that he is more a minor deity than a flesh-and-blood human. I'm always so conscious of how superior he is to me in every way that I can never think of anything cool enough to say, and so walk around uttering the most inane garbage you can imagine and then hating myself.

Josh decided many years ago that he despised both my brother and Cecilia. He didn't have the nerve to forbid me to see my brother, but he sure didn't make it easy. The last time my mother was in town, we all went out to dinner and Josh actually started shouting at Seth, something to do with the Bush administration's handling of 9/11—right there over ceviche at this Peruvian restaurant on Fifth Avenue. He kept shouting, "You can't bully me! You can't bully me!" while Seth just sat there, as if frozen in his seat. And I thought, now it's out, they know what my life is; they know I live under the thumb of a hideous tyrant. And it was worse than that because I'd also flashed to my brother when we were little, approaching my father with something he'd been saving up to tell him, something he thought would win that man's love, only to find himself snarled at or, worse, ignored. Me thinking, you don't want his love anyway. Me not knowing how to protect him. When Cecilia started shouting back at Josh to shut up, I remember dimly thinking, oh, you can do that? And then, before drowning again in my own sorrow, thank God for Cecilia, thank God for Cecilia. She will protect my brother.

Saturday, June 17, 2006

Eleanor's wedding.

"Are you happy now?" Eleanor says. "My parents are spending sixty thousand dollars so you can be a bridesmaid."

"Yes," I say. I'm wearing a gold-colored tissue-papery Miu Miu dress I bought at a Barneys Warehouse sale in another lifetime and pink patent-leather peep-toe pumps. I'm not so sad I can't appreci-ate a good outfit.

"You really wish you'd been born into the French nobility, don't you," Eleanor says, in her wedding dress, sneaking a cigarette out the bathroom window. "Living it up at Versailles."

"World-famous courtesan," I say.

"Right, I forgot," she says. "So you're always saying. Control over their own money and whatnot."

"Showered with gifts," I say.

I help Eleanor put on her grandmother's jade-and-diamond earrings. Make sure the hydrangeas in her hair are set right. But I cannot make her stop counting the minutes until the whole thing is over. I'm thinking, what part of wearing a beautiful, floor-length satin gown and carrying a bouquet don't you like? But Eleanor is just not like that. Sigh. If only I'd been born a Stein.

When the ceremony starts, I'm watching her about-to-be hus-band and he looks so in love, so moved, that I find myself wanting to retch. I mean literally, I feel like I could vomit. How could you think getting married was a good idea? I'm thinking. Don't you know what's going to happen?

And then I am struck by such a feeling of aloneness that I al-most drop to my knees.

After the party, I crawl back to my hotel room and curl up in the bathtub. I can hear Eleanor outside the door wondering where I am, but I can't move.

I tried to be a good bridesmaid. I swear to God I did.

Sunday, July 9, 2006

June has turned into July and still Josh hasn't left. We talk. We talk. We talk. Or rather he talks. I have nothing left to say, but I feel I owe it to him to listen.

The one good thing in my life right now is the crush I have on my insanely cute French yoga teacher. He's got thick brown hair that always seems on the verge of needing a cut, soulful brown eyes with sensitive, sun-touched creases along the edges, and a catlike body. My friend thinks he has a crush on me too. I love that she thinks this, but I know nothing that good would ever happen to me. That's just not how the universe works.

Wednesday, July 12, 2006

Josh has decided to move to Los Angeles.

Thursday, July 27, 2006

It's now been more than two months since I told Josh I wanted a separation, and still he hasn't left. I've been moving from friend's place to friend's place. Now Eleanor's aunt and uncle are letting me stay with them in Brooklyn Heights. They have a room on the top floor of their brownstone they don't use. They're so nice to me it makes me nervous. I tiptoe around and try not to make any noise or take up any space. They're both chain-smokers, so mostly I sit in my room and smoke and look out the window and wonder if I'll ever participate in life again.

Yesterday, after yoga, my friend came back here with me to watch *Deadwood* and eat soul food from this great place on Atlantic Avenue. But Josh had been so weird earlier in the afternoon, weeping and apologizing. I couldn't make him stop. As we put *Deadwood* on, I kept imagining going back to the house in the morning and finding a corpse.

I stopped the show and called him. No answer. I called again. No answer. I thought, this is it. He's doing it right now. If you don't go home right this minute Josh is going to commit suicide. You will have to live with it for the rest of your life. The air in the room felt as if it were pulsating around me. But if you do go home, there will never be an escape.

I couldn't concentrate on the show. I couldn't eat my macaroni and greens. I kept saying to myself, it won't be your fault. It won't be your fault. It won't be your fault.

In the morning I call again. "Oh sorry," Josh says, "my phone died." *Please get out of my life! Please.*

Friday, July 28, 2006

The cute Frenchman does seem to be interested in me. But he's so beautiful. Also, I think he's gay. But I don't care. My heart beats faster when he does a correction on me.

Monday, August 14, 2006

It's mid-August and still Josh hasn't left. I'm living in a friend of a friend of a friend's apartment on Fifteenth Street, cat-sitting for her disgusting, smelly cat. I live increasingly in my imagination. My real life of getting out of bed, failing to do any work, getting stoned, going to yoga, and going back to bed feels distant. As though it's the dream. In my imagination, I'm with Mike Talese. We run into each other unexpectedly, hold hands, stroke each other's hair. They're so pathetic, my fantasies. But I long so much for even these tiny tokens of affection that the lack of them feels like the breath is being pushed out of me. It's real physical pain in my chest.

This is my primary Mike Talese fantasy:

I'm in a café in Los Angeles wearing sunglasses and my hair is pulled back in a loose ponytail.

Mike arrives.

He takes off his sunglasses; his hazel eyes are clouded with caution. They're not open to me.

As we sit, though, he falls under my spell and his eyes light up.

We finish our coffee—or meal, I don't know, I haven't worked that part out—and Mike stands up to go.

I put out my hand.

He looks at me.

"I don't want to say good-bye," I say.

He's about to give his spiel about me being a married woman, but I cut him off.

"Mike," I say. "Let's have one night. Not to have sex"—my fantasy is way too precious to be mauled by lustful hands—"but just to be close. I want one night not to pretend."

In this fantasy, I look incredibly beautiful as I say these things, and although the sun is shining right on me, I have no pores.

"Don't walk out of my life," I say.

Even in my fantasy, I find myself wanting to cry.

"Okay, Heather," Mike says. "Let's get out of here." He tosses some money on the table and together we leave the café, his arm around my shoulders, me huddling against him. We walk to his little silver BMW and then he wraps both arms around me and says my name over and over while the traffic flows down Santa Monica Boulevard.

That is my fantasy.

Tuesday, August 15, 2006

I email my brother and tell him Josh and I are separating. "I'm sorry," he writes back. "That can't be easy. I guess I can't say I'm completely surprised. Do you need anything? You should come join me on tour. We just played Barcelona. It was amazing. Come."

I'm sure he doesn't mean it. But it's nice of him to say.

I email my mother. She calls me on the phone. "What happened?" she cries. My mother has always been crazy about Josh. I think, um, he treated me like shit for a decade? My mother gives a big sigh. "Poor Josh," she says. "He's had such a rough time of it. He just never stood a chance, did he?"

I don't know what I was expecting, but I find this crushing. I get off the phone as fast as I can so she won't see how hurt I am.

Today is August 15—my father's birthday. I wonder as I always do on this day what it would be like to have a father you'd be willing to call.

Thursday, August 17, 2006

The cute Frenchman and I have taken to sitting on a bench outside the yoga studio and smoking hand-rolled cigarettes together. He just broke up with his boyfriend of eight years. Yes, I know: boyfriend. But I really don't care. Frankly, it feels like a relief. We talk about taking care of ourselves and healing and all kinds of New Age crap. It's very relaxing, and he's so beautiful to look at. This is my bright spot.

Wednesday, August 23, 2006

Josh needs a car for Los Angeles, and as far as I can tell has spent the past several weeks doing nothing but obsessing over what to buy. I offer him forty-five hundred dollars. He says he needs at least nine thousand. He says he'll pay me back over monthly installments, which I know he won't.

I sign the papers.

He has a car. There are no excuses left.

Thursday, August 31, 2006

It's only been a week since I last wrote, but how different I feel! I'm flying from San Francisco, where I was at a wedding, to Los Angeles to visit Summer, and you know what? I'm actually feeling pretty good. I survived another wedding! I didn't die of misery this summer! Sure, I get stoned and drunk every afternoon, but I can almost see another life waiting for me over the horizon. Also, I weigh

107 pounds. And let's be honest for just a second. The one upside of heartbreak is the weight loss. I don't think I've weighed this little since I was born. I'm not a little on the slim side. I'm really, truly thin. I keep looking in the mirror and turning round and round just to see the lack of fat from all angles. Even my *ass* is small. Do you hear what I'm saying here? When I was young and taking ballet, my teacher told me I should weigh a hundred pounds. And I was like yeah, right, maybe if you cut off one of my legs. But now I'm at least in the ballpark. So sure, my life is crumbling around me, but then again, I'm nearly as small as a ballerina.

Thursday, September 7, 2006
Los Angeles

My Real-Life Encounter with Mike Talese

I wear green cotton pants that used to be tight but now have to be belted at the waist, a tiny silk camisole edged with lace, and red flip-flops. I feel very California chic. My hair is kind of wild from the ocean dip Summer and I took yesterday, and it flies out from my head in spiraling curls. I ring his doorbell. He comes out, picks me up, and spins me around. We're both laughing. And I'm thinking, Oh God, you are so cute.

In his apartment, I wander around. I look at his DVD collection—*Star Wars*, *Indiana Jones*, Steve McQueen and Clint Eastwood films, *Girls Gone Wild*, Bruce Springsteen Live. In his fridge, there's nothing but a six-pack of Corona in the crisper, a door full of condiments, and a freezer full of vodka and frozen dinners.

"Jeez, you do need a girlfriend," I say.

We change into beach clothes and then head out. There are women shaped liked Barbie dolls in workout gear stretching on the grassy knolls at the edge of the Pacific Coast Highway and a trio of elderly Chinese women in big bamboo sun hats practicing tai chi.

We walk across the pedestrian overpass, down under the stairs, and onto the sand.

What do you want, Heather? I ask myself. What do you want out of this situation?

I lie back, luxuriate under the sun. I have this feeling, though, that Mike is going to think I'm a terrible wife for being out here with him lolling around in the sand instead of home with my husband. I can't bear for him to think anything bad about me, so I blurt it out.

"Josh and I are getting separated," I say. "He leaves the day I get back."

I don't know what I was expecting, but Mike is incredibly nice about it. Sympathetic. We don't discuss it for long.

Heather, I think, what do you want from this situation?

I stand up. "Let's go into the water."

Mike squints up at me. "It's freezing in there."

I'm wearing a little jean skirt I'd put on at Mike's place. I start to unzip it. "I told you I wanted to go swimming in the ocean," I say, pulling it down, kicking it off. "Did you think I was fucking around?"

"Nooo."

"Then don't be a pussy about it."

I start to back away from the blanket.

Mike scrambles up to his feet and comes after me.

When I hit the water, it feels so good, I almost can't believe it. I dive beneath the waves. I float on my back. It's all blue around me. Blue ocean. Blue sky. I just lie there, floating, seeing how good I'm capable of feeling. Mike comes paddling up. I think, this sure beats sitting by the window in Brooklyn. Then I come up with a plan.

"Mike?"

"Yes, Heather?"

He tosses the wet hair back from his face.

This is my moment.

"You know that scene in *Lost in Translation*," I say. "The one where Scarlett Johansson and Bill Murray sit in the bar and hold hands and just admit they're crazy about each other, just for that night?"

Mike doesn't say anything. He's just watching me.

"Well, I think we should have that scene. Just admit that right now, at this particular moment in time, we're crazy about each other."

Mike looks as if something hasn't quite computed in his brain. I can see the upload wheel spinning. Then he smiles, a long, slow smile. "So you admit you're crazy about me!" he says, and splashes water with the flat of his hand.

That's not your line, I think.

"Ha!" I say, and I start to swim away from him. But Mike is right behind me and he catches me, pulling me toward him. I feel his arms wrap around my waist underwater. I feel his breath on my neck. I think, oh my God, this is actually happening. But when he pulls me even closer, I feel something else too. I feel something stiff protruding into the back of my thigh. Hold everything! There are no boners in my fantasy!

I get away as fast as I can. I run out of the water.

"It's too cold! It's too cold!" I shout.

Back at the blanket, Mike wraps his arms tight around me.

His face is so close to mine I can see how thick his black eyelashes are, the creases around his eyes, the bristle from his beard. I think, I didn't know your hair would feel this way. I haven't seen anyone but Josh up this close since I was twenty years old.

"Say you're crazy about me," I say.

"I'm crazy about you," Mike says.

"Say it again."

"I'm crazy about you!"

This is better than I'd even dreamed.

When we finally get up, we're both in a daze. There's been no kissing, but we've been holding each other for nearly an hour. Back at his apartment, though, something changes. Mike pulls me toward him, sort of fiercely, and before I can turn away, he reaches a hand up under my shirt, into my bikini top, and over my breast. I feel something like an electrical current shoot through my body.

"Mike!" It's a plea for mercy. I can feel his desire like some kind of giant wave and suddenly have a terror that it will subsume me, drench me in blackness.

He lets go. Runs a hand through his hair. Straightens his shirt. I don't so much step away as stagger back.

"Okay, well, then I'm going to take a shower," he says.

After his shower, Mike drives me to my car. When we get there, we sit for a moment. Mike is staring straight ahead of him.

"Mike?"

"Yes?"

"You are crazy about me, aren't you?"

Mike sighs and when he turns toward me I'm surprised to see that he looks tired, defeated almost. Then he cups my chin with his hand and kisses me very gently, right on the lips. "Yes, I'm crazy about you," he says. And he is so cute with his black hair brushed away from his face and his tired hazel eyes that I almost can't stand it.

I smile as I slip out of the car.

When Mike drives off down Washington Boulevard, I get into my own car. I sit there not sure what to do with myself. I'm shaking. I'm cold. I'm hot. I'm ecstatic. I want to vomit. I could scream with joy and weep for the loveliness of it all. You did it! I think. You fucking rule! And I lean my head against the car seat and laugh out loud. I feel so alive. I think about calling him and begging him to come back. I pick up my cell, put it back down, pick it up, put it back down. I sit with my face in my hands, laughing and blushing and letting the waves of delight and revulsion pass over me.

The sun is going down. It's one of those magnificent LA sunsets where the sky is crisscrossed with long streaks of burning pinks and deep burgundies. I'm not sure how long I sit there. But it's dark by the time I put the key in the ignition. And I think, this is me, driving off into the rest of my life.

Friday, September, 8, 2006

The next morning after next.

"So listen." It's Summer talking. I have to leave for the airport in like half an hour, but I've swung by the Pilates studio she manages to say good-bye on my way back from . . . Mike Talese's apartment, where I spent the night!

I slept in a pair of his boxers and a T-shirt. No clothes came off, but we kissed all night long and I made him tell me he was crazy about me like fifteen more times.

"Mike is not going to react to this in the same way you are," Summer is saying.

"Okay."

"After men have let themselves become vulnerable, they need to retreat."

"Okay."

"So, don't be offended, don't try to stop him. Definitely, definitely don't be in touch with him. Let him go off into his cave and then just be there, chilling, ready for him, when he comes back."

I'd told Mike that I would call him the minute I got back to New York, but Summer has been dating for like twenty years, so I figure she knows more about men then I do. "Okay," I say. "Got it. Don't contact him."

Summer hugs me. "You're glowing," she says. "You look beautiful."

I feel beautiful.

Saturday, September 9, 2006

"What happened to your nose?"

It's Josh talking to me. We're sitting on the stoop in front of the coffee shop on Eleventh Street.

"It looks like in the old days when we used to make out so much it would peel."

I frown and shrug. There's a second where I think I might panic. I can't tell if Josh is going to pursue the matter. I have no idea what I'll say if he does. But he doesn't.

We walk back to the apartment.

I'm helping him get the last of his things together.

"Okay, let's get this thing *going*," Josh says, a bag over each shoulder. "The sooner I go, the sooner this will be over."

We've decided on a six-month trial separation. At times I feel horribly guilty I'm soft-pedaling the fact that I never want to see him again. At other times I believe what we tell each other. I think, yes, he'll go out to LA, get his shit together, and then he'll come back and we can go on with the life we were supposed to have.

We stand together by the car. We put the two suitcases he's taking into the trunk. We attach his surfboard to the roof. Then Josh and I are standing on the curb. He gives me this little smile that I haven't seen in a long time. It's incredibly tender, like he gets pleasure just from the sight of me. I forgot how tender he could be.

"I love you, Heather," he says. "Little one."

"I love you too," I say, and I actually mean it. I'm thinking, I know you, and suddenly I am near-frozen by the realization that I am throwing away someone's love.

We stand by the car, holding each other for a long time. I can't let go of him. What am I doing? I think. It's Josh who pulls away.

"Okay!" He claps his hands together and climbs into the front seat.

In another instant, he's gone. Just like that. After thirteen years. After the last three months. Just a key in the ignition and Josh is gone.

Later

The cleaning lady comes at one.

She packs up Josh's Pez collection, his Japanese toys, the stacks of philosophy books bought in moments of self-improvement and then left to gather dust and dog hair.

Sakura sits bolt upright in the hallway, triangular ears erect, watching. I go to the back of the house.

And when I come back to the front, I shudder, because Josh's office is empty. It's as if he'd never been there.

Sunday, September 10, 2006

Cleaning.

I have four full-sized garbage bags of computer cords. Random press materials dating back to 2002. Motherboards, flash drives, wireless mouses. I dump everything into bags with no attempt at organization. I fill up an entire bag with game controllers, thick with dust. There are keys that belong to no locks, stacks of disks for programs I've never heard of. All over the house, these little piles of crap—manuals, receipts, empty boxes. I go around with a trash bag, dumping everything in it. I stick a piece of masking tape on the bag and write "Stuff."

Tuesday, September 12, 2006

I pick up all the books all over the whole apartment and rearrange our enormous, and dangerously sloping, bookshelves so they all fit in. I'm crossing my fingers the additional books won't cause the whole thing to come crashing down.

Wednesday, September, 13, 2006

I go grocery shopping and almost become hysterical in aisle three when I realize I don't have to buy all the stupid stuff I usually buy for Josh. Like Gatorade. It's in front of the Gatorade that I almost lose it. Yeah, you sure need some electrolytes with all that remote control action, I used to think. But now my pile of cottage cheese, yogurt, almonds, and carrots looks so small and pitiful on the conveyer belt. These aha moments really aren't what they're cracked up to be.

Thursday, September 14, 2006

Email from Mike: "What the fuck happened to you? Where are you? Are you okay? Is there a reason you didn't call me?"

So much for the cave theory.

Friday, September 15, 2006

Tonight when I was coming home from yoga in my Uggs and sweatpants, I passed a group of people about my age, all dressed up for a night out. I used to pass these people and think, ha, fools, walking around in uncomfortable shoes, desperate to meet someone. And I'd feel smug that I was married and thus had the privilege of schlepping around in Uggs and sweatpants, going home to watch TV and eat tofu pups on a Friday night, secure in the knowledge that I was loved. Suddenly I felt humiliated by my Uggs and the fact that I was going home early on a Friday night to eat cold tofu pups and watch TV. But I like tofu pups, I thought. And then, what if being alone really is as bad as everyone says? What if everything you've convinced yourself of isn't true? What if an awful husband is better than no husband?

Saturday, September 16, 2006

The silence in the house is like nothing I've ever heard. There was a moment today when I was sitting at my desk just going through some papers, and it crept up on me like a living thing. I have this ceramic bunny that sits on my desk—I looked at it and it seemed more still than it had before. I looked at the books on my bookshelves. They seemed stiller. Don't get me wrong, I know these are inanimate objects we're talking about, but I could have sworn that just the moment before I looked, they'd been vibrating. I sat there for like an hour, with my eyes closed, listening to the silence. I had the mad thought that I would never again let anyone into my house to break that silence. It's all-encompassing—gorgeous and dreadful at the same time.

Wednesday, September 20, 2006

Mike was supposed to have arrived in New York the day before yesterday. He'd told me the morning I left LA that we'd see each other that night. Even after the whole cave fiasco, he said he'd see me in New York. He promised me.

I waited for his call all day—and all night.

Finally, at 11 p.m., I left him the most pathetic message in the history of pathetic messages. "Um, hi, it's me. Are you here? Okay, good-bye."

He doesn't call me back. Not that day. Not the next one, or the one after that. The disappointment is crushing. I sit in stone-cold shock for two days. I don't leave the house. I don't really move. Sakura is beside me, but I don't even try to pet him. Like Josh used to, I let him out in the backyard rather than walk him. The silence is impenetrable.

What have I done? What have I done?

Finally I get up because I'm freezing cold. I go into the bathroom and run a tub of hot water. I get in and the strangest feeling overcomes me. Remember my policy of nonviolent resistance, how I used that to get through telling Josh I wanted a separation? That my material body sort of ceased to matter? Well, this feeling comes back to me while I'm in the bath, only more so. I feel myself separating from my self. My body, the bathtub, the water—the boundaries between us seem to blur. I feel like my *self* goes floating up out of my body into the larger atmosphere.

It stays with me as I get out of the bath. I don't feel earthbound. I feel as if someone has come along and untethered me and now I'm just floating in space. Except it doesn't feel scary or lonely. It feels fantastically peaceful.

Monday, September 25, 2006

"It's like I've ceased to exist," I say to Eleanor on the phone.

I can't even explain how strangely relaxed I feel.

"That doesn't actually sound good to me," Eleanor says. "It actually sounds kind of like a psychotic break."

We laugh. And then I try to explain again. "You don't understand," I say. "It's great. I feel totally diffuse. You know how drunk people don't get hurt in car accidents because they're so loose? I feel like that. Like I could just walk through things."

"Let's make a deal," Eleanor says. "If it doesn't go away, you'll tell me. And if it really doesn't go away, you'll call a doctor. You have to take care of yourself, Heather."

I agree to this.

The next day, I'm talking to Summer while I walk Sakura in Prospect Park and I'm telling her about the feeling.

"I think it sounds like enlightenment," she says. "I mean, isn't that what they're always talking about in yoga—letting go of the ego?"

I like the sound of this much better.

"Exactly," I say. "I always had this notion of Heather as this solid thing. As something I could describe or show you. Something you could hold on to. And now it's just gone. There is no Heather. And since there's no Heather, I don't have to do anything to be like her. I can just be."

Lately I've been having conversations with people on the street and finding myself thinking that I love them, passionately. I feel so much warmth for everyone. Amazement at their existence—at their brilliant, flawed humanness. I hope I'm not losing my mind.

Sunday, October 8, 2006

The contractors came today. I'm using the last of my money from the billionaire to have flagstone put down in the backyard and flower beds built. One day, I will have a garden.

Friday, November 10, 2006

So much time has passed and I haven't been keeping up-to-date. September became October, and then October, November. It gets darker earlier. I don't like that.

Talese finally called me. In October, from LAX on his way to Tokyo. He's sooo sorry he missed me in New York. Noooo, it wasn't anything weird at all. He just got busy.

Fucking pussy.

"Mike," I say. "My girlfriends tell me that when a man doesn't call, it's because he doesn't want to talk to you. Why didn't you want to talk to me?"

This seems like a good question to my mind. Straightforward, to the point.

But suddenly Mike needs to go because his flight is leaving right now, right this very minute, got to go, have to rush, so sorry, bye, bye.

"Why did you ask him that?" Summer says. "I told you to keep it light!"

"But why would he have just disappeared?" I say. "I don't understand."

I can hear Summer holding up her hand across the country. "Do not even go there," she says. "Expect nothing and take nothing personally."

I start hanging out with a game designer I know. A little guy, with a puffed-up chest and a strut like a peacock's. He's supersmart and really fun to hang out with. One night we go dancing and end up making out like crazy on the dance floor. I haven't kissed someone my own size since high school. I spend the night at his house and we stay up all night, not taking off any of our clothes, but kissing until the light breaks. I had to cancel another date I had the next afternoon, because I was so pooped. And that very night, he sends me an email telling me what a great time he had and how awesome I am, and that kissing me was "heavenly."

"See, that's what you're looking for in a man," Eleanor says.

At my coffee shop I meet a beautiful dark-skinned Israeli

with long dreadlocks, an electronic musician. He's so lovely in a millennial-generation, Benetton kind of way that I can't believe when he starts calling me and wants to take me out. We go to a bar in the neighborhood. He tells me how his best friend was killed in a car accident. I think, why me? We make out a bit. The next morning he calls and asks me to come to his house. I live just down the block, so I say, sure, and head over.

"I just think you should know I live here with my girlfriend," he says. "Oh God, now you're going to hate me. You hate me, don't you?"

"I don't know you well enough to hate you," I say. And then, as I walk out, "Dude, you are crazy."

Eleanor sets me up with a somewhat well-known writer who is in New York to give a talk titled "Depression: Is Suffering Useful?" I say, "I'm kind of done with suffering for a while." But Eleanor says he's "one of us," so I go for it. I meet him at the lecture, and then he takes me to Angel's Share bar above Ninth Street at Bowery.

He's sitting next to me, not looking at me, with the palm of one hand cupped over his left eye, his right eye staring into space in front of him. He confesses that he's a sex addict.

"Boy, were you set up with the wrong person," I say.

"No one understands," he complains. "It's not like we're running around all the time with our tongues lolling out of our heads. It's not like that at all. It's just a need. A need to connect. It makes the pain go away."

"Oh, I get it," I say. "You're a seducer. Me too. Only I don't care about the sex part. I just need to get my hooks in a person, then I'm pretty much done."

He looks at me for the first time all evening.

"What?" he says.

"It's about getting high, right?" I say. "Me, personally, I get high off seeing someone unable to resist me. Then I go home and I'm depressed."

The writer puts his finger on his nose, then points it at me.

"Now you're talking," he says.

"It's bottomless," I say. "There's no amount of sex you can have that will fill you up. It's futile. Don't you know this?"

Then we go back to the Carlyle, where he's staying, and fool around on his big hotel bed. I don't know if it's all the practice or what, but the sex addict gets me seriously hot. He even got my shirt off, which is more progress than the game designer has made in three weeks.

"I think all the machinery is working," I say to Summer the next day on the phone. "I got wet. A little. I'm pretty sure."

"That's great news!" Summer says.

I've been to the gynecologist many times over the last decade to investigate my lack of sexual interest and failure to *ever* get wet. I thought it was a medical problem. Josh always said it was my "issues."

I've been making out so much, the skin around my mouth and nose is in tatters. It's constantly peeling off.

I FUCKING LOVE BEING SINGLE.

Finally I decide I ought to have sex. But I don't know who it should be. The sex addict disappeared back to Virginia or wherever he lives. There's an AP photographer I've been going on walks with. And an amateur boxer I met at the coffee shop. But I think he might be on drugs, or maybe just crazy. Also, he has very long nose hair.

I decide on the game designer, because he's such a nice guy. I let him take my clothes off. I let him go down on me. At one point he raises his head and says, "You know, feel free to make noise at any time."

Somehow I get through the whole thing without ever touching his penis.

Josh never even comes into my mind. It's Mike Talese I feel I'm betraying.

The next day I am miserable. I feel gross and lonely and violated. I curl up in a little ball on the back of my couch. Sakura is sitting in his sphinx posture on the window ledge.

"Sakura," I say. "Do you love me?"

Sakura blinks his white eyelashes. His eyes are black and mournful in the dim light. I first saw Sakura in a pet shop window in a mall in New Jersey, never having even thought about getting a dog before. He'd been looking at me with his soulful eyes, as if saying, please get me out of here, don't you see this isn't where I belong? And I took him home with me that day. I wonder what he did as a pharaoh that has him back on earth as a dog. I imagine he had a favorite mistress in his harem and when he discovered she had a secret lover he had the young man killed—beheaded in a rose-filled courtyard while fountains bubbled, hummingbirds buzzed, and his lovely mistress wept.

"Sakura, what did you do? Talk to me."

But he just sits there looking impossibly elegant. And I think, you and me, dog, dropped into the wrong lives.

Thursday, November 16, 2006

Ben Green and I are having sushi, on him, since, technically, he's my agent. Ben has softly curling red hair, very white skin, and a mouth that always seems to be about to laugh out loud. It's so good to see him, it's like a physical rush.

I don't say, my husband forbade me to see you. I don't say, I'm sorry I allowed myself to be forbidden. I don't say, I not only failed to defend you but also started bad-mouthing you myself so I wouldn't have to admit how insane my husband was. I just try not to be completely silenced by my own shame.

All I get out is, "Look. I'm really sorry about all the, ah, weirdness."

I'm thinking that Ben and his wife, Marie, have had not one but two children since I took the book deal and that I've never been to meet them. I'm thinking that I wouldn't blame Ben if he never wanted to speak to me again.

But he says, "Hey, Heath, that's okay. Books are hard."

"I want to meet them," I say. "Your sons. Eli and Alex. Will you invite me over soon so I can do that?"

"Definitely, Heath," he says. "Next week. Or the week after."

And I think, okay, the past does not determine the future. I will rebuild my family. There is redemption for me.

Thursday, November 16, 2006

Something sort of momentous happened tonight.

I was out to dinner at this upscale empanada place on Fifth Avenue for a friend's birthday. I was sitting between her boyfriend and this aspiring novelist with a shaved head and shy eyes, who I was thinking should be my next conquest. I have no real evidence of it, but I've decided he has a crush on me and have been considering working my magic on him for a couple of weeks now.

Somehow the Rock Star my brother is playing with came up.

"Oh yeah," I said. "My brother is with him now. They're touring Europe."

Suddenly everyone turned to look at me. It was twelve or so faces, just staring in my direction. I always forget how impressed people are by this Rock Star thing.

"He keeps telling me to come meet him somewhere, but the tour is almost over," I said. And then I kept going, because everyone looked so expectant. "Dublin is their last stop, and then they're coming back. Should I go? I don't even have any work right now and I have like five million frequent-flyer miles and a zillion Starwood points. The whole thing would be free."

And then I looked over at the aspiring novelist, my future conquest. And he was looking at me with this expression on his face that was not shy. He was looking at me like, what the fuck is the matter with you? And suddenly I thought, what the fuck is the matter with me? Why on earth aren't I flying to Europe to hang out with my brother, who is on tour with one of the biggest rock-and-roll stars in the world? Why aren't I doing so right this very minute? If I can reconnect with Ben Green, surely I can reconnect with Seth, my brother. I watched the aspiring novelist watching me, and I thought, I can do anything I want. The world is mine for the taking. I'm going to fucking Dublin.

BOOK TWO

DUBLIN

Sunday, November 19, 2006
Dublin

It's pouring rain out of a flat, white sky. It's about 7 a.m. and I'm on the bus from the airport into Dublin. I can't believe it's only been three days since it even occurred to me to come.

I got an Americano at the airport. It came out inky black with a delicious-looking film of light brown on top.

"Do you have cream?" I asked the guy behind the counter, meaning half-and-half. He pulled out a bowl of real cream, freshly whipped.

"Wow," I said.

"See, I knew you were coming," he said, and winked at me.

I gave him two euros and thought, I love it here.

Later

I thought I was immune to nice hotels, but apparently not. I have French doors opening onto a balcony from which I can see the roofs of the old part of Dublin, and a wrought-iron spiral staircase leading up to a sitting room with book-lined walls and a working fireplace. I have a bed that's big enough to land a small aircraft on, all in white, with plump white pillows the size of small settees. My bathroom is the size of a tennis court, with a glisteningly white tub like a swimming pool at one end and a separate shower stall big as a studio apartment at the other.

Viva the George Bernard Shaw Suite at the Westin, which I got for free with my Starwood points, and to which the receptionist upgraded me for no reason I can think of except the Universe has changed its mind about me.

Later

The band flew in from Bristol last night and I know better than to wake my brother before noon. Rock-and-roll hours and all. Went in search of an umbrella. Took me a good hour to find one without a leprechaun, a four-leaf clover, a harp, or a glass of Guinness on it. Walked south through sheets of rain and black clouds. Walked down winding, rain-slick cobblestones with tinsel Christmas decorations swinging overhead and buildings of orange Victorian brick on either side. Walked under a massive stone archway and through a park of tidy flower beds, crisscrossing pathways, a lake with swans floating in it, and a small waterfall cascading down a slope of slippery silver stones. Down a long block of Georgian town houses right out of a Jane Austen adaptation. Across a canal lined with weeping willows. Through an Indian neighborhood with saris and bangles in bright pinks and blues in the windows—who knew there were Indians in Dublin?

Rambled in no particular direction but just following a green brass dome that rose and disappeared, and rose and disappeared, over the rooftops. Found the dome belonged to a church with a high robin-egg-blue ceiling, rows of wooden pews, and linoleum floors. The smell of Lysol permeated everything. Knelt and closed my eyes and thought, yes, yes, yes.

Went into a department store and flirted with a tube of red lipstick.

You know that feeling I told you about, of not being tethered to anything, not even my own body? It's so strong today that I feel as if the outlines of my physical form have disappeared and I could expand to be as big as the city itself. I keep bursting into laughter for no reason at all. "My cup runneth over!" I shout to the Dublin sky.

Later

Seth needs a new pair of shoes. We head out together into the pissing rain. We don't say a word about the fact that I've just left my husband. Josh's name never even comes up. Seth tells me that traveling with the Rock Star is really boring because usually you spend your free time on tour complaining, but the Rock Star is so nice and treats them so well that nobody has anything negative to say.

This is Seth saying the tour has been fantastic.

Then Seth says he's glad I finally got off my ass to come to meet him. I don't even know how to respond to this, because it never occurred to me for a second that my brother cared whether I came or not. When he says this, I feel tears spring up in my eyes.

We go back to the department store I was in earlier.

In the men's section, I pull out a navy-blue velvet blazer and hold it toward my brother. This is a bold move on my part. I half expect him to pull away or make a snarky comment. But instead he looks down at it and sort of pets one of the sleeves. "That *is* nice," he says.

A salesman comes over, helps Seth into the jacket, and asks what he's doing in Dublin. My brother responds in perfect Seth fashion, which is to say he gives a tiny, slightly embarrassed laugh and says quietly, "I'm with a band." When the salesman asks where they're playing, and Seth says The Royal Hall, the salesman says, "But . . ." Then there's a long pause. And then the salesman stands up taller and his eyes change entirely and he says, "Ohhh." Then Seth looks really embarrassed, and I refrain from doing a backflip, because (a) I probably would have broken something, and (b) Seth would have killed me. One thing about my brother is that he's the most modest person you'll ever meet in your life. In fact, his modesty borders on secrecy. He could be elected president of the United States and not tell you. As Josh used to say, if Seth played his cards any closer to his chest they'd melt into his skin.

Instead I smooth down the back of the velvet jacket, examine the arms, the shoulder seams, the cuffs. Really it's just an excuse to touch my brother. I want to hurl myself into his arms and hug him until he pries me off. I'm thinking that in the navy blazer, with his dark hair, deep-set hazel eyes, movie-star-white teeth—just like my mother's—and long Virginia Woolf nose, he looks incredibly handsome. I'm amazed that he's not swatting me away but instead seems shyly pleased. I'm trying not to cry tears of pride. An image of my father comes into my mind, and I shove it away as if with my fist. I think, check us out, *Dad*, on top of the world despite you.

Seth looks at the jacket's price tag.

"It'll be a cold day in hell when I pay nine hundred euros for a piece of clothing," he says. Which is good, because otherwise I would have thought playing for the Rock Star had changed his personality entirely.

On the way out, I hand over fifteen euros and scoop up the red lipstick.

Monday, November 20, 2006

I just woke up from a dream so simultaneously terrifying and absurd that I don't know what to do except record it exactly and let you judge for yourself. If you're one of those people who find other people's dreams intolerably boring, don't even bother. This isn't for you.

I dreamed that I couldn't find where I lived. Or rather, I no longer knew where I lived. Summer was there and we were in a filthy kitchen with dirty windows and greasy bottles of spices on the countertops—like the communes my father lived on when we were little. I knew it wasn't my house, but I couldn't remember where my house was—or if I'd been keeping up with the mortgage payments. I had a vague image of a dark red wall—like the one in my actual living room—and I kept thinking that if I could find this wall I'd be home again. But I had no idea where it was.

Then my boyfriend from high school was there and we were going up a long mahogany staircase. He had his arm around me and I thought, did I make a terrible mistake? Would I have been safe if I'd married this man?

Then I was in my childhood house in Baltimore—that looming Victorian with the high ceilings and constantly leaking roof. But I couldn't see clearly and nothing was where it should have been. Suddenly these ephemeral beings—I don't know what else to call them—swept down from the ceiling and over the staircase. They whooshed over me with great gushes of air and no sound at all. The silence was so petrifying my face grew hot and little pinpricks of fear raced across my body. Then, from behind the closed door of a room down the hallway, I heard breathing. I crept closer. I knew something terrible was happening, and I knew I should find out what it was, but instead I started screaming as loud as I could and listened as no sound came out.

The next thing I knew I was in another apartment, this time with Josh. The place seemed to be made up entirely of cabinets. We were emptying them out, filling enormous trash bags with stainless steel pots of all different sizes—one for boiling lobster, another for sautéing, a third for simmering sauces. There were molds in the shape of fish and spatulas and a whole bag full of giant plastic spoons. In the dream, I closed my eyes because the waste was so painful to me. When I opened them I was alone. The place had become completely dark and my heart was pounding. My breath came out in frozen particles. I was slithering myself along the wall so that no one could sneak up and grab me. I was thinking, please don't let this be where I live.

Then I was back on the commune with Summer, and it wasn't so much filthy as covered with grime. Linoleum floors that would never shine again, cabinet shelves covered in peeling contact paper, years' worth of finger marks on all surfaces. There were bean sprouts and old tea bags on the counters; the refrigerator was filled with glass dishes of leftover vegetarian food. Summer told me there was a policeman to see me. It turned out there'd been an anonymous complaint against me. Something terrible had happened to a small child and I was accused of doing it.

Josh was in front of me, swelling up to enormous proportions before my eyes like a helium balloon version of himself. He put his hands around my neck and the next thing I knew he had thrown me to the ground and was strangling me. I was hoping someone would notice but no one did. Josh's eyes turned red. They were glowing at me like those of a demon in a bad horror movie. And I looked into his eyes and I thought, *it's him*.

When I woke up in my big bed in Dublin, I was covered in sweat. My first thought went something like this: thank you, Lord, thank you for letting that have just been a dream, I promise to worship you forever. My second thought was: is it really Josh? And then: if it is, and now I've left him, am I safe?

Later

North Dublin. No map. Just wandering. Down one cobblestone alley and then another. I stumble on an old produce-and-flower market in a beautiful Victorian structure of glass and wrought iron—every stall is O'Connor and Sons, or O'Donnell and Sons, or O'Sullivan and Sons. I can't stop laughing at the Irishness of the Irish.

The north is not touristy. There are long blocks of squat brick row houses with doors that open onto the sidewalk and so small it seems hardly possible that grown-ups live there. A middle-aged woman with deep wrinkles in her face and a cigarette dangling out of her mouth scowls at me. There are guys in tracksuits and buzz cuts talking into their cells; young women with bad skin and lots of makeup push baby strollers. I think, I love it here.

South again, and a bit to the east. It's as if orders had been given to spruce up the place. This must be the new prosperity I've read about. Two corners in a row have brand-new-looking coffee shops—there's something wistful about them, like they're fantasies based on a picture someone saw once of San Francisco. They're empty, both of them, but sparkling clean. I nod at a young proprietor in a crisp white apron leaning in his doorframe and he nods back at me. There's something otherworldly about these coffee shops, as if they exist somewhere that hasn't come into being yet, geographically trapped between the old and the new. They seem to be waiting. Waiting for a sign that the gamble will pay off—that the future can be something other than what the past would seem to have foretold.

But perhaps I'm projecting here.

Later

Topshop. I'm a size 26 jeans. Tried them on with a pair of enormous, bitterly uncomfortable high heels and my jaw nearly fell off my face. This not-eating thing is great, I don't care what anyone says. I'm thin! Thin, thin, thin! Thin at last!

Stroll with Seth. He's acting as if he likes me. He laughed at one of my jokes. This trip is a miracle.

Tonight I'm supposed to go out to dinner with Seth, Cecilia (who is flying over from Thailand, where she's been organizing AIDS-infected sex workers), and some of the guys from the band. I'm so jet-lagged, I may just go to sleep. I could go home tomorrow morning and the whole trip would have been worth it.

Thursday, November 21, 2006
Last night

"What do you say to impress a girl from New York?" the Irishman shouts in my ear.

"Hello?" I shout back. And then it's all gobbledygook—something about having been a gardener in New York, and being a manager at a place called Temple Bar. I really can't understand him.

Then he's shouting, "Your name, girl! What's your name?"

And I'm shouting, "Heather," but he doesn't understand me, so I shout, "You know, like the purple brush that grows in Scotland!" And he says, "Ahhh, Heather!" except it sounds like Heddderrr, with the most beautiful rolling r at the end.

When we finish dancing, he gives me a half bow and makes a little flourish with his hands. It's charming in a sort of old-fashioned, awkward way. He's tall with a long neck, sloping shoulders, and dark hair tucked behind his ears. I think, a little dorky, but cute enough. I bow back to him and give him an extra-dazzling smile to make up for the fact that I didn't understand a word he said.

My brother's old friend Leah, who now lives in Dublin, is at the bar, chugging a pint of Guinness. When I reach her, she puts down her glass and rubs her hands together. "He's a bartender or something," I say, and shrug. Then I pull out from the front of my new size-26 jeans four slips of paper with four phone numbers on them. Leah throws back her head and guffaws. I execute a small turn. Then I take Leah by the shoulders.

"I FUCKING LOVE DUBLIN!"

Leah rubs her hands together and says, "Excellent, excellent!"

It's about two in the morning and Seth and Cecilia and all the rest of the band have long gone back to the hotel. But something happened inside me when it was time to leave—I don't know how to describe it exactly except to say that I was overcome with a feeling like I might die if I didn't get to stay.

See, we'd all been at dinner when Seth said he'd seen a flyer for a Jimmy Cliff show. All the guys in the band had started talking at once because apparently the Rock Star had just been teaching them some Cliff tunes. Bob the drummer had stepped outside to call Billy the tour manager, and Billy the tour manager had arranged for us to get into the show even though it was sold-out. "Ah, life with the Rock Star," Cecilia had said, and then we'd all headed over in a big laughing pack—gotten there just in time to hear Cliff belt out "Rivers of Babylon" with his six backup singers and dreadlocks flying. We'd all stood at the back of the crowd, mesmerized, Cecilia singing along in her beautiful voice, and me stepping out of my mesmerized state long enough to think, my, there are a lot of cute guys here—and then the show was over, because really we'd only caught the tail end, and everyone had started to say good-bye and head back to the hotel, and I'd been like, Hello? Rock-and-roll hours?

"Surely, *you're* not going home," I'd said to Leah.

Leah had work in the morning; she'd just gotten back from Amsterdam. What would her boyfriend say?

I have to be completely honest here. I did not care at that moment what was best for Leah. All I cared about was getting back into the room we'd passed on the way out with a DJ setting up and people about to dance. So I'd played my last card, arms spread wide. "Leah—when's the last time we hung out?"

And Leah had relented. "You buying the first round?"

"Dude, I'm buying *all* the rounds!"

Then we'd stepped back in and I'd had the feeling that I could, and perhaps would, devour the whole club in one enormous, life-affirming gulp.

At the bar, I stripped. Off came my coat, a sweater, and two long-sleeved shirts. I had a sports bra under my tank top that I knew showed—and not in a sexy, imagine-me-naked kind of way but rather in a big-blob-of-white-spandex way—but I did not care. My armpits were unshaved and my hair was dirty, pulled off my face with a ponytail holder. All I had going for me was the red lipstick. But let me repeat: I—did—not—care.

You know how every now and then dancing can be a transcendent experience? You feel the music creep into your body and you find yourself moving without being aware that your brain is even giving instructions to your muscles. Maybe you don't. But that's what it felt like to me. I felt like everyone was smiling at me. I have no idea if they were, but I went ahead and smiled back. I had that feeling again, that I wasn't so much a body as moving energy. I felt as if I were lit from within.

I noticed the Irishman before we danced together, and now, an hour or so later, I see his head bobbing above the crowd, watching me with a little half smile on his lips and curious eyes. I don't pay him much attention, though, because I'm watching a guy in a green soccer jersey with a near-shaved head and mean-looking green eyes.

I'm waiting for the mean-eyed guy in the green soccer jersey to make his move, but then he drains his beer, kisses the girl standing next to him full on the lips, and they leave the club together.

Well, fuck me, I think, and head to the bathroom.

Just as I'm coming out of my stall, an extremely inebriated man in a suit vest over a shirt with flowing, white sleeves stumbles in the bathroom door. In the most good-natured way imaginable he says, "And what are you doing here, girl?" I say, "This is the women's room." And he insists on escorting me—quite gallantly though not exactly in a straight line—back to the entranceway of the dance floor. And there is the Irishman—as if waiting for me, or about to leave.

He's wearing a blue Fred Perry zip-up now, and his hair is no longer tucked behind his ears. I think, he's cute.

"So, would you like to see a bit of Dublin while you're here?" he says.

I know he doesn't mean now and probably not with a friend in tow, but I don't care and I say, "Yes!" and grab Leah.

Outside, it's inky black. The cobblestones on the street are slick and gleaming from the rain. Streetlamps make little pools of light all around us. I'm stunned by the beauty of the evening. As we walk, the Irishman—who tells us his name is Kieran—points out everything we're passing. I still can't make out all his words, but it doesn't matter because his voice is so beautiful it sounds like a song to me. I don't know if you've ever found yourself serenaded by an Irish accent—but if you haven't, let me warn you. It does funny things to your insides.

When we hit the River Liffey, Kieran makes us stop and look at all the bridges that run over the water. They stand out from the river beneath like gleaming arches. The sky is full of stars.

I think, How could my life have gotten so beautiful? Am I dreaming all of this?

When Leah says she lives on a street called Lotts just on the other side of the river, Kieran puts a hand over his forehead and says, "Jaysus, girl. I thought you were a visitor too—and here I am telling you all about your own neighborhood."

I think, oh, he's nice.

After we drop Leah off, I slip my hand through the crook of his arm. I think that surely nothing bad can happen to me if I don't even exist. The moon comes out as we walk back across the River Liffey. It just barely breaks through the rolling clouds, more like a hazy light than any kind of solid thing. Then we're standing in front of a hotel that says Westbury in big letters over its front awning. I can't stop laughing.

"No, *the Westin!*" I say. *"The Westin!"*

Kieran looks totally mortified and puts his hand over his forehead.

"It's okay," I say. "I don't understand a word you're saying either." There's a pause, and then Kieran starts laughing too.

"Right," he says, and he takes my arm and turns me around in the opposite direction.

I tap him on the shoulder. "By the way," I say. "I'm just a person. You don't have to do anything to impress me. Honestly, I'm just so happy to be here, you have no idea."

Something passes across his face. I don't know what it is exactly, but it's like his gaze refocuses to see me more closely. I smile at him, because I just can't stop smiling since I got to Dublin. "Really," I say. "You have no idea."

We walk back to the Westin, and when we get there, I figure, what the fuck, and say, "So, do you want to kiss a little?" And Kieran says, "Yes," in this breathy voice and kind of swoops down on me. The next thing I know, I'm up against the front of the Westin, my arms wrapped around this guy's neck, his arms around my waist, and we're making out like a couple of complete maniacs.

Now, there are kisses, and then there are kisses. Remember that scene in *Lord of the Rings* where Frodo throws the ring into the pit of molten gold or whatever that substance was? Have you ever seen steel brought to the boiling point? Silver melted down? Perhaps you've watched an egg fry on Southern asphalt in the summertime? This Irishman, this Kieran, kisses me and the world bursts into flames. I am engulfed in liquefying, molecule-scrambling heat.

If I could have come down to earth long enough to think, I probably would have thought something along the lines of, what the hell is going on here? But I don't come back down to earth. I just think, oh. Oh. OH.

Kieran reaches under my bulky sweater, under the two long-sleeved shirts, under the tank top, pulls aside the white spandex sports bra, and grazes my breast with his fingertips. We both catch our breaths so hard we nearly topple over onto the sidewalk.

He kisses my lips, my neck, and the top of my head. He strokes the hair off my face as if we've been lovers for years. He lifts me up so my feet are not even touching the ground.

"Beautiful girl," he's saying over and over. "Beautiful, beautiful girl."

I am too stunned, too liquefied, to speak.

Finally we pull apart. Kieran brings his face down so it's level with mine. He's looking at me so searchingly that I can't meet his gaze.

"My God, girl," he says. "Do you make out like this with everyone?"

"No," I breathe. "Do you?"

"No." He's looking right at me, as if he can see into me. "No. No."

Half an hour goes by. An hour? Two hours? I have no idea. I've lost track of time. Finally Kieran pulls away, rubs his face with his hands. "Jaysus Christ, girl," he says. "It's nearly five in the morning."

Kieran is holding my hands in his. He says, "I have to go now. But I'm going to be back here tomorrow to take you to lunch. What do you say to that, chick?"

I'm overcome by such a feeling of happiness that I can't speak. Really, I think? You want to see me again? Really? I nod.

Kieran tosses his hair back and holds his index finger up in the air as he starts to back away from me. "One o'clock," he says. "I'll be here for you then, Heather Chaplin. Will I find you?"

I'm smiling so hard, it's like my face is going to split in two. This Heather Chaplin? I'm thinking. The one standing right in front of the Westin? "Yes, I'll be here," I say.

"One o'clock," he says.

I put my index finger up too. "One o'clock," I say.

We're both cracking up as if this were the funniest thing in the world.

To say I'm giddy as I go back inside the Westin would be an understatement. It might be more accurate to say I am carbonated from the inside out.

Later

The dim Dublin light is splattering across the pavement, endlessly shifting shapes as the clouds form and reform and drift apart above my head. I'm hanging out in north Dublin and thinking about God. Not God in the sense of a man with a bushy white beard, but more God in the sense of what some people would call "the Universe." Although, really, I'm not exactly sure what that means either.

I'll tell you right now, I've never been a big fan of the Universe, or whatever you want to call it. I've always thought life was just completely random or maybe worse. Sometimes I've suspected there *is* a larger force out there, but it's not the kindly, gentle force people who talk about the Universe seem to mean. I would have to describe the force I've always imagined as malignant. Cruel. Petty. Treacherous. Those are some of the words that come to mind.

Really, my whole life, it's been as if I were in one of those indoor swimming pools with the built-in current, endlessly swimming as hard as I could and never budging an inch. You could say that's what I thought the Universe was—the thing that holds you back, that keeps good things from happening, that squashes any dreams you're foolish enough to have. There have been times in my life I've felt hopeful, but I've always kept very quiet at these moments. It used to drive Josh crazy. I just always suspected that the way to get around God—or the Universe, or whatever—was to keep secret what you wanted. In other words, sometimes good things can happen, but only when the Universe isn't paying close attention.

Mac and Gabriel's grandfather used to say, "The thing about life, kid, is it doesn't give a shit." And I'd always nod when he said this, and think, don't I just know it.

But now I'm not sure. Since that day in my bathtub when I ceased to exist, everything has been different. I feel like someone has turned off the current. I'm no longer swimming as hard as I can to get nowhere—and suddenly it's like I'm getting everywhere. The whole pool is mine. I'm just floating around, as relaxed as you please, smiling up at the sun, having a daiquiri. I keep getting this feeling almost as if I can will things to happen—but not with any effort. That's the funny part: somehow by *not* making any effort, everything I want to happen keeps happening.

Can the Universe change its mind about a person? Say, okay, you've suffered enough, now you get to be happy. I feel like I slipped out of the universe in which I used to reside into another, better universe.

I have this sense that I'm surrounded by light, or that light is illuminating me from within. I feel like my feet aren't touching the ground but rather I'm suspended by a web of infinitely stretching and ceaselessly malleable threads. What could the glory of God possibly mean except how I felt last night making out with my Irishman?

Later

When I walk into the lobby of the Westin at 12:55, the Irishman looks up from the newspaper and I get a horrible feeling in my chest. This is not some random, sweaty guy from a nightclub. This is perhaps the handsomest man I've ever seen in my life. How in the euphoria of last night did I not catch this?

He's up in a second, laughing this fantastic loose laugh and saying, "Hullo, hullo, did you sleep, girl? I got none at all myself," and kissing me on the cheek.

And I'm thinking, I definitely should have gotten back to the hotel earlier. But here's the thing, I hadn't thought he'd actually show up. My relationship with the Universe is still so new! And even when I did get back, I didn't get into the shower until twelve forty-five, just to prove that I didn't care whether he showed or not. Then, when I got out of the shower and there was a message that he was waiting in the lobby, I put on jeans, the same sweater from last night, and my puffy jacket, which Josh always said made me look like Fat Albert, just to prove I didn't care that he'd shown up.

But the man before me! He's tall and moves in my direction like he's liquid. He shakes his hair away from his face and gives me the most wonderful smile I've ever seen. I think, your eyes are the blue of a summer night just before the sky turns to black. I think, what have I done? I am standing face-to-face with the handsomest man in Ireland, and I have wet hair, no makeup and am dressed like an overweight animated TV character.

I don't know if it shows on the outside, but on the inside, I totally lose my shit.

In a little shop across from the stone arch leading into St Stephen's Green, we get sandwiches wrapped in plastic and cups of hot tea. Kieran insists on paying. The store is very crowded, so he carries the sandwiches over his head on the way to the cash register. He is long and lean, like the soccer players you see on TV. I follow behind with the tea, trying to breathe normally.

We sit on a park bench and I say, just to say something, "I saw the pub where you work this morning. Near where the show was last night. Red paint with shiny black trim?"

Kieran looks up from unwrapping his sandwich. He wrinkles his forehead. "Temple Bar Pub?" he says. "On Temple Bar?"

"Yes! That's it," I say. I'm thinking, Why is everything called Temple Bar? I'm thinking, I want to put my hand in your hair; I want to touch your face. I'm thinking, why am I having these thoughts? "You're a manager there?" I say.

Kieran smiles at me, and his eyes seem to shine and grow warm all at once.

"Well, no, not really," he says.

Turns out Kieran runs a documentary film company called Temple Bar Documentary Film Co., which is in the old part of town, which is called Temple Bar but is not the same thing as Temple Bar the pub or Temple Bar the street. No, it's *in* Temple Bar the neighborhood, *near* Temple Bar the pub, *on* Temple Bar the street.

Kieran finds my confusion highly entertaining. "And you still agreed to go out with me?" he says. "I'm chuffed."

I don't know what that means, but I don't really have time to ponder, because Kieran is moving closer to me, and I barely have time to say, "I try to be an equal opportunist," before we're kissing again. At first we're kissing lightly, and then, the next thing I know, we're kissing like mad, our arms wrapped around each other's necks, and I'm starting to get that feeling again like my molecules are being scrambled.

We break apart, panting slightly. As if we aren't two adults on a park bench in broad daylight.

"What is going on here?" I say.

Kieran's face is just a few inches from mine, and I see that his blue eyes have dark gray starbursts shooting out from the pupils. His eyes so familiar. "I don't know, girl," he says. "I don't know."

"So, you got big plans tonight?" I say. Just to say something. To distract myself from the sense that though he is technically a stranger, I know every single thing about him. I'm wanting to reach out and say, *I know. It'll all be okay.* Even though I have no idea what wouldn't be okay.

"Oh, I'm *in* tonight," Kieran says.

I laugh.

He says, "No, I'm really in. I've got my girls tonight."

Girls? I think. Girls as in children? As in married with children? Oh, fuck you, Universe.

I slide sideways, away from him on the bench. "You're married. How charming."

Kieran is chewing a bite of sandwich. He shakes his head again. "No," he says. "But I was." And when he turns to look at me, there is nothing devious in his eyes—just a blue so deep I think I could happily drown in it.

I say, "I used to be married too."

We look at each other for a long minute.

"I wasn't going to tell you because I thought you might not approve," I say.

Kieran throws back his head and laughs. "You thought I'd be a strict Catholic?" he says. "Ha! No way, girl. I've known too many priests for that."

I slide back toward him. And then what else is there to do but resume kissing, wildly, on this public park bench in the bright sun?

When we come up for air, I find myself telling him about Josh's long decline. How I tried everything. How alone I felt. Then he tells me that his younger daughter is severely autistic, that when she was just two, she stopped responding entirely, that life became surreal and full of a kind of pain he can't even describe. That the marriage fell apart.

We kiss for what seems like hours. I feel a kind of excitement— real, genuine physical excitement, like I can't remember feeling since my early twenties.

He tells me his ex-wife and he still live in the same house to take care of their autistic daughter. I say, "Are you sure you're not married anymore?"

He says, "It would be a pretty complicated story to make up, don't you think?"

I say, "Are you over it?"

Kieran is looking straight ahead of him. "It took me a while to get my head around it," he says. And then he turns and peers at me with those eyes. "But my head's around it now, girl. Believe me. My head's around it."

I walk him back to work. Everywhere, he points things out, especially when we get to Temple Bar.

"See that there, that's the children's art center. We work with the kids there." And, "That's the Temple Bar Music Centre, where we met last night." And when we pass a public square: "See this here, girl? We helped the city start a farmer's market there."

I think about Josh, ashen-faced and afraid to go outside. When I look at Kieran, I imagine a sunflower unfurling toward the sun.

"Listen," he says. "If I can get out of work early, will you meet for a drink? Will you do that, chick?"

"Yes, Kieran, yes," I say.

After he's gone, I keep walking west. I'm in a daze, but not a foggy daze. I'm in a daze of blazing stars. I am not walking. I am floating. The Universe, or whatever, is inside me.

Wednesday, November 22, 2006
Last night

I don't know if you've ever experienced a crowd of thousands cheering for someone you love, but let me tell you, it is an awesome experience.

When the band takes the stage, the crowd goes completely nuts. There's wild cheering, people clapping their hands over their heads, fists pumping the air, and feet stomping. When Seth comes out right next to the Rock Star, swinging his bass and smiling from ear to ear, which I've never seen him do onstage before, I think I might die of joy. Cecilia and I clutch each other and shout and we both have tears pouring down our faces.

The truth is I barely made it to the show. I'd been in this pub with Kieran called the Palace right on the edge of Temple Bar where Fleet Street's cobblestones meet the zooming three-lane traffic of Westmoreland. The Rock Star had arranged a bus for friends and family of the band to go from the front of the Westin to the show at seven thirty. When Kieran and I stepped outside, I could see it across all those lanes of traffic, which meant there was time for a few more kisses, and then Kieran had all these gifts he'd brought me, which meant I had to kiss him more, and really I just couldn't seem to unwind my arms from around his neck. But then, when we pulled apart, I turned around just in time to see the bus pull into traffic.

I am not kidding, I ran across three lanes of traffic after that bus and down two city blocks, weaving in and out between cars, people staring at me and honking their horns and shouting, and all in three-inch platform shoes and carrying a gift basket's worth of sundry goods. I'd had to pound on the side of the bus and scream and then run in front of it before the driver saw me and paused long enough to let me get in. "Well, there you are," Cecilia had called out. "Impressive," I heard someone mutter. I'd stood there in the bus's stairwell, bent over and panting. My brother would not have been pleased if the bus had arrived without me on it. He is not into drama. And then there it was again—the smile that won't leave my face. Really, I thought, everything is going my way in Dublin.

Anyway, I did make it to the show, and I was hanging out backstage in the greenroom that's set aside for friends and family of the band. We were all drinking beer out of goblet-like glasses and I was telling Cecilia and the keyboard player's wife that I made out with the handsomest man in Ireland last night, and they were filled with envy because they're married and never make out with anyone anymore. At first I'd felt superior and pleased they were jealous, but then I was so happy I couldn't even maintain the snottiness, so I let it drift away and we just stood around beaming at each other.

Then Seth came bursting into the room, such an energy in his step and openness in his eye that I almost couldn't believe it was my brother. Where was his caginess, his reserve? Because let me tell you, as much as I love my brother, he can have a real edge to him. He can be viciously cutting, cold as ice in opposition, ruthless in argument, stiff in the face of emotion, and quietly furious. But now he was none of these things.

"Come with me," Seth said, handing me a laminate to wear around my neck with a picture of the album and my name on it. I followed him down a long corridor. People raced past us talking into headsets, wheeling racks of clothes, pushing huge lights with purple, pink, and blue gels over them. Seth was wearing a black shirt with embroidered red roses over each pocket. He told me the Rock Star gave it to him.

I couldn't stop laughing and neither could Seth.

I had an image of him, aged seven maybe, running toward my father. We were in the hallway outside a concert my father was playing. I hadn't wanted to go. Seth hadn't been able to wait. We saw my father coming down the corridor and Seth's eyes had brightened, the way they are now. But when he ran toward my father, my father ran right past him to me, taking me in a bone-crushing hug. I hadn't looked at him because I could feel his eyes glowing, in that way his eyes glowed at me sometimes. And I'd thought, you don't want his love anyway.

I went for a closer examination of the embroidered roses on Seth's shirt and said, "That's beautiful, Seth. Unbelievable."

Seth introduced me to everyone we passed. I met Billy, the tour manager. Janis, the backup singer. It was all hustle and bustle and energy like electric currents running through the maze of hallways backstage. Gingerly, tentatively, I put my arm around my brother. Gingerly, tentatively, he put his arm around me. And it was like this, arm in arm, that we stepped out of the darkness of the backstage corridors into the bright lights and loud laughter of the greenroom.

Later

I'm sitting here in a little tea shop covered in floral prints and lace doilies, drinking tea from a teacup covered in red roses and preparing myself for Kieran not to show up tonight. I imagine the call to my hotel, the apologies. I imagine him not bothering to call and me waiting as eight becomes nine and nine ten and how I'll be pretending I don't care.

When I saw Kieran at the Palace yesterday, before Seth's show, he'd told me a minor miracle had happened. At lunch, he'd told me he was going to see the Flaming Lips on Saturday, which is now tonight, and how he wished he had a ticket for me but there were none to be had in the whole city.

When I got to the Palace last night, Kieran had kissed me full on the mouth as if we'd been meeting each other in pubs for years. He'd steered me to a table in the back and then went off to buy me a Guinness. When he got back, he said a woman at his office had walked up to his desk with an extra ticket. He said he'd almost fallen out of his chair. Then he took my hands in his. "That ticket is for you, Heather. Will you come with me? Will you go out with me Saturday night?"

I said, "Kieran, do you ever feel that maybe there is a God?"

And Kieran said, "All the time."

I had no idea how to respond to that, so I didn't say anything.

At the Palace, with its stained-glass windows and men in windbreakers drinking beer, Kieran and I held hands. He told me about going to raves in Galway, where he grew up, and about the cliffs and wild ocean of his childhood summers in Connemara. He told me about going hiking by himself for five days in the mountains there after his wife said she didn't love him anymore. He said the rugged countryside, wild ponies, and sharp-edged wildflowers had saved him. He told me that Liverpool was his favorite soccer team. He told me he was hoping to go to West Africa in January to produce a documentary about indigenous music.

"Dublin is my favorite place on the planet," I said.

Then we talked about how evil George Bush was and how Dick Cheney was even eviler.

"Kieran," I said. "If I can get a ticket, do you want to come see my brother's show on Sunday?"

Kieran looked solemn. "I'd be honored."

But suddenly, I got nervous. I thought, what are you doing?

"Kieran," I said. "What if we don't like each other anymore by Sunday?"

Kieran continued looking solemn.

"I don't think there's much chance of that, do you?" he said.

I wondered, will I have such faith from now on?

Kieran's eyes were glowing in that way men's eyes can glow, but suddenly I was aware not just of a conquest but of actual pleasure in his physical presence. The sight of his wrists and forearms protruding from his rolled-up shirtsleeves was giving me that liquefying sensation, like I could have melted right out of my seat onto the floor. He was wearing a dark blue button-down shirt with the top three buttons undone, and I realized I was staring at the triangle of exposed skin at the top of his chest. Then, I couldn't help myself. I lifted my hand and actually placed it there. Kieran closed his eyes. We both breathed out.

"Jesus Christ, girl," Kieran said.

This morning around eleven, Seth and Cecilia and I went to the farmer's market that Kieran had shown me. It wasn't raining. In fact, the sun was hot on our faces. Seth had just rolled out of bed. His hair was still tousled.

"Did you have a good time? Did you enjoy the show? You like it?" Seth asked as we walked over from the Westin. Or sauntered. I should say we sauntered, because really we did. Like Dublin was ours—but not in a mean way.

"It was amazing," I said. I'd already answered these questions on the bus back from the Royal Academy last night, but I was happy to answer again. Seth might not seem like he'd care what other people think, but he's always very solicitous after a show.

At the farmer's market, we admired the abundance of vegetables, fruits, and grains piled almost as high as our heads. We
watched a man shucking oysters beside a table covered with a red-
and-white-checked oilcloth. All the Irish people had rope bags or
straw baskets with them. Seth and Cecilia had their arms around
each other.

I told Cecilia I'd had lunch with her brother before I left. I
dread to think what he's said about me over these last few years.
I don't know if Cecilia and Seth realize I've never met Ben's sons.
God, I hope not. If you're ever tempted to think my brother is hard,
all you have to do is hear him talk about Eli. He dotes on that child.
Dotes. My brother saves his chilliness for adults. He's all warmth
when it comes to children.

"We should all get together when we're back," I said.

I thought, being in a bad marriage turns life into such a lie that
you hide from everyone. You don't want anyone to see what your
life is actually like. But then, when you're out, you stick your head
up and realize there are all these people you've been avoiding who
are probably willing to love you and let you love them if given the
chance.

After the farmer's market, we wandered over to Dublin Castle, where the British presided over the Irish for all those hundreds
of years. I had no idea that Ireland only became independent this
century. I laid my back against the stone walls of the castle and
let the sun warm my face, and thought, you and me, Dublin, you
and me.

Then Seth had to go off for a sound check, Cecilia went back
to the hotel for a nap, and I went off to meet up with Leah. Now
I'm sitting here in this tea shop with the floral prints and lace doilies and soon it'll be time to go back to the hotel and get ready
for tonight—if tonight is actually going to happen. At my feet I
have a bag of stuff I borrowed from Leah, somewhat against my
better judgment—a razor, body scrubs, two kinds of moisturiz-
ers, a face mask, eye cream, and several serums for combating fine

wrinkles and dark spots. I'm thinking when I get back to the hotel I'm going to do it—I'm going to stare the Fates in the eyes, tempt the Universe, risk the wrath of God. I'm going to shave every inch of myself and then exfoliate until I'm just this side of raw. I'm going to slather on moisturizer until my body is soft and dewy and scented like the wind blowing over a distant rose garden. I'm going to powder my nose and make my eyelashes long and black, and primp until there's no hair left to pluck and no blackhead daring to show itself. I will be primped down to the pair of pink mesh panties I just happen to have brought along. I'm putting my new belief system to the test. If he doesn't show up, the joke will be on me.

Thursday, November 23, 2006
Last night

The phone in my room rings at 7:51 p.m. The operator says Kieran O'Shea is in the lobby. I nearly drop to my knees in gratitude.

The look in his eyes when I come into the lobby makes me feel as if little men are doing somersaults in my stomach. Again I think of Josh, gray-faced in our living room, refusing to answer the phone or go outside. I watch Kieran with his sparkling eyes and un-self-conscious movement stride across the lobby to kiss me on the lips. Then he takes my hand. The sensation of my hand slipping into his makes me feel as if I might suddenly weep. I'm overcome with a sense of being cared for, like a little girl with her father— well, not *my* father but some kind of platonic ideal father. Kieran leads me down Westmorland, past Trinity College on the left and the Bank of Ireland on the right, and I'm so happy not to be leading for once and to feel I can actually trust the man I'm following that I find myself entirely mute.

After about a block, Kieran pulls out a perfect joint—half

tobacco, half pot, rolled with a little cardboard filter—and I think, what, have I met my soul mate here?

At Vicar Street, where the show is, people are gathered outside in little clusters, smoking and talking. Kieran seems to know everyone. It's all, "Hiya, girl," and "How's it going?" and kisses on the cheek. He doesn't introduce me around, and I have a horrible second where I think, he *is* separated, isn't he? But it passes because then we're inside and he's ordering me a Guinness and when I try to give him some money, he shoos me away.

"Let me spoil you a little bit," he whispers in my ear. "What do you say, girl?"

I say, God bless you and all of your descendants and all of their descendants, but only in my mind.

Kieran takes me by the hand and leads us out of the bar, back through the crowded lobby, and into the music hall, which is already packed from the front of the stage all the way to the back where the soundman stands.

We dump all of our coats and scarves and sweaters and bags in one of the plush red seats that ring the outside of the floor. Holding my hand, Kieran leads me through the crowd toward the stage. I keep my eyes on the dark curls falling to the nape of his neck. I think, Heather, pay attention, because this is one of the best times of your life.

And then just as we're saying, okay, this is a good spot, isn't it? Should we stay here?—the room goes dark. There's about a second of silence as if everyone were holding their breath—then, bam, the room explodes in a phantasm of whirling red lights and soaring music and everyone crying out all at once and lifting their hands in the air. There's a beautiful man onstage with an amazing head of just-going-gray hair and a sharp white suit with blood splattered on it. He's got what looks like a papier-mâché grenade launcher on his shoulder, and when he aims it at the ceiling and pulls the trigger, long streams of confetti come pouring down on the audience. People dressed like glittering Martians are flocking out of the wings onto the sides of the stage. They're dancing as if the party's already at its peak and singing through bullhorns. They're tossing plastic balls into the air that are translucently pale and nearly weightless like bubbles blown through a kid's bubble ring. They fly high into the air in slow-motion arcs of shimmering pale color from one pair of outstretched hands to another. My beer glass fills with brightly colored shards of confetti.

Behind me I can hear Kieran laugh this fantastic loose laugh, and I turn to see him moving in this fantastic liquid way. *Exquisite*, writes itself in my mind. I feel I am living in a series of crystallized moments, as if each one contains all life has to offer. I am not a body; I am moving energy. I am as open and wide and free as the galaxy. I feel like the past has disappeared and why would I even worry about the future? I'm in *this* moment, and it is the most beautiful moment, and I don't care what anyone says.

I put my hands on Kieran's shoulders and stand up on tiptoe so my mouth is against his ear.

"I'm happy, Kieran. I'm happy. Do you feel it too?"

Kieran stops dancing and brings his face level to mine. He's peering at me, and I'm running out of adjectives to describe his eyes. They're bright, they're glowing, they're sparkling, they're intelligent, they're familiar, they're sensitive, they're emotive, they have light pouring out of them. You choose. You pick. Imagine it however you want. I don't care. "It's strange like I can't even explain," he says. "It feels so right that you're here." And he pulls me to him in such a tight embrace that I almost can't breathe. We stand together like that while the crowd dances around us.

Then we're dancing again too. And the confetti is pouring down. Kieran's got his hands around my waist. On a screen at the back of the show, enormous robots are battling enormous Japanese schoolgirls in tiny skirts. I've got my hands around Kieran's waist. A woman dressed like Wonder Woman comes out and shakes her glittery bottom at the audience. Kieran lights another joint, passes it to a group of guys standing near us. They offer us gum, and do we want a pint, they're just off to get one, no, but thanks, ta-ta.

Then the show is almost over. The room gets quiet and the man in the white suit is talking. This is what he says: He says, look, I want to be serious for a minute. I want everyone in the audience to do something. I want you to turn to the person you came with tonight. I don't care if this person is a friend, someone you just met, or your wife. And it might feel awkward or strange or whatever, but do it anyway. Turn to the person you came with and say I love you. Because it's true. Right now, at this moment, you love this person.

This is not happening, I think. Then, this is the Universe making a point.

Unfortunately, this is not a novel or a movie, and I don't have even the beginning of the nerve to throw myself at Kieran and cry, "I love you!" The truth is I turn around and bury my face in his armpit.

"What do you think, girl?" Kieran whispers in my ear. "Is two days too soon?"

I lift my head out of his armpit. "Kieran," I say. "Do you get the feeling that we're being set up here—I mean by, like, some sort of God-like being?"

Kieran doesn't say anything but he picks me up so that my feet are dangling above the ground. The most beautiful song I've ever heard in my life starts to play. "Do you realize that you have the most beautiful face," the man in the white suit sings. "Do you realize that happiness makes you cry. Do you realize that everyone you know someday will die . . ." I'm not good with lyrics but I catch these lines. And I know that henceforth this will be my favorite song of all time. Kieran and I hold each other and kiss. And you know how it is—all the people around us fade into a distant blur.

The VIP party, which Kieran has passes for, isn't much of a much. When it becomes clear no actual Lips are going to show I say, "Let's blow this pop stand."

In an after-hours club we huddle together over pints and bread with tapenade. I reach up and touch an angry red scratch Kieran's got on his forehead. It's from his younger daughter, the autistic one.

"I tried to get the little thing from behind when she wasn't expecting me," Kieran says.

We talk about autism. About separation. About the fact that Kieran's ex-wife is a writer too. We talk about the destruction of the planet (he's the director of an ocean conservation nonprofit in his spare time) and then back to the evilness of Dick Cheney. I tell Kieran about taking ballet when I was a kid and how I wanted to be a ballerina. He tells me that he wanted to study literature in college but there were only scholarships for business, so he did that instead. We talk about my being Jewish, which Kieran finds hilarious, because he's never known any Jews before, which I in turn find hilarious, because how could you go through life without knowing any Jews?

Finally we head back to the Westin. Up in my room, I pull open the French doors to show Kieran the view. We look out together over Westmoreland Street and the roofs of Temple Bar. It's dark except for the streetlights and a pale glimmer of moon, its beams muted by clouds. Kieran has his arms wrapped around my waist and his head buried in my neck.

"Let me show you the duplex," I say, and take his hand as we start up the stairs. But we don't make it to the top. It must be the sight of my new-and-improved ass in those skinny jeans, because Kieran grabs me from behind and the next thing I know our lips are pressed together, and he's on top of me on the second-floor landing while our legs dangle down the stairs. My top comes off. His top comes off. The feel of his skin on mine is like a revelation.

I kick off my shoes. He tears open my belt and pulls off the skinny jeans. He's kissing me all over my chest and belly, his shoulder blades rising up above me, his long hair falling over his face and against my skin. Then, "Come on," and he takes my hand and leads me back downstairs to bed.

Thirteen years and two weeks ago, I ran off from a Halloween party with Josh Reed. What happened that night was like nothing I'd ever experienced before. In high school and college, everyone had been all sex, sex, sex. I'd been fine with kissing, but as soon as hands started getting up in each other's business I always found it pretty disgusting. I was always doing it because *he* wanted to—whoever the he of the moment was. But then I'd run off with Josh from that party and, what can I say, there was nothing gross about it. I remember it was as if a golden light had been shining down on us. Wherever he touched me felt beautiful. I'm sure you've had a night like this at least once in your life, so you know what I'm talking about. The hands on the clock cease ticking, boundaries blur.

This is how it feels with Kieran on my big bed at the Westin. It's all golden light. I'm so turned on I feel faintly nauseated. We're kneeling together by the headboard and Kieran puts a finger inside me. "You're so wet," he breathes. "Jesus, girl." And I *am* wet—soaking, running-down-my-legs wet. I don't know whether to laugh or cry because, God damn it, the machinery is working!

"I can't let you leave Dublin without making love to you," Kieran says. "It's too beautiful what's happening here, don't you see."

Every time he says something like this, I feel as if I were a little plant, an African violet maybe, being showered with rainwater.

And then I have the most extraordinary feeling, as if my body actually wants him. It's like I can feel myself expanding to include him. You have to understand, for as long as I can ever remember, except those very early days with Josh, I've always associated sex with a terrible chafing feeling, as if my body were rejecting the other person without me having any say in the matter. But with Kieran it feels so natural I start to lose track of there being two of us.

Kieran pulls back the covers. "I need a whole night just to look at you," he says. "Beautiful girl. Beautiful, beautiful girl."

I am an African violet showered with rainwater.

We hold each other tightly and rock back and forth.

We whisper together. Little questions, little bits about our lives. Kieran tells me about his mother, a beautiful woman with jet-black hair like his own. She'd called him her "black-haired beauty," because of all her six children, he was the only one to come out Black Irish like her. She was depressive, he says. There'd been heavy drinking and chain-smoking, endless days of silence, followed by weeks then months in bed. Then lung cancer. Kieran tells me how he'd been with her while she lay dying, holding her hand, no one else in the room with them. He says he'd never felt so alone and sad again in his whole life until his daughter got sick and there was nothing he could do to make her better.

I hold him as close as I possibly can.

Then we're having sex again, this time with even more intensity. Suddenly I want to stop. "Kieran, if we do this, I'll be too vulnerable. I'll be sad when it's time for me to leave."

"Then we won't. Jaysus, I don't want to do anything to make you sad."

I've been dying of thirst in the desert and Kieran is a pool of cool water.

We whisper together again. I tell him that leaving Josh was the hardest thing I'd ever done. I tell him how my mother was so depressed when I was growing up she hardly got out of bed for a year. There are things I don't tell him, but I tell him more than I've told anybody since my early days with Josh.

Kieran holds me close, and we wonder at the miracle of having found one another—just on a dance floor.

The early morning light is already streaming in through the French doors when we fall asleep, our limbs entangled, our faces pressed together, our lips just barely touching.

In the shower the next morning, Kieran asks if he can wash my hair. It makes me feel shy. I don't think anyone but my mother has ever washed my hair except at the hairdresser. I have that feeling again of being a child—but a loved and well-kept one. We're in the shower for ages, and neither of us can stop laughing, although neither of us is saying anything particularly funny.

Kieran dries me off with one of the Westin's enormous white towels. We're looking at each other in the bathroom mirror, both of us with huge smiles. "My God, your eyes," he says, bringing his face down next to mine. "And your smile. You have the most beautiful smile, girl. Do you know that?"

Kieran rubs the towel over my head, tousling my hair. Then he stops and gently brushes a few loose strands back from my face, peering at me in the mirror. "This image," he says, "of your eyes shining at me—this is an image I'll have with me for a long time, I think."

He is beaming at me like he loves me.

Kieran has tickets to a soccer game and while we get dressed, I lobby to be taken along.

"No tickets, girl," he says.

"Then don't go," I say.

"Can't do that, chick."

I pout.

"Do you see me pouting here?" I say.

"I do, girl. It suits you. You have a beautiful pout, like a princess."

On the way to breakfast, we run into Bob the drummer. I'm so flustered to be caught with wet hair in the company of a strange Irishman who also has wet hair, and so worried what my brother will say if this gets back to him, that I forget Kieran's name.

"This is, um, ah . . ." I say. But his name will not come to me. Bob the drummer looks at me expectantly but the name of the man with whom I've been up all night having sex has escaped my mind entirely. Finally, mercifully, Bob excuses himself.

"Jeez, thanks a lot," Kieran says to me when we walk on. But he's not really mad. In fact, in another block he's nearly doubled over laughing.

"Oh, shut up, you," I say.

We eat at a little shop in an open market in a Victorian glass-covered atrium. All the tables are full so we sit at a bar that runs along one side of the room. Kieran knows the guy behind the counter. The guy behind the counter brings us mugs of coffee, on the house.

"Cheers, mate," Kieran says.

We each take a stool, our knees touching. Kieran orders an Irish breakfast, which turns out to be ham, sausage, eggs, and fried mushrooms. I have the banana pancakes.

"I'm still pouting here," I say.

"I see that, princess."

"I don't really approve of this whole running off to soccer games while I'm in town," I say.

"Don't you?" He kisses me and then picks up a copy of the *Irish Times* lying on the bar.

I begin to brood.

"Kieran?"

"Yes?" He lifts his eyes over the top of the paper.

"I'm feeling serious," I say.

"Why's that, girl?"

I push the pancakes around on my plate.

"This whole thing, it's just been so . . ." But I really don't know what it is I want to say.

Kieran puts down the paper. He keeps eating, but he's looking right at me, and I can tell I have his attention. His manner is so gentle, so patient, that I find myself thinking how lucky his kids are.

"This whole thing," I say. "I mean, meeting you so randomly, then last night. Then tomorrow, boom, I'll be gone. I just don't know what to make of it."

"This isn't random," Kieran says.

I'm not sure what he means so I don't say anything.

"Don't you see?" Kieran says. "God put us on that dance floor so we'd meet each other—so we could give each other a helping hand in these black times."

The words "helping hand" offend me a little bit. Don't you

mean so we could fall madly and hopelessly in love? But I'm intrigued by the rest of it. God. There He is again.

Kieran continues. "Don't you see? What happened last night—that's not just a physical thing. That's a spiritual thing."

I'm thinking, Jesus Christ, you are the most wonderful man I've ever met in my life. And then, spiritual, what does that even mean? What is he talking about? And then, maybe spiritual is the golden light.

"Okay," I say. "But tomorrow I'm just gone. What does that mean?"

Kieran is firm, although not in the least worked up.

"We'll see each other again," he says, and bobs his head in an affirmative nod.

I prop my face in my hands, look up into his beautiful eyes.

"What are we going to do?" I say. "Meet on an island in the middle of the Atlantic?" I lean forward and kiss him. "Wanna do that?" I say. "Wanna meet me on an island somewhere?"

"If I have to, yes," Kieran says. He drinks from his cup of tea.

"Kieran, I feel sad," I say. He takes my hand and squeezes it.

"That's okay," he says. "You can feel sad."

And we sit like that, Kieran skimming the paper, me feeling sad, holding hands in a state of silent companionship.

We're running around Grafton Street before Kieran has to go off to his soccer game. I've decided I want a zip-up Liverpool soccer jersey as a souvenir.

We spend an hour running in and out of sporting-goods shops with Kieran's friends texting him the whole time and him muttering, "Patience, lads, patience. I'm on my way." But he keeps not being on his way. Finally, he says, "I *have* to go. I'll be dead if I don't get there with the tickets, girl." And then, after kissing me for a long time on one of the windy side streets off Grafton, "Dear God, you're hard to say good-bye to."

"You'll be at the show tonight, right?" I say.

"I'll be there," he says.

"You promise?"

"I promise, girl."

When the show starts at eight, Kieran isn't there.

I keep hold of myself until nine, and then I borrow a friend of Cecilia's cell phone and call him. No answer.

At nine thirty I have waves of humiliation crashing over me because I told Cecilia he was coming and she keeps wondering aloud what could have happened to him.

At ten I'm fighting back tears. I'm trying to pretend this isn't happening.

Around ten thirty Cecilia stops asking where he is.

By eleven: You're so stupid, Heather. You're so fucking stupid.

When the show ends, I try to run away. I don't want anyone to look at me. Before Cecilia and her friend are even out of their seats, I'm halfway up the aisle and out of our section. Then I hear Cecilia's friend calling out to me. "There's someone on the phone for you," he's saying.

I run back down the stairs and grab it out of his hand.

It's Kieran.

I'm debating whether to pretend I don't care or let him have it.

"Where are you?" he says.

"Where am *I*?" I say. "Where are *you*?"

"I'm not sure," he says, sounding a little confused. "By some escalators. In the lobby, maybe?"

I shove the phone back at Cecilia's friend, run through the balcony and out the double doors that lead to the escalators. When I see him, just standing there, looking all around him, I find that I have to run as fast as I possibly can and throw myself into his arms.

"Shhhh," he says. "I'm here, girl. I'm here."

Billy the tour manager accidentally put Kieran in the seat that would have been next to mine except it was all the way across the auditorium on the other balcony.

Oh, Universe, I think. Thank you. Thank you.

I ride back to the Westin with Kieran. I have my arms around his neck and he is leaning over to kiss me anytime he dares take his eyes off the road and probably a few times when he shouldn't. I feel like I'm in *The Year of Living Dangerously*, which I must have watched twenty-five times as a young teenager. I'm thinking of the scene where Sigourney Weaver finally runs off with Mel Gibson past curfew and they smash through a checkpoint in Indonesia. Bullets fly but they don't care, because Sigourney Weaver has slid herself right beside Mel and is kissing him all over his face and neck while he grins and closes his eyes and tries to kiss her back without running them off the road. They have completely given in to the weight of an enormous and unexpected passion. This is what it feels like driving back to the Westin, though admittedly without the bullets.

"So what's the scoop, kids? You guys boyfriend and girlfriend?" It's Richie the trumpet player in a loose Hawaiian shirt. We're at the bar in the basement of the Westin and I'm introducing Kieran around to the guys in the band. "He sure is good-looking, Heather," Richie says, pointing at Kieran. "Hold on, is this the reason you're in Dublin, or is this a just-met situation? What's the story, Kieran? You coming to New York or what?"

Kieran and I look at each other and then the floor.

"No problem, I got it," Richie says. He gives me a bear hug and shakes Kieran's hand. "Enjoy. God bless."

Seth comes in and the three of us have a drink together. Seth invites us out to dinner with Cecilia and the rest of the band, but we stay because we want to be alone. Kieran makes me promise I will say the words "I don't love you anymore" to Josh. He says it's the best thing I can do. It feels wonderful to promise him something.

"Kieran, my black-haired beauty."

We're lying together on my big bed.

"I love you calling me that," Kieran whispers.

I kiss his ear. "I want to tell you something," I say. "But I don't want you to take it the wrong way."

The thing I want to tell Kieran has to with this Rilke poem I was thinking about while he was at his soccer game. The poem says something to the effect that life is a string of pearls. The idea is that the pearls are precious moments collected throughout your lifetime that will be with you on your deathbed—only, trust me, Rilke says it a lot more poetically. I was thinking about this poem, and what the Flaming Lips guy said, and all these perfect moments I've been having lately. I was imagining telling my girlfriends about Kieran and how they were going to pepper me with questions: Are you going to see him again? What's next? What now? Thinking about this was making me feel kind of infuriated, like, why can't a beautiful lightning-strike of intimacy and joy be enough? Why do I have to dump the whole crushing weight of the future on it? I'll never see Kieran again. I know that. But maybe that's okay. That's what I've been thinking while Kieran was at his soccer game. And when I thought it, when I let go of him in my mind, I felt buoyed up into the atmosphere and filled with joy.

Anyway, the only way I can make sense of these feelings, which I know all of my friends will say is crazy, is to think about Rilke's pearls.

"Kieran," I say. My voice sounds tinny in my own ears, quivering slightly. I'm looking at the headboard rather than him. "I don't think things have to go on forever to have meaning."

Kieran props himself up on his elbows and looks down at me, even as I continue staring at the headboard. "Okay," he says. He sounds trepidatious, like he's steeling himself for something painful.

I steel myself to say, for once, what I really want to say. I tell him about the pearls. Then I say, "I don't actually think it matters if we see each other again. But the guy at the show was right. Right now, at this exact moment, I love you."

There's a second where it's as if Kieran and I are frozen, and then I feel what seems like a sob from Kieran's chest. The arm that was holding him up collapses. He's got the back of my head in the palm of his hand, crushing me against him. "I never in a million years would have found the words," he's whispering. "I feel the same, Heather. I feel exactly the same." Well, then, say it back, I think. But only for a second, because he's holding me so tightly and whispering over and over in my ear: "Thank you. Thank you."

Kieran has to go. He and his ex-wife have a deal that neither of them will spend the night away from the house as long as they're still living under the same roof. She was at her mother's with the kids last night, which is why he was able to stay with me—timing he took as another sign from God. I took it as a sign that he's way too concerned what his stupid ex-wife thinks. I hold my hands behind my back so I won't be tempted to grab him and beg him to stay. He stands at the door for what seems like ages, rubbing his face with his hands and looking neither handsome nor unhandsome, but just like a man who's been running on no sleep and is at the end of his tether. His face is pained. He keeps saying, "I don't want to say good-bye to you." So I'm brave for both of us. I open the door and say, "Good-bye, Kieran." And finally he says, "I will be talking to you very soon, girl," and he slips away.

When Les the percussionist leaps behind the bar and starts serving drinks, Seth figures it's as good a time as any to get going.

I've joined Seth et al at a pub called O'Donoghue's on the edge of St Stephen's Green. There's a sign over the front door with a fiddle on it and "Guinness" written out in gold letters, as if announcing a secret entranceway to good times.

The guys in the band are playing and singing with the regulars. Everyone in the place is dancing. Fans are snapping pictures with their cell phones; the regulars are singing with their mouths wide open and their eyes shut tight. The bartenders—two middle-aged men in collared shirts and ties—are standing on stools behind the bar and waving their arms in the air.

When one of the regulars, a man who looks to be easily eighty years old, stands up and sings "Dirty Old Town" with John the fiddle player accompanying him and everyone in the whole place joining in on the chorus, I have the feeling that I didn't know my heart could hold so much joy. Seth and I are sitting at the bar downing pints that the bartenders insist on sending us. Seth is keeping time with his hand on his knee, and I'm just thinking, I've never been so happy my whole life as in Dublin.

We head out around 2:30 a.m. for Chinese food. We walk along the edge of St Stephen's Green, our steps echoing on the cobblestones, the faintest rain coming down on us, more like mist than rain at all. Keith the mandolin player is with us. Seth and Cecilia have their arms around each other.

"You should see my sister's suite," Seth says to Keith the mandolin player over broccoli with garlic sauce and hot-and-sour soup. "It's far nicer than anything the rest of us have."

Seth's gotten a big kick out of the George Bernard Shaw Suite, which fills me with pride, as if I'd gotten the suite through some merit of my own.

Keith says, "I can't believe the tour is ending tomorrow. I'm going to need a therapist when I get home. How do we go back to real life?"

I think, poor guy, he doesn't understand.

"This is real life," I say.

Keith turns and stares at me like I'm either crazy or stupid. "I'm not kidding here," he says. "This is the happiest I've ever been in my life."

I want to share my wisdom with him. "Nothing lasts, you know, but it's okay that it doesn't."

Keith glares at me.

"Maybe Dublin's not a city," I say. "Maybe it's a state of mind."

We leave the restaurant at almost four in the morning. The streets are empty.

Seth says, "You glad you came, Heath?"

He's on one side of me, and Cecilia is on the other. Keith, who apparently I've alienated very badly, is trailing behind us.

"Seth, you have no idea," I say.

I invite Seth and Cecilia up to the George Bernard Shaw Suite for a drink.

Seth bobs his head. "Now you're talking," he says.

Up in the suite, I pour the Jameson and Seth lights the fire. The wood crackles and the walls glow with the reflected flames.

An hour later, Seth is telling us about visiting the Alhambra in Granada. I'm thinking, love. *Love*. LOVE. I had no idea there was so much love in the world. Then I realize I'm going to miss my plane. As I'm running around scrambling to get my stuff together, I'm filled with such feelings of hope like I don't remember since probably the day I got married.

Friday, November 24, 2006

On the flight from Dublin to Shannon, where I have a stopover, I'm stuck beside a couple who is bickering, viciously, in long-term-relationship shorthand. I don't know the meaning of the little bits they throw at each other, but they sure do. His mouth twitches. Hers tightens. Relationships are like life, I think. The end is inevitable, built into the essence of the thing itself. I'm glad I'll never see Kieran again, I think, because I couldn't bear the day when I looked over and realized I hated him.

Pride in my good judgment sustains me all the way to Shannon.

There's a twenty-minute layover in Shannon before the plane is ready to take us back to New York. I take a seat in a small circular waiting area marked "Gate 18," surrounded by about twenty other passengers. A stewardess in a tight-fitting navy-blue uniform crosses the waiting area and takes up her post next to the gate. She opens the doorway and I see down a long passageway. It's dark, and I can't see the end of it.

It's like something clamps itself around my heart.

I think, You're glad you're never going to see Kieran again? Dublin is a state of mind? Are you high?

I look down that passageway and I shudder at how it seems to have no end.

The clamp around my heart tightens.

Oh my God, it's all been bullshit. Pearls? The meaning of life in the moment? The future doesn't matter? The universe is filled with love? It's like I was brainwashed by some horrible New Age cult. What happened to me? How could I have believed such crap? Me, who has always been so sensible.

I realize that the minute I step onto that plane and it takes off into the air, Dublin will be over. It will be in the *past*. It already *is* the past.

It's as if something cold passes over me—it feels like a sidewise glimpse at death. What was I thinking? I can't leave Dublin. I can't leave Kieran. Going home will be like living without the sun after having learned what it's like to bask in its warmth. Surely no one could expect that of a person.

There's a phone bank in the middle of the waiting area. I run to it. With fingers that are trembling, I punch in Kieran's number. An automated Irish-accented voice says my call can't go through. I dial again. It's my credit card. I bang the receiver against the phone. I dial again. "Fucking work!" I cry.

"We're sorry," says the Irish-accented voice. "This call cannot go through."

I empty my purse out on the floor. I'm searching for coins. But I have no coins. Only a ten-euro note.

I stand up, turn to the room at large. "Does anyone have change?" I shout. People look up from their seats, startled. I've got the ten-euro note in the air over my head. Public spectacle is not my usual modus operandi, but I must speak to Kieran again or I will not walk down that passageway with no end.

Not a person offers me anything. They just stare. I start jogging in a loop around the phone bank, crying out, while still trying to maintain some level of respectability, "Excuse me, excuse me, might you have change?"

Finally, a lady in a pink sweater vest takes mercy on me and extends a handful of euros.

I lunge at the phones again, praying. I dial. I hear ringing. Then, "Hullo?"

I close my eyes. "Oh thank God," I say.

"Jesus," Kieran says. "I've been trying to reach you at the hotel all morning, chick. I can't stop thinking about you. My mind is reeling. I'm completely spun. Heather, I have to tell you . . ."

"Yes, yes . . ."

And the phone goes dead. Kieran's voice is gone and instead there's a dial tone buzzing in my ear. And now it won't accept my euros. I try two, three times. I bang the receiver hard against the wall. I have tears streaming down my face.

I dial again. Please, God, I'm thinking. Please.

Finally, finally he answers, and it's like my legs go out. I slide down to the floor, my back against the phone bank, the receiver clutched against my ear. Kieran is talking, and one by one, people are disappearing down the passageway to the plane.

"Girl, I never thought I could feel anything again."

There are only three people left at the gate.

"Kieran," I cry. "I feel like I can't go back to New York!"

There is horrible crackling on the line.

"I know, girl," he says. I hear him as if from far away. "I know!"

"I need you to tell me something, Kieran. Please. Even if it's not true, I need you to say it. Tell me I'm going to see you again!"

There is one person left in line. The stewardess is squinting at me.

"I promise you will see me again," Kieran says. "I'll meet you on an island in the middle of the Atlantic. Will you do that, chick? Will you meet me on an island somewhere?"

I am nodding, *yes, yes, yes*, and the tears are flowing down my face and into the collar of my jacket.

There's no one left at the gate. The stewardess's squint has turned into a scowl.

"We'll find a way. We have to," he says. "You'll see, beautiful girl. It's all going to work out for us."

Then, softly, "Good-bye, Kieran."

"Good-bye, beautiful girl."

When I hang up the phone, my heart is beating in wild,

tremulous beats, but no longer with fear. *Beautiful girl, beautiful girl.* It echoes in my ears all the way to the gate. The stewardess snatches the ticket out of my hand, but what do I care? I run down the long corridor and onto the plane. Everyone is already in their seats. Everyone is staring at me, but what do I care? I have a huge smile on my face. God, or the Universe, or whatever, is in my chest again. It's all going to be okay. Kieran has told me so.

BOOK THREE
CRASH

Sunday, November 26, 2006

Hello? Are you still out there? Reader. Whoever you are. Are you sick of me yet?

It's two thirty in the morning and I'm drunk. Can you tell? I don't even like to drink. I never was a drinker before this whole thing started. And now here I am, the bottle of whiskey before me, not quite ladling it down my throat, but not that far off either.

I'm listening to the Flaming Lips. I downloaded everything the minute I got home.

I'm so confused. I feel like love and death, the beauty of this world and its horror, are pushed up so close to my face I can't see clearly. I can't breathe.

Do you realize—that you have the most beautiful face. Do you realize—that everyone you know, someday, will die.

Monday, November 27, 2006

There's a strangely festive air at the hospital.

Seth and I go down the long hallways past whiteboards, nurses with stethoscopes around their necks, and patients slumped in wheelchairs against the wall. Everybody is gathered in a small private room. Every surface is covered with food—half-eaten roasted chickens and sides of green beans in plastic to-go containers from Fairway. A paper bag folded back with bagels inside. Boxes of coffee from Starbucks. I remember this from when Gabriel got shot. When tragedy strikes, what is there to do but offer food?

Everybody is talking at the top of their voices. We can hear the din as we come around the corner.

I remember all this from when Gabriel got shot too. All these people who love each other gathered together in a small place, no energy for grudges or faking it or trying to impress. Everybody stripped raw, pretenses left at the door. Everybody's outer shell blasted off by the awe of the unspeakable happening. Everybody building a protective bubble of caring around the survivors. Yes, I've seen this before, I think. And you know what else? I've seen what happens when the awe wears off. When the unspeakable becomes just another fact to live with. I've seen what happens when all the friends and family go home. When people mutate into other versions of themselves. I find myself wanting to scream.

Later

I drive Seth back to Brooklyn from Valhalla, where everyone is going to be camped out for a while.

He hasn't been home in six months. He stepped off the Rock Star's private plane and onto the tarmac at JFK, put on his sunglasses, grabbed his cell, and found seventeen frantic phone calls from Cecilia.

The Seth before me does not even resemble the man I was with in Dublin three days ago. This man has skin that seems to have turned ashen and eyes that seem to have sunk into their sockets. They look as if they're surrounded by freshly made bruises. His shoulders are slumped. *Exhausted* isn't even the right word.

"Seth, you need to get some sleep," I say. He stares at me blankly, and it feels as if someone is hitting me in the chest with a sledgehammer. I think, I would do anything to spare him this.

There's something in my brother's eyes I've never seen before. And suddenly I think, he knows now. He knows now just how badly the world will betray you. I have a flash of self-pity as I think, I've always known this. Now we're even.

Seth is looking around vaguely, like he's seeing so many different things at once he can't focus. This is trauma, I think—when your whole world changes from one second to the next, so fast that the change causes a fracture in your brain, just like a bad fall can cause a fracture to your bones. The fracture is the delineated mark between what your world was and what it is now. The fracture is your mind breaking because it can't compute the disparity between the two worlds.

Seth wants to pay for a car service to take me home. I let him so that he won't feel I've gone too far out of my way, which I know he'd hate.

In the car, I put my head onto my knees. I think, I feel it too. Even though I have no right to. My brain can't compute how last week and this week could exist in the same universe.

It's Ben Green who's been struck. Less than two weeks ago we sat across from each other and made plans to get together when I was back from Dublin. I was going to redeem myself by meeting his sons.

All I have to offer are the facts: While Seth and Cecilia and I were all flying back from Dublin, the Greens were driving to their place upstate. Ben was at the wheel. A swerve to the right, a correction to the left. The tiniest of actions. Took a fraction of a second. And now? Now his wife is in a coma. And Eli, his three-year-old son, is dead.

Tuesday, November 28, 2006

Kieran, can I tell you just one thing? I don't know who else to tell. When I first heard? When my brother said, in that horrible gentle voice that people use when they're about to tell you something terrible, when I picked up my phone and he said, "I have some bad news," you know what went through my mind? Nothing. I mean nobody. Josh Reed, my partner of thirteen years, never even entered my consciousness. It was Seth I was on the phone with so I knew he was safe. I had no instinctual pull to anybody. All I thought was, no, I've been so happy.

Kieran, please don't abandon me. I know it's a terrible thing to do to someone, but you hold all light in your hands.

I was at Katy and Mac's house when my brother called. No, I wasn't just at their house. I was dancing a jig at their house. I was dancing a jig right there on their living room rug, with the Pogues blasting and the morning sunshine streaming in the windows.

I was telling them about Kieran and doing his accent. Katy kept saying, "Oh my God, Heather, you're giving me the shivers."

I was telling them about going backstage with my brother and how nice to me Cecilia and he had been.

I said, "Dublin is the best place in the world."

I'd taken Mac by the shoulders and said, "Your grandfather was wrong, dude. The Universe *does* give a shit, if you just open yourself to it."

And I won't tell you my cell rang at that exact moment, because that would be a lie. But it was close enough. Close enough.

I almost didn't answer. But then I thought, what if it's Kieran? And then I saw it was my brother. But then his voice was so gentle. And he said, "I have some bad news." And I thought, no, no, no.

Mac and Katy and I huddled together. They've known Ben and Marie as long as I have. Katy and I sat on the couch, so close our legs were touching. Mac sat on the coffee table in front of us. We wept. I imagined some ancient tribe while a powerful thunderstorm struck, the kind that ripped up crops and knocked over trees, that set the sky ablaze with lightning and made the earth seem to shake with thunder. They wouldn't have known what thunder was or why lightning happened, or when it would end, or *if* it would end. They would have wondered if it was some kind of punishment, personal and pointed, a rebuke for having done something or for not having done something. Perhaps they'd pissed off the gods because they'd forgotten about them for five minutes. They would have prayed and tried to think of a way to appease these impossible-to-know-or-predict gods. And they would have been afraid because here was something they could never, ever understand. Because just five minutes ago, it had been sunny.

As we sat there huddled together, I looked at Katy but not at Mac, even though it's Mac I've known since before I was born. I felt if I looked into those eyes, which I know so well, the sight of the knowledge in them would break me. Mac is like me. He knows that the things everyone fears but think will never happen actually happen all the time.

I thought, please, God. Please don't have done this. I'll do anything. But there's no bargaining with the Universe. Its actions are irrevocable. And the very minute you let your guard down, the spring you decide not to sacrifice the goat or the virgin because the weather has been so beautiful surely it's not necessary to spill all that blood—that's the season the storm will come and wreck your crops and leave you starving.

We sat there like that all day, shivering as if we were cold, getting steadily drunker, Katy weeping, Mac and I not looking at each other, and me thinking, Ben, Marie, Seth, Cecilia. If I could take you all back in time, I would. And you, Universe—I rage against you.

Thursday, November 30, 2006

I talked to Kieran on the phone last night and it was terrible. His accent is completely insurmountable international cell to cell. I so badly wanted to tell him about the accident and have him comfort me. But he was putting his kids to bed and his "ex-partner," as he calls her, was coming up the stairs. He started whispering and then there was no chance whatsoever that I could understand him let alone be bathed in comfort. Today is Thursday. Last Thursday I was on the phone with him and we couldn't stop laughing and he kept saying, "I'm spun, chick, completely spun." He was texting me nonstop. I know he has his life to live. But could he really have forgotten me in a week? Did he get back together with his ex-wife?

I know it's a terrible thing to do to a person, but without you, Kieran, there is only darkness.

Friday, December 1, 2006

Ben's younger son, Alex, is not yet one. He doesn't talk, although he does gurgle a lot. I'm taking care of him now, because all the Greens and their closest friends are up at the hospital in Valhalla where Marie is still in a coma. Ben and Cecilia's mom has brought Alex over to her apartment in the Lower East Side on Fourth Street between First and Second Avenues, and it's there I go to take care of him. Everyone at the hospital cried and hugged me when I said I'd do this, which I found highly embarrassing. Being able to actually help, as opposed to just standing around helpless—they're giving me a gift.

Alex has soft red curls like his father and slightly bewildered blue eyes. I don't know if this is due to the fact that last week he was breast-feeding and now he's got a stranger handing him a bottle or if that's how he's always looked. We sit together in his grand-mother's living room, the walls filled with photographs. There's a picture of a handsome man who looks like Cecilia, who I imagine is their father. He died when they were little. Had a heart attack one day, just like that. I bet they all thought they were inoculated from further tragedy. But the math starts all over again every day, doesn't it?

Everywhere there are pictures of Ben and Marie with Eli and

Alex. They look so healthy and happy, like they could be in a commercial for yogurt or health insurance. There's a picture of Ben and Marie at their wedding. She was already hugely pregnant with Eli. Her face is away from the camera, her head on Ben's chest. Ben's got his arms wrapped tightly around her, his head resting on the top of her head. It's like they don't know anyone else is there.

I remember that wedding for my own reasons. I remember I was talking to some friend of theirs, an English guy, I have no idea now who it was. But I remember having this really easy, enjoyable conversation and thinking, this guy is so cute. This guy is so nice. I had the sense that it was *him* standing before me, not him and a dozen suitcases of psychological baggage he was lugging around. And it had hit me, this is the kind of guy you're supposed to marry. The nice guy. The guy without the suitcases. Josh? Josh is the guy you have an affair with and then never forget. But you don't marry him.

I sit on the floor with Alex while he takes alphabet blocks out of a big Trader Joe's bag and puts them back in. He has a little Mexican rattle he likes to shake. Mostly, I dance around the living room with him on my hip while he coos and laughs and drools. When he's tired, I give him a bottle and lie him down on his grandmother's bed and sing to him until his breath becomes soft and even. I smooth the hair away from his forehead and watch him even after he's fallen asleep.

I didn't know it would be so easy to love a baby.

After Alex goes to bed for the night, I sit with Ben's mom in her little, cramped kitchen. No one has been back to Ben and Marie's apartment since the accident, so she has been buying things for Alex on an as-needed basis. The counters are piled high with boxes of Teddy Grahams and zwiebacks. All day long people come by to visit. They bring lasagnas and roast chickens and elbow noodle salad. I clean up all the coffee cups from all the visitors and tidy Alex's toys.

Ben's mom cries a lot. She shakes when she cries. I don't say anything to her, because really what is there to say. But I sit, and sometimes I hold her hand.

I crawl home. Whiskey. Smoking.

I don't know where the sun beams end and the starlights begin and it's all a mystery.

I can't stop listening to the Flaming Lips. I can't stop hearing Wayne Coyne—I now know the singer was Wayne Coyne—saying, okay, turn to the person next to you, tell them you love them. Because at this moment you do. I close my eyes and try to will myself back a week and a day under the rain of confetti and shimmering balls ricocheting over my head.

Oh, Kieran. I know you think we met for a reason, and you nearly had me believing the same thing. But we didn't, you know. There's no such thing as reason in this world. You and me meeting was as random as Ben's accident. I think life is made up of millions of squiggling variables, all moving and pushing you along in a certain way until some accident, some random occurrence sends you flying onto some other path. Horrible accidents. Beautiful meetings. They're collisions, is all. Random collisions in space.

I feel such rage in me. Fury at the Universe. Fury at myself for believing for even a minute that things could be different.

And when the rage subsides, it's terror. Dread like something creeping up in the middle of the night.

Later

It's almost 3 a.m. I can't sleep. Kieran, I started you a letter. I wrote more than ten pages. Then I started it again and wrote another ten pages. I could write a hundred pages just marveling at your existence.

He said he'd call today, but he didn't. Today marks the first twenty-four hours of no contact. Please don't do this to me, Kieran.

I think, you still have your pearls.

I think, what are you talking about? You die alone. A few hunks of spun sand from an irritated oyster won't make a difference.

Sunday, December 3, 2006

Summer is chopping beets for a kale-and-brewer's-yeast salad. She's crying a little as she chops. We've been talking about Ben. She's known Ben and Marie almost as long as I have.

"What else you gonna add to that salad?" I say to distract her.

"Sesame seeds and pumpkin seeds," she sobs.

"That sounds good," I say.

"Heath?" she says.

"Yes?"

"I'm scared."

I have an image of Summer at fourteen, slim-hipped and flat-chested, a long-legged beauty with acres of white-blond hair in cut-up punk-rock T-shirts. She'd been living with her ex-stepmother after her mother had abandoned her to her father, and then her father had abandoned her in favor of the next-door neighbor. The ex-stepmother reminded her regularly that she wasn't being paid enough to take care of her, and the ex-stepsister drove around in a convertible and dated an outfielder from the Baltimore Orioles while Summer lived in a tiny side bedroom. Quite the Cinderella story. Although so far, no glass slipper and no prince.

I start to cry.

"Summer?"

"Yes?"

"I'm scared too."

Monday, December 4, 2006

Josh calls. News of Ben's accident has reached him out in LA. He says, "Heather, when I first heard, all I could think was thank God it wasn't you."

I think, this man loves me. What have I done? What have I done?

At night, I dream again that I can't find where I live. I know there's a red wall out there and if I can find it, I will be home. But I don't know where home is. I think, wait, if I have a home out there, have I been paying the mortgage on it? Will I be foreclosed on? I can't afford rent and a mortgage.

There are Indian-print bedspreads in this apartment in my dream. The place is filthy. It's the kind of place where people walk around in their bare feet and don't care that their soles are black with grime. It's the commune my father lived on again. This isn't where I live, I think. And then I'm trying to run but I can't even move. Total terror.

Tuesday, December 5, 2006

On the Amtrak down to DC for Eleanor's baby shower. Ben's mom said she'd be okay without me for two days.

Out the window, the leafless trees fly by in the stark winter afternoon light.

Later

I've never seen Eleanor so happy. When she picks me up at Union Station she is laughing so much she has to rest her head on the steering wheel. "Am I not the most pregnant woman you've ever seen in your life?" she keeps asking me. "Am I not? Am I not?" If you let her, Eleanor will ask you the same question five hundred times. It reminds me of the way I felt in Dublin—when I was smiling so much I'd start laughing. Her cup runneth over, I think. And I can't help it, there's a frozen hostility in my chest that leaves me stiff. Why does she have everything while I have nothing, I think.

When we get to the house, she doesn't even take off her coat or let me take mine off. She's pulling me by the hand to show me the baby's room—there's a white crib and little orange and green circular rugs she's placed all over the floor. And she shows me the dressing table, which she says she made her husband sand down and paint white. And he did. That's the part that amazes me—and it hurts, like someone's knocked me in the head. She married a man who when she didn't like the finish on the baby's dressing table, he sanded it down and painted it white for her. Just like that. Just to make her happy.

I go into the bathroom and put my head in my hands. I can't even count the times I've spent getting my shit together in bathrooms at Stein residences. Everyone in Eleanor's family is a novelist, heading a department at some major university, or having a MoMA retrospective. Their homes are filled with awards and Picasso sketches the way other people's houses are filled with magazines. And I've spent time in almost all of their bathrooms trying to compose myself. I still remember going to Eleanor's house for the first time. I was in first grade. The house was clean. The grass was mowed. The family ate dinner together every night. All those years growing up, I thought, why her and not me? See, I always thought Eleanor and I were the same. Twins, she used to say. We could have been sparring partners, except she'd had the best coaches in the world, while I was just in the ring swinging wildly.

And if the self-pity isn't making you hate me, this will.

All those years I was married and Eleanor was so desperate for a husband and children, I actually felt the Universe had evened things out a bit. What a horrible thing to say, but there it is. She's my best friend, and I didn't want her to have everything.

At the shower, I barely talk. I just work. Pile up cucumber sandwiches on Provençal-style plates. Lay out scones and Danishes. Arrange teacups. Eleanor's mom, who I've known forever, is chain-smoking Parliament cigarettes. She's an impressively thin woman in dark-tinted glasses, and modern jewelry. She was just named president of the American Historical Association. Eleanor keeps saying, "Mom, it's 2006, you can't just go around smoking everywhere." But her mother waves her away. Eleanor whispers to me, "Mom went crazy. She spent nine hundred dollars on baby clothes. I told her to take it all back but she said, no way, it was too much fun."

I more think of her mother cooking coq au vin or delivering personal anecdotes about Derrida than shopping for baby clothes. But I guess all mothers long for grandchildren. Eleanor's aunt, in matte red lipstick, a neat black bob, and a herringbone jacket, comes up and they converse momentarily in French.

Our friend Faith comes. I've barely seen her since her second child was born, and that was more than a year ago. She and I were the kids in the after-school program who'd still be there at five, hoping our parents remembered to pick us up. Faith looks terrible. I can't put my finger on it exactly. Not fat, as Faith is the skinniest person in the world, but it's as if she's given herself a layer of insulation. There's something far away in her eyes.

The bags of baby clothes and teddy bears begin to swim before me as Eleanor opens presents. I can't stop thinking about baby Alex. The way he rests his head on my shoulder. His soft breathing when he falls asleep. I think, you will never have a child, Heather. You weren't destined to have the kind of life other people have. I never wanted children, ever. And then one day I thought maybe I did. But then I looked at Josh and realized if I had a baby I'd be taking care of two people for the rest of my life.

Later

At night, in a room with a sign hanging on it saying "The Heather Chaplin Guest Bedroom," I'm not so much asleep as knocked unconscious. It's like I'm buried underground. And I'm sweating, profusely. I can feel it running down my chest, out my head and through my hair, down my legs, over my ass. It's soaking my T-shirt and pajama bottoms. I have to get up, eyes still closed, shivering as I stand in the darkness and peel them off because they are freezing me. I'm shivering as I climb under the blankets. Then I'm dead asleep again, except I can still feel the sweat pouring out of me.

I wake up again around 4 a.m. I have an image of a shotgun in my mind. It's placed against my forehead, and I let myself indulge, for just a minute, in the sense of peace that would come from pulling the trigger. I think, Kieran, why have you abandoned me? I'm in a room with the lights slowly dimming, and soon it will be dark.

There's not enough love in the world to save you now, Heather.

Thursday, December 7, 2006

Back in New York.

Seth and I stop to eat on Delancey Street. Seth can't stop thanking me for taking care of Alex.

"You have no idea what a relief it is to everyone up at the hospital," he says. "Besides, when did you get so good with children? You're a natural."

Praise from my brother! It's like sun on my face. Did Seth think I would let him go through this alone? Seth is doggedly loyal. Did he not know I am too?

Alex is on my lap and I feed him cream cheese and listen to the couple behind us bickering in Russian. Seth reaches across the table and tickles Alex's belly, making him gurgle and grin his single-toothed grin. He drools a little when he smiles, so I dab at the corners of his mouth with my napkin.

"Remember going out to dinner with Zaidie?" I say, inclining my head toward the old Russian couple. "How he'd chew up all his fish and then regurgitate a little pile of bones on his plate?"

Seth tilts his head to one side and raises his eyebrows.

"Or how he'd drink Shirley Temples all through dinner but still end up singing in Yiddish at the top of his lungs?"

"Thanks for reminding me," Seth says.

"Speaking of crazy old men, does your father know what's going on?" I ask.

"No, I don't think so," Seth says. "But I did talk to your mother."

This is how we speak of our parents.

"She'd like to come and help out, but she isn't feeling herself just now," Seth says.

Our mother hasn't been feeling herself for as long as I can remember.

"Count your blessings," I say.

We're on our way to Ben and Marie's apartment. No one has been back since the accident. Seth's whole face sags as we let ourselves in. He touches the mail, runs a hand over the kitchen counter. There are rotting vegetables in the fridge, which we dump into a trash can that's still got trash in it. I remember helping clean out Gabriel's apartment. His razor in the bathroom with bristles still clinging to it. A coffee cup in the sink.

"Come on, Seth," I say. "Let's just grab their stuff and get out of here."

Seth is wandering around the apartment, half looking at things, picking up a magazine in the living room, tossing a pillow from the floor back onto the sofa.

"Seth," I say. His eyes drift to mine. I walk up to him and put my hand on his back, rubbing in a gentle circle. Somewhat to my surprise he doesn't jump away. I nod encouragingly. "Come on," I say. "I'll help you. Just tell me what we need to get."

Has my brother ever let me help him before?

Even though it's only four, it's dark by the time we're back outside on the pavement in front of Seward Tower. Seth gulps the air, runs a hand over his face. "Jesus fucking Christ," he says.

I put my hand on his back again. "I know, dude," I say. "I know."

Later

Tonight, I'm alone in the house. I'm listening to the Wailers. *This train is bound for glory*, they sing. Oh lord, why is it so hard? I feel so weak and ashamed of my own weakness. I don't want to be a quivering, needy female. Look at me, waiting to be saved by some stranger from across the Atlantic. I should be strong and not long for salvation in the darkness of long nights or spring afternoons I can't touch. *This train is bound for glory*, the Wailers sing. Oh, come to me, salvation, I think. I'm weak, I admit it. I want to feel this glory. The glory of your light. I think God only means not feeling alone.

Friday, December 8, 2006

This morning, Ben's mom came home from running errands and just totally broke down, collapsed into her easy chair, her coat still on, her purchases on her lap, sobbing. She said, Go! Go! And I went. I suddenly, desperately, needed to get out of there. Sometimes the depths of this tragedy, the darkness of it, the horror that can't be mitigated no matter how I turn it over in my mind feels like it's sucking the air out of me. So I admit it, I fled. And now I'm sitting in a vegetarian Chinese restaurant on Avenue A listening to the chop, chop, chop of a knife against a butcher's block from somewhere deep in the recesses of the kitchen.

I have this sense today that if I accidentally open my mouth the wrong way, the fury in me would cause all of Avenue A to collapse on itself, buildings falling, people screaming, dust reaching up to the sky. I had this feeling a lot when I was a kid. I remember smashing up the tiles in our bathroom with the head of a shower nozzle. I remember throwing all the books in my room against the wall and shrieking until my throat was sore—all the while hearing the dum-dum-dum of Seth's bass from his bedroom next door, steady as a metronome.

By the time I was a grown-up, it hadn't been like that for a long time. When Josh first yelled at me, I'd almost keeled over in horror. I'd never been in a screaming fight in my life. But the fury leaked out. Let's be honest, it must have. Josh would start screaming, I'd be thinking, I hate you, I hate you, I hate you. But not saying a word, completely impassive, with a look on my face that must have been about as friendly as a visit from the Grim Reaper. And that's a kind of anger too, isn't it? Not speaking. I believe it's called withholding.

Sunday, December 10, 2006

I take care of Alex during the day. I long for Kieran at night. What else is there to say? A three-year-old child has been killed. What else is there to say?

Monday, December 11, 2006

Marie is awake. The doctors have been saying for about a week it was possible. But today it actually happened. And now the doctors are saying there may not be any permanent spinal damage. I spin Alex around the room. He gurgles and I say, "Your mommy is going to come home soon. Will you like that?" But he just looks at me with his implacable stare and one-toothed smile and drools a little.

I never knew it would be so easy to love a baby.

Wednesday, December 13, 2006

Last night I finally went out with the game designer. He's been calling since I got back and I've been putting it off and putting it off. Even tonight as I set out from baby Alex's to meet him, I say in my head, Kieran, are you sure? Is this what you want? Because I don't want it. But I haven't heard from you in twelve days. Every night I run home from taking care of Alex to check my email. My heart pounds. All other messages are like cruel jokes. There's nothing from you, and then it's just emptiness.

I don't understand, Kieran. All those texts just two weeks ago—

"... Chick, chick, are you there, chick? ..."

"... I hope you're smiling, girl, as it is the most beautiful smile ..."

"... Are you sleeping, chick? I wish I were there with you, my hands where they should be and will be again ..."

Me writing, "Kieran, are you a mirage?" You writing back immediately, "Jaysus, girl, I hope not."

I'm writing this down, because I want it in the official record. I was not making Kieran up. This was how it was just two weeks ago. What happened? What did I do wrong?

I meet the game designer on the corner of Franklin and Broadway near his company. It's a gorgeous, strangely warm winter evening. The sky is inky black above the building tops and clear enough that we can see stars. Enormous white clouds roll by, seeming almost to keep pace with us, sometimes obscuring and sometimes parting to reveal a nearly full moon.

We go to a tiny taqueria on a concrete island between the flow of traffic where Lafayette and Centre Streets merge. There's a "secret" restaurant downstairs guarded by a skinny kid in a trucker hat and wifebeater, and I think, oh please, Josh was wearing trucker hats and wifebeaters in the early nineties.

The game designer and I sit at the counter, under the neon glow of pink letters. The game designer is telling me about his ex-fiancée, who jilted him a month before their wedding. He says that people keep telling him how sorry they are but that all he can do is think, thank God.

"If I'd married her, my whole life would have been a nightmare," he says. "I would have spent the rest of my years taking care of her. I feel so lucky."

I'm sitting there thinking how much I like this man—I mean, who gets dumped at the altar and a few months later is talking about how lucky he feels?—when he puts his arm around me. Oh, Kieran, I don't want to kiss him! If I kiss him, I will be admitting that Dublin is really in the past. But then, that's the whole reason I'm here, isn't it?

It's a questioning kiss. I see his eyes soften behind his smudged glasses. I think, thank you for feeling this way about me, but if I could, without being rude, I would run from you, out the door and all the way home. But I stay. And not just out of politeness. Don't you see, Kieran? I have to lay you to rest.

I let the game designer come home with me. The ride over the Manhattan Bridge is spectacular. Still that black, black sky with the fast-moving clouds, now framed by the arching lights of the bridge, Manhattan receding behind us and Brooklyn looming up ahead as we pass over the black expanse of the East River.

Sakura huffs indignantly as the game designer follows me inside. Then, as if offended, he trots off to the back of the apartment while we go to the front.

I roll a joint, pour us whiskey.

"Oh, Heather Chaplin," the game designer says as we start to kiss on my couch. "I forgot how delicious you are."

I roll another joint.

The game designer says, "You're sexy when you smoke."

"Don't say that," I say. "Smoking is bad for you."

"Heather," he says. "I think you should do whatever gives you pleasure in your life right now."

I think, you are the sweetest man I've ever met. Why can't you be someone else entirely?

We kiss more. The game designer says, "Heather, I am so into you."

Christ, to love and be loved, is that so hard? I try to make myself love him, I really do. In my mind, I build a casket. Sides of wood, a top to close it. In my mind, I lower Kieran gently into the ground. I think, I should explain. Tell the game designer I fell madly in love in Dublin and then let him decide if he wants to stay or go. But I don't. I'm too selfish. I want to make love to this man so that the last man I've made love to will no longer be Kieran. I think somehow this will release me.

I turn off the lights when we get into bed. I don't want to see who is actually there. When I first feel his body against mine, all I can think is, it's not Kieran. The thick muscles, the short torso and limbs—this isn't the body I'm looking for.

The game designer is aggressive about pulling my clothes off, tossing me further into the bed. And I submit, sink into the easy luxury of giving into someone else's will—like sinking to the bottom of a dark lagoon, letting the seaweed and other dark matter of the water pull me down. I'd wondered after Dublin if some of this new passion belonged to me, to bestow on whom I chose. And I find it is. But when it's done, when he lies shuddering and moaning beside me, I feel about as close to him as I would a passenger on the subway. I feel like I've always imagined men feel after sex. I wish he were gone so I could be alone. I look at the clock and wonder what time it is in Dublin.

This black lagoon I'd been floating around the bottom of, it starts to feel frighteningly murky. I want to cry, or scream. I want to find you, Kieran, through the drifting seaweed and creeping sea plants that wrap themselves around me. I want to swim up to the light and see you waiting for me up there where the sun is shining. I suddenly don't like it, don't like it at all, in this dark, watery place.

Thursday, December 14, 2006

Things are as good as they possibly could be for Marie. Even the doctors can barely believe it. I'm on the phone all day passing along the good news. Seth and I talk for a long time. He tells me that Ben has told Marie what happened. I try not to imagine. When I get off, I cry for what seems like ages.

Friday, December 15, 2006

After leaving the house and refusing to come home again for the entire day because I think seeing Josh's stuff for one more second in the apartment is going to give me a brain aneurysm, I call Mac and ask him to help me move some of it into the basement. He's there two hours later, their new manny, Peter, in tow.

We all go down the stairs together. The air in the basement is filled with a fine dust, and there's black mold crawling up the walls. A long fluorescent light hangs at an angle from the ceiling as if someone had tried to rip it out but failed.

If I were into Freud, I would say this basement is the subconscious of our marriage. It fills me with such shame. In boxes of disintegrating cardboard are stacks of professional-quality photographic equipment from when Josh decided he wanted to be a photographer. The music equipment from when he was going to be a DJ sits in a pool of water. There are all the boxes we never unpacked when we moved in seven years ago; all the boxes we packed to sell on eBay that never got listed. Broken furniture that we neither threw away nor fixed. Half-assembled IKEA desks and bookshelves.

Mac's face is a grim line as he goes up and down the stairs bringing down bags of clothes, a surfboard, turntables. Peter's eyes are wide.

When Mac has to go, I convince Peter to stay because the thought of being left alone in this apartment is too depressing to contemplate. Peter reminds me of a baby bear—he's pudgy with big, flopping brown hair and a kind of shyness like he'd happily run away into the woods and hide in a tree if it were an option. He's twenty-six, a student at NYU. I almost keel over in joy when he tells me he was in Ireland last summer. He knows the market where Seth and Cecilia and I strolled. "My friend helped the city start that market," I say.

I say, "Do you by any chance know how to fix lightbulbs?" And he says, "Um, do you have a ladder?" And the next thing I know, he's lumbering up and down my ladder, putting new lightbulbs in the fixtures of those ten-foot ceilings that I can't reach even standing on the highest rung of a ladder, and which Josh would never replace for me. It was dark in the apartment since almost the day we moved in.

When Peter leaves, I lie on the floor looking up. There is light in my house.

Later

Eleanor gave birth to a baby boy. Zachary. I am a godmother. How can Ben's son just have died, and now Eleanor's son has just been born? It's total confusion in my mind.

Sunday, December 17, 2006

My mother and her boyfriend, Richard, arrive. They're here for the funeral tomorrow.

My mother sweeps me into her arms. "Oh, you are my best hugger!" she cries. And then she gets down on the floor with Sakura, who, much to my annoyance, has gone into downward dog and is grinning at her through little slanted eyes, his ears flat on his head, his curled tail wagging ferociously. When Josh and I were stranded at their house in Baltimore around September 11, Sakura became very fond of my mother.

"He remembers me!"

"He remembers the roast pork you used to give him."

My mother looks fantastic. She has not lost her beauty, not even deep into her sixties. She wears no makeup and her hair is iron gray, but still she could pass for ten years younger. From a distance, twenty years younger. I don't know how she does it, but I find it spectacularly annoying.

Richard on the other hand looks to have aged about twenty years since I've seen him last. He's carrying thirty-odd FreshDirect bags and two large suitcases. Often I've wondered if my mother is intentionally trying to run him into an early grave.

"Let me get those for you, Richard," I say.

"Oh, aren't you a dear," he says. "What a wonderful daughter. And such a wonderful person. How did we get so lucky? What if she had ended up a Republican?" And he staggers away down my hallway, heaving enormous breaths into his lungs.

"Mom, did you make Richard drive?"

"Richard loves to drive."

I make them steamed broccoli and miso soup for lunch. "Oh, Heather, this is the most wonderful lunch I've ever had," Richard says, which I find hard to believe considering it's steamed broccoli and miso soup.

"Oh, damn it," my mother says. "I left my air cleaner in the car. Richard, can you run and get it?"

"Of course, dear heart," he says, though he looks like he can barely stand.

"Give me the keys to the car," I say.

When I get back, staggering under the weight of this fifty-pound machine my mother carries with her everywhere, they're both in my living room reading the *New York Times*. Yet it's as if the newspaper exploded and now is taking over every available surface in my house. I wonder if they've brought several months' worth of *Times* to catch up on.

"Just plug that in for me, will you?" my mother says.

I plug it in. The thing starts whirring.

"I packed up all your things and put them on the back porch," my mother says. "That stuff is very dangerous."

I go out to the back porch. Sitting out there is a plastic bag containing all my soaps, shampoo, conditioner, dishwasher detergent, laundry detergent, perfumes, candles, and assorted hair products.

I sit down on my couch in the back of the house and get very stoned.

"Still smoking?" says Richard when I come back into the living room. "Thatta girl." And he raises his fist in the air. Power to the people? Black power? And chomps away on his nicotine gum.

"Honey, can you fetch me a cup of hot water?" my mother says.

I bring her a cup of hot water. I can't remember when exactly herbal tea got added to the list of things she can't consume or be around. She sloshes the water around in her mouth as if she were at the dentist's office and puts her feet up on my coffee table.

I sit down at the dining room table and watch them for a while. In my mind, I say, oh, I'm okay. The separation has been a little rough. Thanks for the concern, though, guys. Really, it's touching.

Thursday, December 21, 2006

Today is the funeral. I didn't go. Seth asked if I would stay with Alex instead. When I arrive, Cecilia is helping her mom into her coat. I get the feeling they don't even see me. They barely register my presence. They head out the front door, eyes staring, zombie-like. Has there ever been a day more terrible than today?

Friday, December 22, 2006

When I wake up there's an email from Kieran. Full of apologies. "Sorry for being out of touch, chick. Getting ready to go to West Africa for the film I told you about. Will be delighted when all is sorted. How are things in the Big Smoke? Still holding that weekend precious in mind. xxxxxxxxxxxxxxxxxxxxxxxxxxxxxx."

Oh, thank you, God, I think. Thank you. And then, the Big Smoke? London is the Big Smoke. I live in the Big Apple. Does he not even know where I live? But never has the phrase *beggars can't be choosers* seemed more apropos.

I send him a picture of myself from a couple of years ago with my hair pulled away from my face in a ponytail, kind of blown out, making my skin flawless and my eyes enormous and very blue. What a difference a few years make. I lie and say someone took it yesterday. And then the emails really start to fly. I'm gorgeous. My mouth is luscious. He remembers the first time he saw me with my hair pulled back like that. How beautiful I'd been on that dance floor. How low he's been since I left. Much better, I think. Much better.

And then from his BlackBerry, "I will get over to New York in 2007, chick. That is a promise xxxxxxxxxxxxxxxxxxxxx."

It's all going to be okay, I think. My fantasies of having him here are going to come true. I will *make* them come true. The Universe is not just a place that kills small children.

Saturday, December 23, 2006
Washington, DC

In DC for baby Zack's bris. As his godmother, I hand him to the rabbi for snipping. Even though the Steins make me feel like a piece of crumpled trash, they also make me feel like maybe I am part of a family.

Later

Had the worst phone call in the history of worst phone calls with Kieran. I tried to keep it light. I swear I did. What did I do wrong?

I show his last email to everyone. "Heather, I'll always be there, girl. May the clouds lift and float away for both of us. Take care, beautiful girl. How I would love to lie down with you, our skin meshed together once again . . ."

It's proof, right? Proof that he loves me.

Mac clears his throat. "Quite a poetic fellow," he says.

Summer says, "I get it. Remember my vegan chef? I didn't really know him either. It's pheromones."

Eleanor says, "Look, I understand that it's very intense and everything, but you don't really know this guy, do you?"

I think, I don't care what any of them say. He's coming to New York next year. I mean it. He's *coming* to New York. He promised.

Sunday, December 24, 2006

It's Christmas Eve and I'm sitting in an empty Starbucks in Baltimore on York Road between two out-of-business storefronts and across from a failing movie theater, drinking a lukewarm decaffeinated cappuccino.

Have you ever read a more depressing sentence in your life?

I'm staying with Faith now.

Every year I do this. Come down to see my mother for Christmas and then spend the whole time hiding at my friends' houses. Seth didn't come down this year, because he's up with the Greens. We've agreed between us to split these responsibilities.

Today was one of those glorious thank-God-for-global-warming days. High sixties. Warmest December 24 in recorded history. I sat outside with Faith and her husband, Derrick, and their two kids. Since I've seen him last, Derrick has covered himself with tattoos. At one point when Derrick was talking, I looked over at Faith and she was looking at him, her eyes narrowed to little slits. I thought, holy shit, she hates him as much as I hated Josh. I almost felt sorry for Derrick being on the receiving end of that look. Is it just inevitable that after a certain period of time you grow to hate your spouse?

I tried to make eye contact with Faith, but she wouldn't look at me. I tried to think of something to say, but all I could think of was what she used to look like when she looked at Derrick. Her face use to light up with some internal glow when he walked into the room. She used to hang on his every word, quote him in conversations. It was like she'd aged one hundred years since then. This stern woman, rigid with contempt, didn't seem to have anything to do with the pretty girl who used to be so crazy in love.

So this is it, I thought, looking at Faith not looking at me. This is what happened to us. This is the end of our story. And—scene! Right here in this lousy neighborhood in Baltimore. We had crappy childhoods and we chose crappy men and now we have crappy lives. I wouldn't have been surprised if the Grim Reaper had stepped into the living room, leaned his scythe up against the wall, and asked for a cup of tea.

I sat there not saying anything, while Faith sat there not saying anything back, and finally I got up and walked the three blocks to Starbucks, where you find me now.

I'm looking at the four pictures I have of Kieran on my computer. Nothing since yesterday's phone call. I had him, but I lost him again. Driven him away by my inability to make light conversation.

My phone rings. It's Josh.

I'm feeling so desperately alone that even talking to Josh seems preferable to sitting here in this deserted Starbucks scrolling through the same four pictures and listening to Bing Crosby sing "White Christmas" for the ninth time.

"Hey, I'm so glad to reach you!" he says. I think, he wants something.

He starts to tell me how great everything is for him. "Heath, I feel better than I have in like ten years," he says.

He has a whole litany: He's looking for a job. He's lost thirty pounds. He's stopped smoking pot. He's reading a book about how to maintain friendships. He's thinking about buying a bicycle. He's eating vegetables.

And I don't know, maybe if I were a better person, I'd be thinking, great, you're happier now. You're as better off without me as I am without you. Mazel tov. But I don't. Instead I'm thinking, go fuck yourself. While living with me, you didn't feel any need for self-improvement, or, say, getting a job, but now you're going and doing all the things I spent the last ten years begging you to do? Great. Thanks. Fuck off.

Plus, I don't even buy it. I've heard it so many times.

"Aha," I say. "Aha." I'm looking at my pictures of Kieran, thinking, you're so handsome. You're so trustworthy. I bet you're such a great dad. Why didn't you email me today?

Finally, after maybe twenty minutes, I say, "Look, I gotta run."

"Right," Josh says. "Listen, I forgot, there was one thing I want to ask you about."

There's about five minutes of hemming and hawing and throat clearing and then he blurts it out. "I've met someone."

And action! There's Ingmar Bergman and the Grim Reaper, cloak billowing, scythe freshly sharpened. Bergman asks for a shot of espresso. The Grim Reaper orders a latte. "White Christmas" comes on for the eleventh time. Kieran continues to stare at me from my computer screen and fails entirely to walk into Starbucks and save me like he's supposed to.

Then Josh starts to blather about how he doesn't know whether to pursue this relationship because, ah, um, cough, cough, he doesn't know where he stands with me.

I'm thinking, wait, you're calling me on Christmas Eve to ask me for advice on your love life?

Then it hits me. Not the fact of the girlfriend but that I don't care. I have no hot pin-prickles of pain, no sense of my heart breaking, just a confirmation that this enormous love, which ruled so much of my adult life, is dead. Oh, hello, Ingmar, thanks for coming. Mr. Reaper, just lay your scythe there. Make yourselves comfortable, please. Another latte?

Finally, through clenched teeth, I say, "Do you really think I'm the right person to be asking about this?"

Josh sounds so sad after I say that. I can just see his face sag. His voice takes on that brave-child quality of trying not to cry. Then all of a sudden it brightens, gets overly, inappropriately cheery, as if I won't know it's an act. As if I don't know all the modulations of his voice and the instincts and tiny internal decisions that lead to those modulations as well as I know my own.

When I get off the phone, I think, how can it be that I live in a world so unfair and absurd that Josh, *Josh*, already has someone new while I, in all my glory, am going to be alone for the rest of my life?

Then it's just emptiness. Like I'm a husk. I think, it doesn't matter if I live or die. No one needs me. I have no children, no lovers, no friends whose lives would change if I dropped dead right here in Starbucks, cold decaf spilling onto the floor. I think, maybe I should just walk out onto York Road into traffic. I wonder, is there enough traffic out there that eventually some dumb Baltimorean would manage to hit me?

I think, I'm thirty-five and have no reason for being alive.

And then, when this moment comes, really, ought one kill oneself?

Wednesday, December 27, 2006

Back in NY. I rushed back up to resume taking care of Alex, but now I'm sick. Sakura is curled up in a ball at the corner of the bed. He is the most perfect creature. I could never share my bed with some slobbering, hairy dog breathing on my face. Sakura is the only thing that makes being in this apartment bearable.

I lie in bed and long for Kieran to be here bringing me soup and stroking my hair. I calculate the time difference between New York and Dublin over and over in my mind.

Oh, the sympathy I have for my single friends. I had no idea. I used to listen to them going on about this guy or that, dissecting phone calls and emails, parsing conversations like they were lawyers in discovery. And I used to think, oh Christ, get a grip. Have a little perspective. He called; he didn't call. He's more affectionate one day and less the next. So it goes. Get some self-respect and think about something else for a while. And now, here I am, in the midst of this horrible tragedy, and I'm going over every word Kieran ever uttered, rereading every line of every email exchanged, cringing over a single phone call days ago—all as if there were some secret code that with enough study I could crack to explain why I'm lying here alone.

Dear Single Friends, I apologize for my lack of sympathy. I apologize for my smugness. It's true. I thought I was better. More evolved. Cooler and smarter. Forgive me, Single Friends. I plead ignorance.

Why won't he let me lavish him with love? I have so much love to give if only he wanted it.

Thursday, December 28, 2006

Marie is going to be let out of the hospital in two weeks. I haven't heard my brother's voice sound so strong in weeks. It's like warmth spreading in my chest.

Later

I have to get out of my house, so I go to the coffee shop across the street.

The amateur pugilist comes in. He's got stains on his coat and is wearing baggy wrestler's pants. I can't believe I considered even for a fraction of a second going on a date with him.

"Hey, Heather. How were your holidays?" he says.

The amateur pugilist has very close-set eyes and a tremendous amount of nose hair. I always wonder, doesn't he see it when he looks in the mirror?

"I considered suicide," I say.

"No shit," he says. "How were you going to do it?"

"I have this fantasy of walking out into traffic."

The amateur pugilist waves his arms wildly in front of him. "What, are you crazy?" he says. "You wouldn't die. You'd just break a leg or something. It would be a total disaster."

"I don't know then. Poison?"

"What, so someone could find you and rush you to the hospital where they'd pump your stomach?"

"It's funny," I say. "I think there are two kinds of people in the world, homicides and suicides. Me, I was always a dedicated homicide. But now I'm starting to see the upside of suicide."

"Oh yeah, definitely," the amateur pugilist says. "No competition. But it's got to be a gun to the head." And he makes the motion with his hand, forefinger at his temple, thumb pulling back an imaginary trigger. "There's no other way."

"Well then, I'm out," I say. "I'd never have the nerve for that."

He shrugs, as if to say, your loss. Then he wanders out of the coffee shop, and I go back to my paper.

Saturday, December 30, 2006

Shit is falling apart.

Down in Baltimore, Faith has locked herself in her bedroom with the children. I'm panicking because she's panicking and Faith never panics. Faith may look sweet in her sweater sets and matching jewelry, but don't let it fool you—she is tough. The woman was a union negotiator and then a social worker specializing in violent children in the South Bronx.

Yesterday she called me, ecstatic. She'd kicked Derrick out of the house. "I want to be an emancipated woman like you," she'd cried. I'd thought, emancipated. I can barely get out of bed in the morning. Turns out Derrick had been having an affair. Also, last month she'd discovered receipts for a number of guns. *Guns.*

"Why didn't you tell me any of this?" I nearly shouted at her. "Faith, you have to talk to people!"

She'd been too euphoric, though, to do anything but laugh. "I did it, Heath! I did it!" she kept saying.

But now she's just called and Derrick is, she thinks, coked up and threatening to come to the house and take the kids. I've never heard Faith sound so scared. I don't know what to do. I'm running up and down the hallway, trying to figure out if I should go down there. She won't call any of her friends who live in Baltimore. She doesn't want anyone to know. I say, Faith, you can't live like that. Her father is in DC but she's too ashamed to call him. I can't think of what else to do, though. I call her mother and get her mother to call her father, who agrees to go spend the night with her. I stay on the phone with Faith until he arrives.

I can't stop running up and down my hallway, though. Even after Faith's father calls to tell me she's gone to sleep. What has happened to us all? What has happened?

Monday, January 1, 2007

Last night was New Year's Eve.

Before my friends come over, I'm on the phone with Seth. They're all up at Valhalla with Marie, who is beginning to eat a bit. Ben has brought Alex up for the first time. When I ask Seth how it's going, he says, "It's going okay, Heath. It's going okay."

When my friends get here, we order Chinese food and drink champagne. We're coming up with slogans for the next year.

"Care less about other people: 2007," I say.

The aspiring novelist says, "That's funny." But I'm not kidding.

Then I say, "Oh Christ, I just need a sign. A sign that next year will be different."

They groan because I've been talking about signs all night.

We realize it's 11:55 and we're going to miss the fireworks in Prospect Park. The others are for blowing them off, but I say, no way.

"Every year I miss them, and every year I say, eh, next year. I cannot start another year knowing I've already failed in the very first thing I wanted to do," I say. "Off your asses, everyone."

We hear the fireworks start just as we're crossing Sixth Avenue. That's when I start running. At first we're all in a pack, but one by one the others fall off until it's just me, sprinting up Eleventh Street. My breath starts to feel raspy, scratchy in my throat. I can hear myself wheezing, and my thigh muscles burn from the sudden expenditure of effort. But I feel somehow as if the whole of my next year depends on me making it to the top of the hill and seeing those fireworks. I don't care if I make myself sicker.

Right as I hit Prospect Park West and my breath is near entirely gone, a round goes up into the air. There are lights in the sky, erupting over the trees before me. Dazzling and bright, halos of color, sparkling and whirring and fizzing. I'm panting so hard I have to bend over, hands on knees. I'm light-headed, everything spinning around me, but I'm also laughing out loud. My friends trot up behind me just as the fireworks are finishing. We all cheer and jump up and down.

Lying on a blanket looking up at the stars in Prospect Park, I think, if my neighbor weren't here, I'd *definitely* make my move on the aspiring novelist. But as a five-some, it would be awkward.

We get back to my house around 1:30 a.m. to finish off the Chinese takeout and down the last of the champagne. I see something shiny and purple hanging from the front door of my apartment building. It's a cone-shaped hat with the words "Happy New Year" written in silver glitter on it. I turn to the right. I turn to the left. I look behind me. No other door has a hat like this on it. I think, is this my sign? When I was about six, I woke up New Year's morning to find my mother had brought me back a hat just like this—same color, same writing, same everything. I remember this hat, because I'd been desperately jealous of my mother getting dressed up to go out for the night, while I was just a child who had to stay home. It had been like a souvenir from another world; it told me that out there, beyond our crumbling house, beyond the nightmares and terrors, beyond the loneliness of nights without my mother and the sheer disappointment of being only me and not Ginger Rogers in *Top Hat*, there was something else, a place where someday I would go and words would be written in silver glitter.

My friends are stamping their feet in the cold and clamoring for me to open the door. I take the hat and turn to them.

"Do you see this?" I say. "It's a sign."

"Oh, shut up!" they cry. "We're freezing out here!"

Inside, we drink the remaining champagne and crack open our fortune cookies. I pull my slip of paper out. It reads, "It's always darkest before the dawn." I have the sudden feeling of tears welling up in my eyes. I know what you're thinking. A fortune cookie? She has had a psychotic break. But I don't care what you think. I think of Ben and Marie and my brother and Cecilia and the horror of the last month. And I feel a tremendous surge of optimism in my chest—a glimmer of the light that shone in Dublin. I put the slip of paper on my refrigerator with a rose-shaped magnet. I don't care if it's from a fortune cookie. I believe it. Surely the dawn is near ready to rise for me.

BOOK FOUR

SUMMERTIME

Friday, June 1, 2007

I have not been keeping up. It's been six months since I last wrote. You will just have to forgive me. What can I say, first I was too miserable and then I was too busy—and now? Now I'm just too psyched to make any promises about anything. It's SUMMER-TIME! Summertime. Do you know what this means? It means the flowers are blooming, the sun is shining, and the days are long. I can go swimming every day at the Red Hook Pool, and I've got more cute boys on my tip than I can handle. There are seven guys on my bench. That's right, count 'em up, seven. And after several months literally thinking I was going to be foreclosed on, I have managed to eke out enough money writing magazine stories to pay my bills. Oh, and I'm now a contributor to *All Things Considered*. Hey. Hey. Hey. How you like me now?

Tuesday, June 12, 2007

My garden, as of today:

  1 pink rosebush
  2 pink hydrangeas
  1 border of purple and yellow pansies (not yet bordering
      anything, but soon)
  1 purple azalea bush
  1 blueberry bush
  6 sweet-smelling thyme bushes (planted between the flag-
      stones)

6 ivy vines (planted to hang over raised flower beds)
2 foxgloves
1 dogwood tree, so beautiful, it hurts me to look at it. (And
  now I know why we make prisoners dig ditches. It fucking sucks. I nearly broke my back getting that thing into
  the ground.)
1 redbud tree (ditto, my back)
1 white butterfly bush

All, all glorious

Wednesday, June 13, 2007

I saw Josh this spring. In LA, when I was there for a story. We went to
the Griffith Observatory, a creamy-white fascist-looking monstrosity
atop a hill overlooking the city. The sun was enormously bright
and there was no escaping it up there. Josh and I walked around in
sunglasses, squinting, our hands up to our foreheads shading our faces.
Josh told me not only the history of the place but also the history of all
telescopes—how a guy named Hans Lippershey patented the earliest
one and may or may not have also invented the microscope. We
talked about man's endless quest to stretch beyond his own physical
and mental limitations. It was so interesting I lost all track of everything except what Josh and I were saying. Then there was a pause,
and I was back in the sun on top of that hill, standing next to Josh, my
ex-husband, who's lost thirty pounds, gotten a job, and knows everything in the world there is to know. I found myself wondering what it
would be like to kiss him. The curiosity felt like it could have burned
a hole in me so I ran away into the observatory's café.

In the café, Josh was drinking orange juice. Then he tilted his
head to one side and shook it at me. Then we were both clutching
each other with laughter, because this is a joke from the first week
we met, back at Gabriel's funeral, and no one knows the joke but
Josh and me and Mac.

We both had to wipe the tears from our faces we were laughing so hard. Josh was looking at me with his brilliantly green eyes, and there was love coming out of them that takes a lifetime to build. I thought, you broke my heart with your negligence and abuse. I will never meet another person as fascinating and wonderful. I hate you.

Thursday, June 14, 2007
Yesterday

At Shea Stadium with the hacker—he's an Indian guy with a firm little potbelly and big metal glasses I met at a party last week. I'm reading the *New York Times* and eating some vegan snacks I brought along. We're talking about the effects of globalization on advanced capitalism. The hacker says, "I'd sure like to scan God's database and see if anyone else here is having the same conversation. What do you think?"

To get home, we sneak our way onto a water taxi.

Then we go to the Red Hook Pool and practice flip turns.

Then we go back to my place and watch *Deadwood*. Sitting on my couch with the flickering of the TV for light, I'm waiting for the hacker to make his move. But he's focused on the TV like it's the most interesting thing he's ever seen. He's all, "wow, great shot," and "interesting choice." I'm thinking, man, your priorities are messed up.

At the door, he finally goes in for the kiss. Our teeth knock, but otherwise it's nice. Then when he pulls away he seems really shy all of a sudden. He says, "I'm scared, but I want to try." I'm thinking, try what? We're not going to have a relationship here.

Oh yes. Summer 2007.

Friday, June 15, 2007

"No, no, you've got it all wrong. Men don't want to be reassured you like them. They like not knowing."

It's Eleanor berating me. I'd been thinking about the hacker after our day of fun and how he was kind of nerdy and probably didn't go out with that many women, especially such stunningly hot women like myself. So I'd written him this really nice, long email to let him know I thought he was awesome. I told him I'd love to see him again and as long as he didn't try and have any relationship conversations with me I'd be happy to date him.

"You are so crazy," Eleanor says. "Of course he didn't write back. You probably totally freaked him out."

"What are you talking about?" I say. "I was being straightforward. And I just felt sorry for him. He's obviously such a great guy."

Eleanor can't stop laughing at me.

Sunday, June 17, 2007

Joined a softball league today. Never been interested in softball in my life, but my writers' space has a team in the New York Media league, and I figured it would be good for meeting new people, especially the kind of people who are boy people.

And oh my, is it.

There's this guy on the other team with the most incredible jawline—like something a superhero would have. I'm trying to give him the eye from across the field, and then the next thing I know one of our batters slides into second base and everyone is laughing and joking about whether he's out or not—but this guy, the guy with the jawline, starts screaming, "Come on! Give me a break! He's out!" And the next thing I know he's almost coming to blows with our second baseman. I'm thinking, what a dick. Who comes to a softball game of *writers* and almost gets in a fistfight? But I'm torn, because, you know, the jawline and everything. And then the game is over, and he's taking off his baseball hat and under it is a head of dark hair so thick it's hard not to walk up and run your hands through it. And oh my goodness, he's got blue eyes like the

Pacific Ocean on a bright day. So I'm like, that's fine, you can be a dick, and I slide him my number on the way out.

Monday, June 18, 2007

Summer says I'm on a roll. And I laugh, but inside I'm thinking, this ain't no roll. This is *me*. Turns out I am smarter and cooler than all those other single women after all. Oh yes.

Sunday, June 24, 2007

Sixty people showed up for my barbecue last night even though I only sent out the invite on Tuesday.

I made gazpacho, cucumber yogurt soup, and cold potato soup. It's terrible party food, but it was so much fun to welcome people with "Let me show you the soup bar."

The economics reporter for NPR got into a heated discussion with the Middle Eastern correspondent from the *Nation* about drone policy on top of my pansy border, and I had to yell at them to move before they destroyed the whole thing.

The game designer came.

The hacker came.

Both softball teams came.

I hadn't noticed before what a square chest and nice forearms the hot dick has.

My neighbor came up to me and said, "Who is that *hot* guy out there? Blue eyes? Thick brown hair? Square chest?" Her husband said, "Oh, I talked to that guy. He's a dick."

The aspiring novelist, who I never got around to conquering, was there. Handing him a bowl of cold potato soup, I thought, I should give that another go.

I had the Flaming Lips on shuffle. Some guy who just moved here from Seattle to host a new radio show—I have no idea who brought him—congratulated me on the excellent music. I thought, oh, you're cute.

By 2 a.m., there were just four of us left in the backyard. The hacker, me, one of my good friends from the neighborhood, and her horrible geek-hipster crush. The geek-hipster crush and the hacker got into an argument about whether or not Tupac was an authentic hip-hop artist despite his commercial success. I was thinking, oh my God, why are you both so annoying? Hacker, hello, can we just move to the part where we're making out?

At 3 a.m., my friend and her asshole crush left and the hacker started acting like, oh, maybe I should go too. I said, "Don't be ridiculous. Of course you're spending the night." But by the time we lay down I was so tired, I really only had the energy for a couple of kisses and then I fell asleep.

Monday, June 25, 2007

It's 3:30 a.m. I admit it: my sleep is kind of messed up.

I was up almost all last night and now everything is screwy. I went to the Loft party with some friends. If you're into DJ culture, you know that's a really cool thing. I'm not particularly, so I didn't. But my friend is on the special guest list so I figured, why not. They all did ecstasy, which I most certainly did not. The last time I did ecstasy, I couldn't sleep for three days and then fell into a major depression for like a month. After that I started seeing this shrink who turned out to be the best shrink I've ever had, and believe me, I've had some bad ones—since I was thirteen I've been schlepping in and out of psychiatrists' offices. He told me ecstasy was the worst possible thing I could ever do. Something about plummeting serotonin levels. He said I had to learn to *manage my personality* and that meant three things primarily, besides, of course, taking my meds. He said I had to eat, I had to sleep, and I should never do drugs. I didn't tell him how after Josh's mother died, I administered myself spoonfuls of her liquid morphine and ran through her family-sized bottle of Percocet in less than a year. I didn't tell him about the way time sometimes shifts its tempo around me, or the terrible images that get stuck in my mind. I was just like, yeah, totally, of course.

Now, though, I stick to those rules as if they were the gospel. Well, not really the eating one. I find it hard to believe eating is really that important—I'm still in the ballerina range and frankly I have no intention of ever getting out of it. And I guess if I'm really honest with myself, I'm not great on the sleeping one. I mean, here I am wide-awake at nearly four in the morning. But I am good on the drug prohibition. Nothing illicit has passed my lips since that day except weed, which doesn't count.

They're so basic, his rules, and so strangely hard to follow.

Wednesday, June 27, 2007

Every night the same dream. I know there's an apartment somewhere with a red wall, but I can't remember where it is or if I've remembered to pay the mortgage on it. I'm always screaming but no sound comes out. I keep thinking, why can't I find the place where I live? And I'm running and running, but I can't even move, and the sweat soaks the sheets beneath me.

Friday, June 29, 2007

Mac and Katy's manny, Peter, comes over. I'm making him dinner because he watched Sakura while I was traveling so much this spring. I was in San Francisco, Los Angeles, Miami, Utah, and Las Vegas. Eleanor kept saying I was using travel to jack myself up so I wouldn't have to face my life at home. Which of course is partially true and thus doubly annoying to hear. But on the other hand, I was like, hello, I'm trying to make a living here. When I get an assignment, I go.

Anyway, Peter comes over. I make him look at my hydrangea and peer into my dogwood blooms and admit they're the most beautiful things he's ever seen.

He says he loved my book.

I say, "Did you hear my story on *All Things Considered* about video games as complex dynamic systems? Did you know complexity isn't the opposite of simple? It's the level of interconnectedness. Did you know if you take that to its furthest conclusion, you reach Buddhism or Hinduism?"

And totally to my surprise, Peter's says, "Yeah, I know."

"Oh," I say.

"Yeah," he says. "I read your book. Also I've been reading about complex adaptive systems and the RAND Corporation trying to predict human behavior on the first supercomputers back during the Cold War."

There's silence between us for a minute.

"Oh," I say.

"Plus," he says, "I think people have known for a while that contemporary physics maps over the Dalai Lama."

There's another pause.

"Hey, you're really smart," I say.

Peter laughs, a surprisingly frank laugh for a guy who seems eager to take up as little space as possible. "No shit, dude," he says.

The game designer comes up and Peter can't believe I know him. I forget that the game designer is a god to lots of people. Suddenly I feel very conscious that Peter is young. It hits me how easy it is for older people to take advantage of younger people—how easy it would be to make myself enormous in Peter's eyes and then get off seeing my bloated image reflected back at me. I have a flash of my father leaning in close so his face was near mine, talking to me about Wittgenstein or Nietzsche or Paul Robeson or Buckminster Fuller and how it was just a given that he was a genius bestowing his wisdom on my lucky self—but that now, as an adult, I have no idea if he knew anything more than any college freshman knows. It gives me a feeling like there's a trail of slime on me.

Friday, June 29, 2007

Afternoon with my friend Daphne. She's older than me. A screen-writer and novelist who I know because she optioned a story I did for the *Times* styles section many years ago. I've never understood why she gives me the time of day, but I adore her. Adore her.

We have lunch at the Odeon and then go to Issey Miyake. When I come out of the dressing room in this black skirt and navy-blue top, Daphne is like, "Oh my God, Heather. You look so gorgeous since you left your husband. I'm afraid someone is going to abduct you on the street."

I tell her about my bench. I tell her I met this guy in Prospect Park who then started calling and wanted to buy me a ticket to fly first-class with him to Australia.

"Do you think I should go?" I say as we walk through Tribeca up toward SoHo.

"What, with a stranger?" she says. "Are you insane?"

"I always wanted to be the kind of woman men bought first-class tickets for," I say.

"You are an adventuress, Heather," Daphne says. And then, "But no, don't go off to a foreign country with someone you don't know. That is not a good idea."

Monday, July 2, 2007

It's 2:25 a.m., and I just got home.

1. Coffee Saturday morning with friends from San Francisco.

2. Wedding dress shopping that afternoon with a friend who's getting remarried. (I told her not to do it, but she's determined.)

3. Badminton in Prospect Park with friends. (Brought the hacker. He's really growing on me; he's having an existential

crisis, but I find it sort of charming. On the way over we talked about the meaning of happiness. I took his hand and told him again how awesome he is. I don't care what my girlfriends say, if someone is awesome, you should tell them. When we got to Prospect Park, Mac was there, looking extremely dapper in blue Tretorn sneakers, blue-and-white-striped seersucker pants, and a white polo shirt with the collar turned up. I said to him, "You're looking very George Plimpton. What, you got a tennis match after this?" Then our host came up and said "Ready to play badminton?" "I've never played before," I said, to which Mac looked heavenward. "Next she'll be offering bets to liven up the game," he said. "Don't trust her. They brought her in as a character study for *The Sting*." As I pummeled him, he kept saying, "Eye of the tiger, Chaplin. Don't deny it." I don't even know what he's talking about.)

4. Ditched the hacker. (Actually, I invited him to come with me karaoking in the city, but the existential crisis was weighing on him too heavily. He's a strange creature. I keep thinking he must be so into me, because, well, I'm me, but then when I give him a chance, he's always running off.)

5. Karaoking in the city. (When I get there, it's as if the hot dick has been waiting for me. I can't believe that someone so handsome could be as if waiting for *me*. He's a stringer for the *New York Times*. Just back from Israel. He's trying to write a screenplay now. "I'm not really a writer, though," he says. "I'm not smart enough to be a writer." When I begin to protest, he says, "No, really, I'm not that smart. If you get to know me, you'll see." I have to admit, he doesn't seem that smart. But when you're that handsome, I'm not sure it matters. Plus, he's got this sort of self-effacing smile that I find endearing. Then it's four hours later, and that thing had happened

when suddenly everyone is smashed and everything becomes heightened—people singing louder, laughing louder, shouting in each other's ear. Drinks flow. Pizza is ordered. Copious sweating. It's 1 a.m., then two. Then three. People are busting out dance moves, doubling over laughing. The stringer and I are together the whole time, leaning against the wall, leaning in toward each other.)

6. Kicked out at 4 a.m. (The stringer, his stand-up comic buddy, and me stand outside the karaoke place. The stringer is exclaiming over the muscles in my back, feeling the muscles in my arm. "You're so strong," he keeps saying. "And so tiny. What do you weigh? Like a hundred pounds?" And I'm thinking, you are literally the most delightful man I've ever met, when his stand-up comic buddy booms, "No way, she's at least 110!" Which is exactly right, but still I think, fuck you, asshole. Then he says, "Come on. Stop touching Heather. Let's go get falafel." The stringer and I ditch him and saunter down Second Avenue, past wriggling fields of yellow taxis coming in and out of the steam rising from manholes. Dip into a brand-new hotel on Bowery with dark wood paneling, pillars made of Moroccan tile, Persian carpets on the floor, and palm trees in the corner. Like somewhere Rudolph Valentino would have lived. We go through the lobby to the balcony—more palm trees, wicker furniture, and the Lower East Side rising up like black shadows against the just-beginning-to-lighten sky. "Come on," the stringer says. "If you don't mind spending the night with a stranger, I'll get us a room.")

7. Staying at the Bowery Hotel. (Thick white robes. Not fooling around at all, but naked under the terry cloth. Half kissing, arms wrapped around each other. So much hotter than actually doing anything. Ordering room service and lounging about on that big bed all the next day and evening. The

stringer has two primary topics of conversation: ice hockey and all the assholes in his life. Note to self: don't become this guy's girlfriend. But hang around on a hotel bed in a bathrobe with him? Absolutely.)

8. Chinatown at midnight. (Before we leave the hotel the next night, the stringer says, "I'm sorry I didn't satisfy you. You're obviously this really deeply sexual woman. It's just I'm new out of a relationship." Me, dying laughing. Him: "What?" Me: "Trust me. Don't sweat it." And then I say, "Aren't you having the time of your life?" And I get a real smile from him, for the first time a real smile. There's something very sweet about the stringer. "Yeah," he says. "I am. I actually am." Then we walk to Chinatown and have greasy noodles and Tsingtao beer while all around us people shout in Cantonese.)

9. A kiss under the Manhattan Bridge. (Right as the stringer calls me a taxi, I take him behind his neck and pull his face to mine and kiss him right on the lips. Then I slide into the taxi without a backward glance. I've never done anything like that in my life. The whole ride over the bridge, I'm rolling around on the backseat guffawing to myself, thinking, you rule, HC!)

10. Home at dawn. (I know this is bad, but come on. A girl's got to live, doesn't she?)

Saturday, August 4, 2007

Sorry, I haven't written anything in almost a month. My sleep is seriously messed up. It's four in the morning. I fell asleep at my desk today and didn't get any work done. I should go upstate and see my brother and the Greens. Through the winter and into the spring, I was seeing them every couple days. And we all had dinner together like once a week. And when Seth looks at me there's something different in his eyes—it's as if first so much happiness and then so much pain has softened him. I never imagined my brother would actually be my ally. But now it's like he is. He emails all the time saying, come on, come upstate. What are you waiting for? But the thing is, I'm having too much fun in the city to give up, even for my brother.

Sunday, August 5, 2007

"So what are you hoping to achieve?"

"Achieve?"

"Well, I'm assuming you're hoping something will work out with one of these guys?"

It's Eleanor. I feel like she's berating me, and I start to bristle.

"What do you mean, work out?" I say. "I just want things to go on exactly as they are."

"Well, eventually you're going to want to be in a relationship with one of them."

"No," I say. "I never want to be in a relationship again. Being single is obviously the best possible state. I just didn't know it before."

Then we talk about baby Zack, and I try to be a good friend and care about his sleep patterns. But the truth? The truth is, right at this moment, I don't really care about other people's children.

Monday, August 6, 2007

Oy, I didn't even go out tonight and still I'm awake at four thirty in the morning. This is not ideal. But you know what, really, my sleep has been messed up since about the day I was born. You want to hear something? When I was a little kid, I was afraid to go to sleep. When I'd feel myself start to drift off, I'd jolt myself out of it. I've always thought the phrase *falling asleep* was particularly apt. It feels like falling to me. Falling off the highest building you can imagine, arms and legs flailing in the air, not knowing what to fear—the bottom, or that there won't be any bottom. And I could not tolerate going to bed alone. I always had the heart-pounding, air-quivering, terrifying sense that there was someone outside my door or window. I could not escape this sensation no matter how hard I tried, and the terror would mount in me until it became uncontrollable. Sometimes my mother would sit with me. Sometimes she'd pay my brother to sit with me—forty cents an hour, I think, was the going rate. I always kept a foot on Seth's back so I'd know if he tried to leave. I was petrified of the thought that I'd accidentally fall asleep, he would leave, and then all would be over for me. To keep this from happening I'd make little noises and movements to let him know I was still awake. Sometimes I think I trained myself to be an insomniac.

And then there were the visions. Well, maybe *visions* is too strong a word. You know those images I mentioned that I didn't tell my old shrink about? Well, the other reason I didn't like to close my eyes at night was I'd see horrible things—serrated knives plunging into my abdomen. A leering man with talons for fingernails outside my door. My eyeballs being ripped out of their sockets. I still get them sometimes, though now they're just flashes out of the corner of my eye, and only when I'm superstressed or very tired. But at times they've been bad, like one of those movies about Vietnam, where the vet is back home but bombarded with images of dead Vietnamese children and palm trees and shouting soldiers, and blood splatters the camera. Except of course the horrors in my mind take place in Baltimore, not Vietnam.

I remember telling my mother about the images and how I couldn't make them go away. And she said, imagine that they're on a train and when the caboose goes by, that's the last of them. And I remember a feeling of total and complete aloneness came over me, because if she thought these images were going to drift peacefully out of my mind, she truly had no idea what I was telling her.

Tuesday, August 7, 2007

My Apartment: Peter is staying at my place to use the AC because there's a major heat wave on. He brought me a book about complex adaptive systems and another about the Vikings. He and Sakura sit panting, companionably, in front of the unit.

Tenth Street and Broadway: Lobster rolls and champagne with Daphne and her husband. (They are beyond lovely. Why, why on earth are they interested in me?) Got quite tipsy. They say leaving my husband was clearly the best thing that ever happened to me. They invite me to go to Hawaii with them in September. I can already hear Eleanor in my head, but on the other hand—Hawaii.

NoHo: Meet the stringer at a crowded wine bar. Turns out he's a Zionist. Should have known. In an alley behind the bar, I kiss him anyway.

Some Rich Guy's Balcony in the West Village: Mac texts. He's at a party for *Radar*, which is relaunching. I go meet him at this ridiculously swank apartment. We stand on the balcony overlooking the Hudson. We toast each other and say, "Not too bad for a couple of scrubs from Baltimore, not too bad."

Home at 3 a.m.

Wednesday, August 8, 2007

"Why do you think he disappeared?"

"I don't know," Summer says. "They just do. Men disappear."

I'm talking about he-who-cannot-be-named.

The Irishman.

I cannot write his name. It hurts too much.

In April, he sent me a care package with a pageboy's hat, a T-shirt that said "Connemara Republic of Ireland," and a long letter of unintelligible scrawl signed "all my love" beside a long row of *X*s. He called to make sure I'd gotten it. Then he disappeared. I won't bore you with the pain.

Thursday, August 9, 2007
Baltimore

My budget is tight so I've taken the bus down to Baltimore to help Faith move. How I Went from Private Plane to Chinatown Bus in Less than a Year, I think. The Heather Chaplin Story.

I know I have my bench to tend to, but no one should go through what she's going through alone. Faith is *down*. Seriously down.

"You couldn't have known that Derrick would go the way he went," I say.

"I guess," she says.

"Look, it was inevitable," I say. "Of course we married shattered people. That's all we knew. You left him the minute you were psychologically able to."

Of course I'm talking to myself as much as her.

"I guess," Faith says. Then, "Why did you do it, Heath? Really, why did you marry Josh?"

"I wanted a diamond ring," I say.

Faith doesn't say anything.

"Okay, also Accutane."

"What?"

"My skin was clear. I was a size two. I wanted a diamond ring and a big dress and to be surrounded by flowers with everyone standing around admiring me for just one day in my life. Is that so wrong?"

Faith keeps staring at me.

"I've said it a million times," I say. "I'm very shallow. It's not my fault no one believes me."

"You weren't in love with him?"

We sit in silence.

"What about you?" I say. "Why did you marry Derrick?"

Faith looks right at me and she narrows her eyes and they are fairly glistening with a kind of shrewd fierceness. "Fear," she says. "I married Derrick because I was afraid no one else would want me."

"Jesus Christ, Faith."

"It's true. I knew I wasn't in love with him. I hadn't been for years. But he wanted to get married and I was too afraid to say no."

Then she drops her head into her hands, and soon her body is heaving with sobs. "I feel so ashamed," she cries. "Of what I let my life become."

I don't know what to do except put my arms around her. I don't have a good response, because when I think about my life with Josh, I'm too ashamed to even move. I think, what did we do to ourselves? And dear God, what did we do to our husbands?

Went by my mother's before taking the bus back to New York. She wants to move to Florida. I was like, How are you going to support yourself in Florida? My mother has a photography business in Baltimore, and when I mentioned that her customers might not relocate with her, she made noises like how could I be so boring and pedantic. Then she showed me pictures of mansions on the beach and tried to convince me to buy one with her, telling me what a good financial move it would be. This made me cry. Why would she want me to do something that would be ruinous for me? She's already digging up her garden and giving away her flowers. She gave me some daylilies. At the first rest stop, I called Seth and told him I was going to throw those lilies away but he was like, "Well, you might as well put them in your garden."

Saturday, August 11, 2007
Los Angeles

I'm just back from the best date of my life. In fact, it might be the first official "date" I've ever been on.

Daphne is in LA too, having a book party, and while I was there, just hanging around munching on a cucumber sandwich, this cute guy with a mop of dark hair made a beeline for me. A movie director. A minor one, but still.

He takes me to an Italian restaurant on Sunset Boulevard where we meet up with these guys he's writing a movie about. One of the guys is an ex-mobster who went into the witness protection program, then jail, and now runs a chain of limo services. There's a woman there too who used to run strip clubs in Chicago. Her name is Scarlett so I say, "Were you named after Scarlett O'Hara?" And she says, "Honey, Scarlett O'Hara was named after me."

The mobster says he knows I'm from New York because of my "confident swagger." Which makes me think, confident swagger? Who are you talking about?

The mobster asks us when we are getting married. I say next June. Then they won't stop toasting us. The minor director bites his bottom lip when he's pleased. It's cute.

The mobster leans into the minor director. "She's intense. You know that, right?"

Now, it's not like no one has ever described me as intense before. But I can't imagine what I'm doing at this moment that is intense. How does he know this about me? Is it that obvious? I try so hard to be light.

The waitresses, who all have boobs bigger than my head, keep coming to check on us and bring us bottles of Chianti wine. Then the guys from Cypress Hill come and sit down at the next table and start ordering lobster tails and rolling fat joints.

When the director drops me off, he insists on walking me to the door. I keep thinking, who are you? Are you the kind of man I should be looking for? If I could be with someone this respectable, this well-mannered, should I grab it?

The problem is, Summer says, it sounds like it was actually the mobster I liked. And God damn it if she isn't right.

Sunday, August 12, 2007

Summer decides she wants to go on a date so we head out to Huntington Beach in search of surfers. It's hard not to think of Josh growing up in this horrible place. The first time we went there together, I'd almost wept, thinking of him as a little flower trying to grow up between the inhospitable cracks of a Huntington Beach sidewalk.

"Hello, Richard Nixon. Hello, Ronald Reagan," I cry out the passenger window. "Hello, land of rich people with no values!"

At the beach, Summer plays along the surf's edge while I sit on a hill of sand. I notice she seems to be frolicking in the direction of a guy in mirror sunglasses and low-slung swimming trunks.

Then she runs to me.

"I see what you're doing down there," I say.

"Oh my God, am I some monstrous middle-aged lady with cellulite jiggling everywhere? Am I totally making a fool of myself?"

"No fucking way," I say. "You're gorgeous. You're like Cameron Diaz out there. I'm not even kidding."

"Really? Really?" she says, and then she's back out on the water's edge.

The next thing I know the two of them are rolling around on the sand, like something out of *From Here to Eternity*. Personally, I don't think I could enjoy making out while getting sand all over me, but I'm impressed nonetheless. Then they're up again and walking toward me. Summer's cheeks are rosy and her hair is sticking up in the back of her head.

"George, this is my friend Heather," she says.

George still has his shades on. He's slouching gorgeously. "Heath, man, what's up?" he says.

Then they're off hububbing together, and finally George saunters off in the opposite direction and Summer sits down next to me.

"Hey, I can go sit in a café," I say.

"No," Summer says. "I only needed a few kisses. I've had just the right amount of George."

Then we're pounding our fists into the sand and weeping with laughter.

Later

Back in her apartment, Summer is having a semipornographic text exchange with George. Then she sighs and tosses away her phone.

"I don't understand," she says. "How do you do it, Heath? You are the living embodiment of the four-man plan."

One of Summer's self-help books advocates dating four men at once.

I'm quite pleased. I don't think anyone has ever asked my advice on dating before. "It's beyond obvious," I say. "Why would you ever trust only one man?"

"But don't you get attached?" Summer asks.

"No," I say. "Why would I get attached? I'm just looking for a certain amount of male attention—if it's scattered across the field, I have a better chance of getting my daily allotment."

"Do you care about any of them, at all?"

"I care about all of them," I say. "Each guy gives something different. It's naive to think one man could be everything."

"Wow, you are advanced," Summer says.

"No," I say. "Just realistic. If you don't have kids there's no reason to have only one partner."

"What about with the Irishman?"

"What Irishman?" I say.

Later

The minor movie director emailed me to thank me for going out with him. Who is this guy? Should I go for it? Yes, I think I will. I will not be the kind of girl who likes the mobster. I will give the minor director a chance.

Monday, August 13, 2007

Last night I did not dream about the red wall. Last night I dreamed—of Kieran.

Did I not just yesterday decide to give the minor director a chance? Why is Kieran back to haunt me? Why does just writing his name cause my heart to turn over? I *just* stopped calculating the time difference between Dublin and New York.

I can kiss all the boys in the world, and none of them will kiss me like Kieran kissed me. When I wake up, it's with a sob.

Later

Party on Thirteenth Street. Lots of disco music and men putting makeup on each other. Not really my scene.

Pop into Barnes & Noble at Union Square on the way home. This guy comes up to me and tells me how beautiful I am. This has never happened to me before. People used to stop me on the street and say things like "Why don't you try smiling?" or "Hey, life can't be that bad." This is much better. He's with a woman friend who's perusing a Noam Chomsky book so I figure, how dangerous can he be? I give him my phone number. Summer says I'm no longer on a roll. She says I'm on a streak. I say, "Oh, I see." But inside, I think, this isn't a streak, this is *me*.

Tuesday, August 14, 2007

The hacker is back. He was gone for a while. Turns out he'd decided to be silent for a week. He was meditating. And finishing a commission from Maker Faire to build a TV controller out of an Altoids box.

We sit outside on his steps and drink fine red wine that his friend, who runs a wine shop, brings us. "I tried meditating once," I tell the hacker. "But I accidentally got so relaxed I pissed myself."

"Chaplin—"

"I'm not kidding," I say.

And I'm not. I'd been in Costa Rica with Josh and, just to see what it was like, I'd signed up for a meditation lesson. Cut to a week later, and I'd had pee running down my leg on a public bus.

The hacker has his head between his knees, he's laughing so hard.

"It's not funny," I say. "It was very embarrassing. It was like I'd been holding myself so tightly for so long that the second I let go, I lost control of my bladder."

What I don't tell him is how during the second week of meditation, I'd been sitting there, visualizing each one of my organs, as instructed, and settling into a state of relaxation like I'd never felt in my whole life. And then, suddenly, it was as if all the little hairs on the back of my neck had stood up. It was fear as I imagine animals experience fear. Fear beyond intellectual reasoning, beyond the reach of language. It was no longer just the two of us in the room. There was another presence there, a breathing in my ear. I was huge and tiny at the same time. The breathing was next to me and inside of me. It filled up to be the whole room. I filled up to be the whole room. I disappeared into being not even a speck on a dust mite. Boundaries disappeared. It was the oldest feeling I'd ever had or could ever remember having, ancient and in my bones, as much a part of me as the marrow in my bones and as terrifying as if someone were dishing that marrow out to me in a spoon.

"Chaplin, are you okay?" The hacker is peering at me.

"I'm fine."

"It's funny," he says. "I get the feeling that you're always pushing—trying to get somewhere. Like you think something is going to sneak up behind you."

I gulp the rest of my wine. "I've got to go home and walk my dog," I say.

Then I hop on my bike and pedal away home as fast as I can.

Wednesday, August 15, 2007

I'm making out with the stringer at an afternoon pool party in Jersey City when my cell phone rings. I don't bother to answer it, because, you know, I'm making out.

On the way to the PATH train to meet my date for the evening, I check my messages.

"Hullo, beautiful girl. Hullo, sweetheart. I'm sorry I've been out of touch. How are you, girl? How are you? Let's talk soon, chick. Very soon, sweetheart, okay, very soon . . ."

Please don't do this to me, goes through my mind. Leave me alone, leave me alone. And then, he loves me! He does!

I run through the streets of Manhattan as if running were an entirely effortless act. On my date, I'm fairly buzzing with excitement, but none of it is for the man in front of me.

Sunday, August 19, 2007

Summer sighs. "I get it," she says. "He's your vegan chef."

"No, this is different," I say. "It's like he knows. How could it be that I have a dream about him, and then two days later he calls?"

"Yeah, that's how it was with the vegan chef," she says. "Men have spidey-sense. That's just the way it works."

"Do I call him back?"

"I wouldn't," she says. And then, "Well, that's not true. I would. But my advice is you shouldn't. Make him suffer. He'll only want you more."

Eleanor says the exact same thing about the spidey-sense. She says men know the minute you're slipping away and that's the very minute they step in to reel you back. Is this something all women know, except me, because I was the dumb one who hooked up at age twenty?

"I can't stop thinking about him," I wail.

"I know," Eleanor says. "The brightest sparks are the most dangerous."

Monday, August 20, 2007

The minor director disappeared.

I do not understand men.

Tuesday, August 21, 2007

I slept with the hacker last night. What a disgusting business sex is. Two grown people sweating and grunting and pushing themselves up against each other. It started hurting midway through but I didn't want to make him feel bad so I didn't say anything. He's such a lovely guy. After he fell asleep, I talked to myself between my legs. I said, it's okay. There, there. And I squeezed my eyes shut and scrunched up my face against the feeling of violation and loneliness that settled in around me.

I had to wake up at the crack of dawn to get to the Omni in Midtown, where I interviewed Colm McCullough. Colm starred in that movie about the Irish real estate developer in Dublin who falls in love with a Ukrainian governess, which my neighbor took me to see the night before last. I nearly wept through the whole thing. I kept thinking—that's St Stephen's Green, where I had lunch with you-know-who. That's Grafton Street, where I went shopping with Seth. That's the Northside, where I wandered around and felt so happy. There's the market where you-know-who helped the city start a farmer's market.

Why is it that happiness remembered feels like despair?

Afterward, I spent the whole day on the phone tracking McCullough down. In real life he's a rock star. (Well, an Irish rock star. I'd never heard of him.) And then it turned out he was in New York doing a show and I bullied his PR person into getting me an interview.

We talk for three hours. Every time he says my name, with the *th* turned into a *d*, and the long rolling *r* at the end, my heart contracts and then goes to jelly. When I'm leaving, Colm scribbles his number in my notebook and says to call him anytime. He says, "I feel like I'll be seeing you again soon." Maybe I just like Irishmen?

Later

It's 3:30 a.m. I just got home. I met the Ukrainian governess from the movie. She's only twenty-two and Colm McCullough's girlfriend in real life. They fell in love while making the movie. I wanted to punch her in the face. She's so tiny and pretty. Why does she get to live a fairy tale? Colm told me to come visit backstage after his show, but Miss Fairytale put the ixnay on it saying she didn't want any press around. So I headed out with the rest of the band to this bar the Scratcher on Fifth Street and drank Guinness with them and basked in the sounds of all those lilting voices and thought, why, why, why. I was so happy in Dublin.

It's strange, isn't it, how Josh never even crosses my mind? How can it be I was with him for thirteen years and then one day he's just gone and I don't even seem to care?

I will not call Kieran back. I will not call Kieran back. I will not call Kieran back.

Friday, August 24, 2007

Should I go upstate? Am I a terrible person for being here having the summer of my life while they're all upstate recovering from the worst thing that can happen?

Sunday, August 26, 2007

Friend's baby shower. Lots of exposed brick and high-end Viking kitchen equipment. I am the only single person here. I am surrounded by moms in skinny jeans and oversized tops, all with dainty chains around their necks with little gold circles engraved with the initials of their children. They must hand these out at maternity wards. All the women have rocks on their fingers—not Upper East Side rocks, as no self-respecting Park Slope mom wants to be mistaken for an Upper East Side mom. Rather, the diamonds are just big enough to say "I shop at the food co-op for the organic produce, not the cheap prices." The buffet is artisanal cheeses and figs, chunks of dark chocolate, bunches of red grapes.

I am simultaneously baffled by their need to make their lives look like a magazine spread and trying not to drop to my knees weeping that I've failed to pull it off myself.

Everyone knows I'm recently separated. I'm treated with a kind of gentle deference like I was just in a car accident but no one wants to mention that my face has been disfigured. No one says Josh's name but everyone says, how *are* you? To which I think, better than you, asshole, married to that slob you know you hate, with your brain turned to playdate and diaper-infested mush. I think, you're lucky oversized tops are in right now, because I know what's going on under there. You may have your children, but I have my waist. And I think we both know who got the better end of the stick. And then, oh God, these women look so tired. None of us knows anyone else's pain, do we?

Tuesday, August 28, 2007

My bench has crumbled. It's gone. Totally wiped out. It was here just last week. I don't understand. What happened to everybody? Is it possible I was just on a streak? That I'm not smarter and cooler than everyone else?

I'm going upstate.

Thursday, August 30, 2007
Upstate

Seth wants my advice on hanging a few pictures.

Seth is not the fastest decision maker in the world. "Here?" he says, holding them up above the couch.

"Sure," I say.

"Or what about here?" Up behind the dining room table.

"That works."

"Or maybe here?" Up over the easy chair.

Cecilia comes in through the kitchen door. She puts her hand in her hair. "Oh my God, is this still going on?"

"Is it so wrong that I want the place to look nice?" Seth says. "Is that so wrong?"

"Thank God you're here, Heather," Cecilia says.

Really? I think.

Later

We go for a swim at Crystal Lake. Mark Ruffalo is just leaving with his son when we arrive. I love Mark Ruffalo.

The lake is in a valley surrounded on all sides by hills covered in fir trees. A friend of Cecilia's meets us there; I'm intimidated because he was one of the founders of ACT UP, but I try to act nonchalant. When he asks me if I want to swim around the lake I say, "Yes!?" and then, "Actually, I'm kind of scared of dark water." Around the lake is more than a mile. He says his boyfriend was scared too but that he got over it. I decide I will too. I will not have my life be dictated by irrational fears, I think.

The water is freezing at first, and here's the thing, I truly have a terror about dark water. And in Crystal Lake, you can't even see your toes when you step in. I've scuba dived down as far as 140 feet—I've seen manta rays and sharks, eels and parrot fish, and swam right through a school of ferociously grinning silver barracudas. But that was in clear blue ocean water. It's the *dark* that scares me. I've never done anything at Crystal Lake but putter around the edges. The sky is overcast, so the water is not just murky today but nearly black. Glassy without a ripple on it.

"Maybe I'll hold off, actually," I say.

My brother rolls his eyes. "Oh, shut up," he says. And then to their friend, "She can swim around this whole thing twice if she wants." It reminds me of Mac's comment at the badminton game in Park Slope. What do these people know about me that I don't know?

The first time I put my face into the water, I have the sensation that I am going to lose control of my bowels. It's not a pleasant feeling. I make myself do three lengths, but then the fear causes me to start to sputter and flail my arms and legs. I think about everything I've ever learned about breathing—how yoga is all about the breath, how in scuba diving your lungs will literally explode if you don't keep breathing—but I can't find my breath at all. Neither, though, will I let myself take my head up out of the water. You will do this, I say to myself. As I keep swimming, I get a feeling like I've lost all sense of where up or down is. I feel like I might vomit into the water. Finally I can't stand it anymore and I break through the surface, gasping for air. I hear the fir trees that rise up from the lake rustling in the breeze.

The first half mile is the worst. I'm thinking, oh, I guess this is what panic attacks are like. But then something shifts. Eventually the vertigo gives way to a state of incredible relaxation, like my body is an aquatic thing, a perfectly calculated machine for doing exactly what it's doing right at this moment. It's effortless, and the ongoing rhythm of my stroke feels like someone comforting me.

As we're heading back to Seth and Cecilia, watching us from their towels, I even put my face in the water and open my eyes without thinking I'm going to be sick.

Seth calls out, "You didn't make any bets with her, did you?"

Later

We go hear Ray Price and Willie Nelson play at Bethel Woods. Seth was on tour recently with a band that opened for Willie Nelson so Cecilia and he head backstage to say hi. I stay in my seat. Josh and I had our first dance to a Ray Price song. I watch the people around me. Lots of older people, the ladies with bouffant hair, the men in cowboy hats. I wonder if any of them had Ray Price as their first dance too. I wonder if they all hate each other now.

Friday, August 31, 2007

Seth is at the grill. Alex Green is leaning on Ben's knee, drinking from a sippy cup. Alex is not only walking but also talking. In my heart I want Alex to run to me like his long-lost mother. But I also don't want him to even recognize me, because I don't want Marie to be reminded of those months when she wasn't there.

I'm amazed at how easy they all seem. I know that the worst thing I could do is only think of their tragedy when I see them, but I can't help it. I find it harder to meet Ben's eye now than when he was on his knees weeping.

After dinner they tell us. Marie is pregnant. Just a few weeks so we can't tell anyone else.

How could they have enough faith in the world to have another child after what happened to them?

Saturday, September 1, 2007

Back in Brooklyn.
     Is it getting dark already?

Sunday, September 2, 2007

Reminder to self: do not agree to be on any more panels about stupid shit you don't care about.

I spent the whole day in Goldman Sachs next to the president of UCLA, a pop-culture academic from MIT, and this video-artist buddy of mine, while they tried to raise money for some new digital media program. It was hours of blathering on about emerging art forms of the future. Blah. Blah. Blah. Blah.

Then, as if that weren't enough, we were whisked uptown in black SUVs with leather seats and tinted windows to a little fete at the Goldman Sachs guy's gazillion-dollar apartment. Private elevator and horrible modern art everywhere. I mean, there was an eyeball as big as my torso blinking at me from the fireplace. And the banker's wife was wearing a gray wool dress with leather cutouts lined with grommets and shoes covered with more grommets. How could her stylist have let her out with so many grommets, I think.

My artist buddy is a big fat man with a trim black beard, one eye that runs off on its own, and some kind of foreign accent. He was psyched because if this program gets approved, he'll be the director. So that's what he was doing there, but what was I doing there? The pop-culture academic, in Tevas, jeans, and red suspenders, was clearly there for the free food—he packed it away like nobody's business, shoving little piles of tuna tartar into the hole behind his beard with a rapidity of motion I've rarely seen from the academic community.

Then I got placed at a table with the editor of *Artforum* and some guy in a cravat with enormous, round, black-rimmed glasses that made me want to laugh out loud in his face. And I know I should have schmoozed and made nice and acted like the fancy, impressive person they'd carted me up here to be, but I was so busy trying not to drive a fork into my hand under the table that I couldn't. Instead I got incredibly drunk, and I must confess I snorted when the president of UCLA congratulated the grommet-covered woman on her art collection.

The last thing I remember is a plate of artisanal cheese and apple slices placed in front of me and a vivid fantasy of smashing my champagne flute into the smooth, oval face of the poor, unsuspecting *Artforum* editor to my left.

In the SUV designated to drive me home, the world spun, and I closed my eyes and tried not to vomit and thought, what a fool you are. What a mess.

Monday, September 3, 2007

It's definitely getting darker earlier. I've decided to go to Hawaii with Daphne and her husband.

Tuesday, September 4, 2007

It's past two in the morning. I should be asleep but I'm not.

Kieran, why did you call me? Should I have called you back? Do you think about me the way I think about you? I still compose love letters to you in my head, you know.

With my bench it was easier not to think about you. Did you know I had such a strong bench? They're all gone now. It doesn't matter anyway, because none of them made me feel the way you did. I only had sex with one of them and only once. It was totally gross. What a disgusting business sex is. Not with you, though. Not with you. I wish you were here, Kieran. I wish you loved me.

Saturday, September 8, 2007

4:32 a.m.—just home.

Faith comes up to visit, and we go to a house party in Prospect Heights where my friend is DJing. The air is thick with marijuana smoke. The host is a tiny Korean guy with a wispy goatee. Highly mellow. We thank him for letting us come. He puts his hand over his heart and thanks us for coming.

Around 2 a.m. we leave to go meet a friend of mine who's in an anarchist marching band, which is hosting an all-night revelry at Grand Army Plaza.

At the circle, we dance with the anarchists and with each other, swinging arm to arm. I grab Faith in an enormous hug.

"Thank you for bringing me here!" she cries. "I needed this."

"I love you," I say. I am determined to bring a little fun into Faith's life. "We'll get through. I promise."

And then, as we whirl around, and the dark sky above us spins: "Oh God, please don't let summer end!"

Faith pulls slightly away. "Heath, summer is already over."

But I don't want to hear it. I swing her around harder until we both fall on the grass.

Tuesday, September 18, 2007

I'm in Prospect Park, and I am sobbing. Right there by the swan pond, in full view of about fifteen Hasidim and a dozen joggers.

Eleanor is saying, "Heather, Heather, it's okay. It's okay."

But I am not able to stop.

"I can't explain," I gasp. "I can feel it. Something very bad is going to happen. There are storm clouds on the horizon. I see them coming."

Thursday, October 11, 2007
Hawaii

1. I love scuba diving. No one else wanted to go so I went by myself. I swam next to turtles that must have been five hundred years old. Hovered right beside one, watching him watching me and thinking the world is a wonderful and beautiful place.

2. I do not like being around famous writers. All the people here are like 500 million times more successful than me, and they all tell amazing stories around the dinner table. I feel tiny and insignificant. I don't even try to get a word in edgewise. I focus on not scowling too ferociously.

3. I do not like insomnia. We're staying in a house atop a cliff overlooking an immense white sand beach—whiter than I knew a beach was capable of being. There's a riptide on this beach, which means it's completely deserted. Just miles of white sand and turquoise water. Every morning before anyone else is up, I walk this beach, my legs sinking knee-deep into the sand. I'm pouring sweat when I get back. Since I got here it's been one nonstop attempt to exhaust myself with swimming, walking, surfing, running, and yoga. But nothing helps. I'm awake. I'm awake. I'm awake.

4. I do not like couples. There are four of them. I hear little snippets all day long. I watch them help each other in little ways—Honey, you want me to pack you a sandwich? Hey, babe, I grabbed a towel for you. It makes me think, really? It could be like that? And then it's a sharp pain in my chest.

5. I do not like Eleanor. Her cousin got married and she didn't invite me. This is the first time I haven't been invited to a Stein event in as long as I can remember. I wasn't part of the family? I was just her stand-in until she found a husband?

6. I do not, it turns out, like the good life. Every evening we all climb into the hot tub, which is off the back deck set right on the cliff edge over that extraordinary expanse of white beach. We bring in cocktails and glasses of champagne and watch the sun set in the most extraordinary displays of rippling pink light. I have a little voice in my head, taunting me, saying, *How you enjoying the good life?* Fuck you, I think back. This *is* the good life. But I can't help it. I seem to be permanently irritated, as if irritation were a living thing, a festering of bugs on my skin.

7. I do not like Kieran. He emailed me yesterday asking when I was going to come visit. This time, I couldn't resist. I wrote him right back, call me please. And to my amazement, and horror, he did. And I wanted to hate him, but the sound of his voice was like butterflies fluttering in the sunlight. I tried to keep it light, but then I couldn't help it and I said, "Why are you inviting me to visit now?" Longing for him to say, *I can't stop thinking about you, girl. I must have you again.* But he said, "Jesus, girl, I don't know. It popped into my head." And I nearly doubled over in pain.

8. I do not like my mother. She is moving to Florida. She hasn't said she'll miss us or that she's sorry to be moving so far away. This feels like a pincer in my chest. I go around acting like I hate her, but whom do I think I'm kidding? What have I ever wanted but to feel loved by her and be capable of loving her back? I'll admit it: I still fantasize about being held by her. And now that Faith is a single mom, I find myself kind of in awe of how she managed when we were little, which pisses me off because it really damages my case against her. Am I

actually supposed to admit that she might have done the best she could—and that, considering the circumstances, her best wasn't so bad? Not today I'm not.

9. I do not like myself. All summer, I've felt so enormous—not diffuse and full of love like those blissful days of Dublin, but big, like a helium balloon at the Macy's Thanksgiving Day Parade. Picture me, or picture yourself if you prefer, blown up to the size of a New York City building. Held in check, but barely, by a team of people, and just cruising down the street, over the heads of all the little folk below. I felt like I imagined kings must have felt in medieval times—anointed superior by God himself. I gotta say, it felt great. But now I feel like the parade is over and I'm being deflated, and somehow it was actually kind of monstrous being that big. And maybe I'm not as cool and awesome as I thought.

Saturday, October 13, 2007

Everyone else is asleep. But I'm awake. I feel haunted by Josh. I find myself in bed at night longing for him to be here so I could curl my feet around his ankles, wrap my arms around his waist, and lay my cheek against his back. I think about him on our wedding day. I think how I wept as he read his vows, not expecting to find myself crying but suddenly completely undone by the realization that this man loved me. *Loved me.* And I could hear everyone in their seats bawling too, because even though that very morning I'd still been nagging him to write them, he'd come up with words so astonishingly eloquent and unusual that what could anyone do but weep?

Even as I long for him, I can't bring his face up clearly before me.

Maybe I will go to Dublin. I've been working on a pitch about Colm McCullough and Dublin's newfound prosperity. It would be a research trip. And if I happened to see Kieran, I'd happen to see Kieran.

Monday, October 15, 2007

Email:

Dear Kieran,

Greetings from Hawaii!! More beautiful than you could possibly imagine! I'm having the best time! Cocktails in the hot tub every night! I'm so lucky that I can work anywhere. In fact, I just may come and visit you as I don't think I'll be able to make myself stay home! Do you know Colm McCullough? I'm doing a story on him and Dublin's newfound prosperity—isn't that funny! Talk soon! Xoxo

He writes back right away. (!!!!)

Email:

Hiya girl, now that sounds utterly fab. You are a lucky girl indeed to live that kind of life. Def come over for a visit if you can, as we would spoil you. It would be so nice to have someone to hold, someone I can trust and relax with, talk as well as make love to—maybe you should definitely come over and quick. Yours, in anticipation, Kieran.

Someone. He means me, doesn't he?

Tuesday, October 16, 2007

Email:

Good morning, girl. Thought I'd give you a wake-up note. Slightly worse for wear this morning myself due to a great night out. Brilliant stuff. Loads going on. Get that lovely ass of yours over here. Xxxxxxxxxxxx

That's two in a row from him. Two. In. A. Row. From him.

Wednesday, October 17, 2007

I've started cutting my meds in half. I have not had an orgasm with anyone else in the room since my early twenties, and I know it's the Paxil. If I decide to go to Dublin, and I'm not saying I have, I at least want the possibility of having an orgasm.

I've also started cutting my food intake in half. If I decide to go to Dublin, and I'm not saying I have, I *will* be as thin as last year.

Later

"This is what I get," I say to Eleanor. "I lost in the husband-and-children lottery, so instead, I get to have adventures. Just to stay home would be a waste of how much freedom I have, don't you think?"

"I do, I get it," Eleanor says. "I really do. And I'm in constant awe of how you live, I really am. It's extraordinary."

"But . . ." I say.

"Look, here's what I'm afraid of," Eleanor says. "You go. You have this amazing time. You get up really, really high, and then, when it's over, you crash back down to earth and are really miserable. I mean, you're already doing so much traveling. I mean, honestly, if I'm completely honest, what I'd like is to see you build a life for yourself where you actually live."

"I don't think you should make decisions based on fear of what might happen afterward," I say.

"I just don't want to see you suffer," Eleanor says.

"Suffering is part of life," I say.

Saturday, November 3, 2007
Montreal

In the lobby of the W Montréal, I can't stop shivering. I'm here doing a story for *All Things Considered*. I haven't eaten since yesterday morning. *All Things Considered* doesn't pay expenses so I'm saving money by not eating.

Peter comes out of the elevator with this guy Billy Santiago, a former Microsoft programmer turned experimental video-game designer with a shaved head, heavily muscled torso, dirty glasses, and a tiny little cupid's bow of a mouth. He's thought to be a genius. A genius and an enormous asshole. Peter is gaga for him. I got Peter a gig covering this conference for Wired.com so he's here with me, sharing a hotel room. His face is glowing, which I take to mean his interview with Billy went well.

Peter takes one look at me and says, "Dude, are you okay?"

"Of course I'm okay," I say. "It's just so cold."

"Cold?" Peter says.

Billy Santiago is looking at me through his glasses with eyes that are like X-ray machines. I feel like he's going to know my hydration levels and chances of getting cancer at the end of this stare.

"I think maybe I'm hungry," I say.

Billy walks away. I think, wow, he is as big an asshole as everyone says. Then I see him walking back, but now he's got three Granny Smith apples in his hand, plucked from a silver bowl on the reception counter. He gives them to me. I bite into one. My hands are shaking.

"Do you want to get dinner?" he says.

"No," I say. "Not really. I mean, it has to be clean. You know, a clean meal."

Peter is looking at me, very concerned. But Billy is nodding.

"I know exactly," he says.

I think, you do? Then I think I might fall on the floor. The next thing I know, Billy Santiago is walking me to a taxi while I lean on his arm, and getting me in the taxi and to a Chinese restaurant where he orders us both plates of steamed vegetables.

Then we have an amazingly fascinating conversation about the nonlinear nature of time.

Also, Billy Santiago says he's been studying subparticle physics in his spare time and that at that level, particles exist only in relation to one another. Literally. There is no such thing as parts, only relations between parts. Then he says that if you brought a microscope down close enough on your finger, the boundaries separating your hand and everything else would begin to blur.

"You as a person are only a social construct," he says.

Wednesday, November 7, 2007

I lost the hat Kieran gave me. I don't know why I brought it to Montreal in the first place. The truth is I couldn't bear to be parted from it. Okay, sometimes I sleep in it. But, I've always been like that, picking up little odds and ends belonging to the people I care about, feathering my nest with flannel shirts and sweatshirts belonging to boyfriends, old maternity dresses of my mother's. Am I really to be punished for such a harmless comfort? I can't stop crying.

It gets dark so early in Montreal.

Thursday, November 8, 2007

I don't know what to think anymore. Today, Kieran wrote me a note full of anguish about his daughter, the autistic one. It was like I could feel his pain across the ocean. Apparently after several months of progress, the girl has regressed badly. I almost had tears in my eyes just reading about it. Then the note got really stiff, and he said he needed me to know his children would be his priority even if I were to come visit, which, okay, I have been leaning toward. In my mind, I was like, no shit, Sherlock. I wrote back right away, saying of course, of course, if now's not a good time for a visit, just say so. And I meant it. But then he wrote even more stiffly saying I wasn't understanding him, that of course he wanted me to come, he just wanted me to know what the deal was.

In order to ease his mind, I sent a picture of Sakura leaping in the air and wrote, "Fret not. This is a representation of how excited I am for the prospect of a trip! All will work out."

And then he wrote back an even stiffer note. This one started, "Dear Heather," and my heart almost sank to my knees. He told me how he'd been seeing someone on and off over the summer and that she wanted to be serious and this "had him running," that with his daughter regressing and his ex-wife screaming at him all the time he "couldn't take anything else on." He needed to know I didn't have any "expectations" of him.

I was so confused and hurt I didn't write back. Wasn't he the one who'd invited me?

Oh God, it wasn't a real invitation, was it. Was it?

Summer said, "Oh, men are the new girls. Why do they think they need to share every passing thought?"

My neighbor said, "He's probably so in love with you that he feels vulnerable, which is making him act weird." But then, she's obsessed with a guy in Bali who's clearly been trying to give her the heave-ho for months. Why do women give each other such bad advice?

Eleanor said, "Just drop the whole thing. Just drop it."

Then Kieran wrote again before I could even think how to respond: "I'm sorry if I pissed you off, girl," He wrote. "I know you're cool, strong, and independent. Come to Dublin. We'll have great craec."

BOOK FIVE

DUBLIN REDUX

Thursday, December 6, 2007
Dublin

When I get off the plane at ten to seven, I go to the same airport café and order an Americano. This time when I ask for cream, the guy behind the counter scowls at me and slides a container of skim milk across the counter.

It's raining in a thin, misty way.

I see the Bus Éireann with its blue upholstered seats and I can't help but feel excitement rise up in my chest. I think, I did it! Because let me tell you, just agonizing over whether or not to come was becoming a full-time job.

First off, my pitch about McCullough and Dublin's newfound prosperity is with an editor at the *New Yorker*. Ben hooked me up. True, the editor didn't call me back last week, but just the week before he said he loved it. And if that editor thinks stonewalling is going to put me off, he doesn't know me.

Then I found my own place to stay. My brother's friend Leah was going to be out of town and she said I could use her apartment as long as I didn't judge her for its messiness.

Then—and this totally threw me—Kieran was offended. (Hadn't he been the one freaking out about expectations?) I said, look, I don't want there to be any pressure for us to be romantic if we didn't feel like it. (Because really, does he not think I'm terrified we'll look at each other and find there's nothing between us anymore?) To which Kieran was all, cool, girl, we should have just told each other we were nervous before. Let's say we start as friends—"special friends"—and take it from there. (To which I was a little hurt but simultaneously like, no duh, dude.)

I got an assignment with the BBC, which means visiting my friend Phil in London and then hitching along on his trip to Morocco over New Year's. (Morocco!)

Then I found someone to rent my place, and Katy and Mac agreed to take Sakura while I'm gone.

In addition, I'm totally off Paxil, and my size 26 jeans need to be belted.

The point of all this? The point is here the fuck I am.

Later

To say Leah's place is "messy" would be like describing Stalin as grouchy. Cockroaches scatter when I turn on the lights. In the kitchen, there are greasy pans piled high on the stove and old wrappers from packaged food overflowing the kitchen trash. Who leaves town and doesn't take out the trash? In the bedroom there are piles of clothes up to my waist. The living room looks like a psychotic robbed a duty-free shop and then used his stolen goods to create spin art. The floor is littered with unopened boxes from Lancôme and Chanel. There are family-sized bags of chocolates as big as eggs, plugs for computers, shoe boxes, boxes of peanut brittle, an upside-down PlayStation, and multiple twenty-four packs of C batteries. Who even uses C batteries anymore?

All I can think is, what happened to this woman? And what's happened to me that I've ended up here?

I go into the bathroom, strip off my airplane clothes, and turn on the water.

After five minutes, the water is still cold.

After ten minutes, the water is still cold.

I'm shivering, my body covered in goose bumps. I can't get the heat to work any more than I can the hot water. I'm wrapped in what I hope is a clean towel.

After fifteen minutes, I take a deep breath and get into the tub and stand under the icy spray. I shout to bear it. I'm shivering even harder when I get out, and I race back to the bedroom still shouting. The carpet feels grimy under my feet, so I wobble to my suitcase, leapfrogging across the enormous piles of clothes that are every- where. I'm back out of the apartment in ten minutes.

As I'm leaving, I catch a glimpse of myself in a hallway mirror. It's not a pretty sight. My damp hair is hanging, uncombed, around my face. I'm wearing a sweater, a sweatshirt, my puffy jacket, and running shoes. My skin is pasty like it's been decades since I saw the sun. Great, I think. Great.

Later

When I get to the River Liffey and step onto the Ha'penny Bridge with its white cast-iron railings and lampposts, it's hard to believe I'm the same person who walked across this bridge last year with Kieran. I know if I keep going straight I'll be in Temple Bar, and I remember having passed a health food store there last year. I'm saying to myself, don't panic. Just get your almonds and everything will look better. There is no room in my budget for food on this trip, so I've decided to go without. Half of my suitcase is filled with Pow- erBars and sandwich bags of Puffins, which I figure I'll carry in my pockets to use as needed. I didn't have time to get any almonds before I left though, and almonds are central to this plan.

I have to pause for a minute as I cross over into Temple Bar, because I'm having the strange sensation both that I know exactly where I am and also that I am completely lost. I know that I've been at this spot before, but it seems like maybe it was in some other lifetime. I turn my head to the left, and then to the right, trying to get my bearings. There's a woman with a stroller looking in a store window to my right, and, to my left, a man in a gray scarf is striding toward me. I'm beginning to think I feel lost in perhaps more than just the geographical sense. Then I find myself becom- ing intensely aware of every detail around me—the precise way the air feels against my skin, the way the light shines through the grimy windows of a fishing supply store. I notice the woman with the stroller to my right is hugely pregnant. I see the man to my left is wearing a pin-striped blue suit with an open-collared shirt and that his hair is black. The thought runs through my mind that he's very handsome. I turn again to the woman and see that she's sucking on a lollipop. Then I turn back to the man—and it's as if the pace of time stops moving by any law of nature I've ever known, grinding me down into sickening slow motion. The handsome man with the gray scarf and black hair striding toward me is Kieran.

I think, No. Universe! My hair. My face in that mirror. I'm in running shoes.

And then I see his whole face light up. He starts to run. From a block away, I see those dazzling blue eyes widen and shine. I see his mouth open and transform into a smile of amazement. I see him running toward me, and I feel for a minute as if all the muscles in my body might give out. It's all going to be okay, I think. It's all, finally, going to be okay. This man is going to sweep me into his arms and hold me and I will, at last, finally, finally be safe.

And then he stops running. Just as I was picking up my feet to start running toward him, he stops running toward me. As if he'd hit a barrier. It's like I'm watching him assert control over himself as if control were the most important thing in the world. His face goes cold. His eyes go flat. He is no longer running. He is sauntering. He is sauntering toward me as if I barely ranked as a casual acquaintance.

"So you're here, are you?" he's says when he reaches me. I have frozen entirely. "When did you get in?" He's looking all around. Anywhere but at me. I cannot find any rational words in my mind to answer him. All that comes to me is, your eyes are so blue.

How can the very first person I see in Dublin be *Kieran*?

The word *no* is running through my mind. And then inane mumblings begin pouring out of my mouth. I have no idea what I'm saying or why I'm giggling like the village idiot.

"Well, I'm on my way to a meeting," Kieran says. "Fancy a drink tonight?"

"No!" Inside my head. Now outside in the world. All I want

is to get away. This is not how this scene is supposed to be played. I must regroup. I must regain control of the situation. I must be wearing mascara for this scene to be played properly.

"Right. Tomorrow then." And he's gone. And I stand there. And I have a terrible feeling in the pit of my stomach—just a tiny thing, but terrible nonetheless. It came into existence in that fraction of a second between when he was running toward me and when he stopped.

Reader. Why did he stop running?

Friday, December 7, 2007

Andrew Dempsey is complaining about the Irish. I'm scribbling down everything he says in my little notebook.

Andrew is the director of the movie about the Irish landlord and the Ukrainian governess. He's thin and tall, gangly like a not-yet-fully-developed teenager, although I think he's about my age. His skin has clearly seen its share of acne. His nose seems to move in several different directions at once before ending in a disjointed knob not far above his top lip. For a guy with a hit movie, he seems remarkably grouchy. I like him immediately.

Just as it was last year, Grafton Street is hung with shimmery silver Christmas decorations lamppost to lamppost.

When I left the apartment this morning I decided I wasn't going to get all dolled up for my drinks with Kieran. I'd said to myself, no, you are cool, strong, and independent. You will face him *again* in running shoes. My nod to vanity is a white aviator's hat that I bought in Montreal. As I'm talking with Andrew Dempsey, I find myself smiling in anticipation of Kieran saying how beautiful I look in my hat.

We've been talking about Dublin's newfound prosperity; Andrew says it's destroying the city. He points to a window display of cheap, slinky party dresses. "All this 'wealth'"—he makes air quotations—"it's bullshit. It'll come crashing down. It's not who the Irish are. Just read the newspapers—did you read about Katy French?"

"Who's Katy French?" I ask.

"Read the papers," Andrew says. "Girl thought she was some kind of socialite celebrity. Reality TV. Modeling in her knickers for the papers. As if Ireland has socialites or celebrities. We have Bono, that's enough. She OD'd three days ago. I'm telling you, this 'prosperity' "—again with the air quotations—"it's not real."

"Well, it is real," I say. "It may be different, but it is happening."

"No," Andrew says. "It's not. It's people at a party thinking the morning will never come. Well, the morning is coming. It came for Katy French, didn't it?"

This gives me a kind of chill.

On the way to meet Kieran, I stop in Bewley's Café at the top of Grafton Street and put on a little mascara and some lipstick in the bathroom—because, you know, while I am cool, strong, and independent, I am also human.

Later

There are plush red banquettes around the bar's edge, high ceilings, dark mahogany–paneled walls, filmy glass chandeliers, and a long marble bar—with Kieran O'Shea sitting at the end of it, head down in a newspaper.

I'm standing there, my eyes adjusting to the light, waiting for him to sense my presence. I start walking. At any minute he will look up, and then he will turn to me, and then I will see his eyes deepen and shine, and then he will open his arms to me and yesterday will be blotted out.

I'm all the way next to him before he looks up.

"Kieran!" I cry. I *will* be the woman of my emails. Cool, strong, and independent. Did I not tell you that those are my middle names?

Kieran is barely looking at me. "Hiya," he says. The first thing I think is that he's afraid, but I don't know of what or why. And I don't have time to contemplate because he says, "What is that on your head?" and he reaches over and takes my hat and drops it onto the bar.

The tiny panic in the pit of my stomach from yesterday spreads up out of my stomach, into my chest and then into my brain. I have an image of curling up in a ball under the bar.

I think, I will have to go through this night with hat hair.

I open my mouth and just start talking.

I'm like, "Kieran, I lost the hat you gave me! I was sooo bummed!" Blah, blah, blah, blah! I'm yammering and trying to be full of mirth.

In my imagination, Kieran says, *Come on, girl, let's go right now and buy you another one.*

In real life, Kieran says, "I'll tell you where I bought it," and drains the last of his pint.

"Ha-ha-ha!" I say, although I have no idea why I'm laughing.

Silence. And then I say, "Okay! Next round on me! This trip you *have* to let me pay my share."

In my imagination, he says, *No way, girl. Your money is no good here. I'm going to spoil you just like last time.*

"Okay," Kieran says, and gestures to the bartender.

While he's ordering, I take a closer look. His eyes are red-rimmed and the set of his jaw is grim. He reminds me of Ray Liotta in *Goodfellas*, all torqued up on coke and driving around in that 1970s car, peering through the windshield at a helicopter that may or may not be following him. Now, just to be clear, I found Ray Liotta in *Goodfellas*, all torqued up on coke, driving around in his 1970s car, incredibly sexy. So I'm not saying he looks bad. He just looks strung out. Like he's suffering. I say, "Kieran, are you okay? You seem kind of tense." And he says, "I'm fab. Totally fab."

I get the feeling that he wants to scratch me. Or is afraid I'm going to scratch him. I think, Kieran, are your claws out? I know what that's like. But you can't just say that to a person.

And then he's drinking the last of his beer, and I think, any minute he's going to walk out the door and this will be the state of things. You will have *lost*. Suddenly I find myself feeling exactly as I had in the Shannon Airport. That if I don't hold on to this man with everything I have, I will die. So, giggling, inanely, I say, "Oh my God, Kieran, you're not going to believe this after all our back-and-forth, but the place I'm staying at has no hot water and no heat and cockroaches everywhere. I need to come stay at your place after all!"

Within thirty seconds I wish I could have taken it back. Kieran is like, "My ex is using my house, which has a trampoline in the back, because it's the only thing keeping my daughter calm right now." And I'm like, "Oh my God, forget I said anything. I'm not your responsibility." But then it's like some moral-principal hospitality thing has kicked in and he keeps saying, "No, I cannot have you staying somewhere like that in Dublin. You *will* come to my house."

I can't even tell you how racked with guilt I feel. But then, something else too. As we leave Stag's Head, it's horrible, I know, but I feel a little spark of excitement in my chest. You haven't lost yet, I think. Got him. A foot in the door.

Later

Through the taxi window, I see Kieran waiting for me in his doorway. He's got one arm up against the frame, the other hanging loosely by his side. From half a block away I can see how strong and lean he is. I find myself flushing with desire, followed closely by shame.

The taxi stops in front of his house. Kieran leaps across the sidewalk and opens my door. He's all smiles, talking to me, talking to the taxi driver. "Here you are, girl. Was starting to worry about you—thanks for bringing her, mate. You find the place all right?

Okay. Good. Good. Ta!" He insists on paying the cabbie and grabs my bag, waving me away with his free hand when I try to protest. "Don't be ridiculous, girl," he says. "Come on, come in. Come see my house."

I'm not sure what to make of this change. Was Stag's Head a bad dream?

Kieran leads me into his house, talking all the way. There are the kids' rooms, that's his bedroom, come up the stairs, here's the kitchen, want a beer? Make yourself at home, sit down, I'll bring it to you.

The living room has blue walls, a Christmas tree flickering with Christmas lights, a stereo, stacks of CDs, and a burgundy-colored couch in two sections against the wall. "I'm a bachelor, as you can see"—laughter, the sound of the refrigerator door opening, a bottle cap being popped off—"but it's mine." He's in the living room with me now, handing me a bottle of beer, throwing himself into a corner of the couch. "Been on my own for five months now. Actually having my own space, girl"—he makes a kind of whistling sound between his teeth—"well, I don't need to tell you what that's like, do I, girl? Mad stuff altogether."

I laugh. I'm so relieved, I could drop to my knees.

I can't help myself, though. I say, "Kieran, I don't understand. You seem so much more relaxed now. You seemed so tense before."

"I was just off work then, girl. Now I'm home."

I think, this is more than the difference between home and work, but I don't pursue it. I'm too relieved. Instead I jump up. "Kieran! I have a present for you!"

Kieran rubs his hands together, cries out, "Amazing! I love surprises."

I pull a package wrapped in red tissue paper from my bag, hand it to him. "I got this for you in Hawaii since you said you'd always wanted to go there," I say.

It's a lie. I bought it off the Internet when I got home. But he'll never know.

Kieran pulls apart the wrapping with a big smile on his face, holds the T-shirt up in front of him. It says "Hawaii" over a 1970s-style image of a surfer riding a wave. "Look at you, girl. Aren't you magic? I love it."

I'm thinking, finally.

"Should I try it on?"

"Absolutely."

Kieran stands up and pulls the T-shirt he's wearing off—in that way guys do, with one hand grabbing the fabric from behind the neck and pulling it over his head. I think, he's showing off his body. And then I think, oh my God, his body.

"Well, girl," he says. "How do I look?"

"You look fantastic," I say. "I'm so pleased."

Kieran comes and sits down right next to me on the couch. "Thank you, Heather," he says. And then he leans toward me and I don't know whether he's going for a peck on the cheek or a full-on kiss until I actually feel his lips pressing against mine.

Half of me is thinking, finally, finally. The other half of me is thinking, don't do it, Heather, if there's one thing you know it's pain. And this man is in PAIN.

But I can't resist him. Or I don't know, maybe that's why I can't resist him.

I feel his arms encircle my waist. I wrap my arms around his neck. He runs a forefinger down my cheek, leans his forehead against mine. "Picking up right where we left off, aren't we, sweetheart?" he says. I nod, too shy suddenly to speak. He lays himself down on the couch and pulls me on top of him.

Saturday, December 8, 2007

Email:

Summer, I slept with Kieran last night. I wasn't going to, but then I did. I said, "Kieran, let's go slow." He said, "why?"

And I said, "because I'm in a foreign country and you seem really tense." Then he said, "well, we don't have much time, girl." And that really hurt. But then it was like a fog descended over me and my vision got blurry. I was wet, Summer. I was so wet. Why does he have this power over me? Then he kept saying, "Yeah, baby." Like it wasn't actually me there but rather some fantasy partner in some amateur porn he was filming in his mind. And Summer—he told me to lick his balls. I don't know what to make of this. He said those exact words—"Lick my balls, baby." Please tell me, has anyone ever said that to you? Is that normal? It felt like a slap. What happened to the man who rhapsodized about my skin in the moonlight? I feel so ashamed when I think about it. Not of doing it—because I did, and actually it was fine. But the way he said it. It was so impersonal.

I hear him moving around upstairs. Please write back.

Later

Kieran makes us eggs and fried tomatoes. It's total silence in the kitchen except the sound of him cooking—pans out of the cabinets, eggs breaking, a knife cutting into soft fruit, oil sizzling. I sit in my chair, feet tucked under me, drinking coffee, watching him, trying not to take up too much space.

He smiles at me for the first time when he deposits our food on the table. I breathe out. He's eating, looking for the sports section and telling me about the day ahead. He's got a friend coming over to hook up speakers for the party he's having tonight, then he's off to watch a soccer match with friends before the show at Temple Bar Music Center he's also got on the roster. I'm thinking, why again are you having a party while I'm here? And why are you going off to watch sports on television while I'm here? He clears his throat and says, "That girl I told you about in my letter, she's probably going to be there tonight. And I am *not*—" he holds his hands up in front of him—"I am *not* going to tell her about you. That is the last thing I need."

I have just taken a mouthful of egg, but when he says this, it refuses to go down my throat. I think, he's not even soft-pedaling here. I can't say anything back because the egg is stuck on my tongue. I find myself thinking, maybe I should get up and spit in the sink. Would that be too disgusting? Could I do it without him noticing? Confusion reigns in my mind. All I can think is, don't let him see you're suffering. I would like to say, fine, sounds good to me, but, because of the egg, I can't. So I just nod in what I hope is a cool, strong, and independent manner, and then I get up and leave the room.

Half an hour later

"You know what? I'm ticked off." It's me talking—talking loudly, not screaming, but heated. I'm talking in a heated manner. To Kieran. "This whole other-girl thing? I would never have done this to you. If you had come to New York, I would never have slept with you and then expected you to hang out with someone I was seeing the next day. That is rude."

I'd sat in the bathroom being cool, strong, and independent by myself for a while and then I had thought, you know what, I am tired of always staying silent. And I'd marched back up the stairs into the kitchen.

"Do you hear me?" I say. Because Kieran has his back to me. He's washing dishes at the sink. "Do you hear me?"

Kieran turns around slowly, and when he does, there is anger on his features like I have never seen on anyone except Josh. He throws the dish towel he was using onto the counter and points a finger at me, and the next thing I know, he's nearly shouting at me. It's as if he's in the middle of a slightly different conversation than the one I thought I just started. "No! No! I will not have this," he is saying. "I have done nothing my whole life except take care of people, and I will not take care of you too. I cannot have this right now!"

I take a step back. In my mind I'd only gotten as far as marching bravely up the stairs. Now I don't know what to do. And I get the strange sensation that Kieran may be talking to other people besides just me.

"Why did you sleep with me last night?" I cry.

"Goddamn it!" Kieran's got his hands in his hair now. "I knew I shouldn't have. I promised myself I wouldn't even touch you!"

It feels like he's swiped at me with a razor. Why wouldn't he have wanted to touch me?

"Well, you did!" I shout.

"Well, too bad!" he shouts back. "I'm selfish and hard-hearted right now. What don't you understand? My daughter, my wife, my mother—and now *you*! I'm done taking care of other people! Do you hear me? I'm done!"

I find myself thinking, who is he talking to? And then, that could be me talking. There is such anguish on his face. All the anger that was sustaining me evaporates. I understand exactly what he's saying, not the specifics of course, but the feeling—the desire to do exactly as you please for once; the ferocious need to protect your freedom after years of enslavement to other people. Care Less About Other People 2007. Turns out it runs both ways. I feel myself visibly deflate.

"She lives here," Kieran cries. "And you're leaving in three days. What do you want from me?"

He's right, I think. What *do* I want from him? Why am I here?

"I get it," I say. I'm deflating so rapidly I might as well be an old balloon hissing its way out of the sky. "Of course you're selfish right now. That's how I've been too since the separation. It's not wrong of you. And your daughter. I understand. You should absolutely do whatever pleases you right now. I totally get it."

Suddenly, I feel so tired, as if I might fall asleep right there on the linoleum floor.

Kieran is staring at me. He looks suspicious, like he thinks I'm faking him out and is waiting for me to spring on him.

"I'm just gonna get going," I say. In my mind, I exit the room and am gone before he's even regained his balance. But I'm so tired, it feels like my eyes are shutting on me. My exit is less than graceful.

"I'm just"—I gesture downstairs—"I'm just gonna lie down for a few minutes. If that's okay. And then I'll go."

Kieran is still as a statue, still in fighting stance, still staring at me. I stumble out of the kitchen. My eyelids are closing on me. I can't be awake anymore.

Later

It's cold in Kieran's bedroom. I have all the covers piled on top of me, even over my head. I'm curled up in the tightest ball I can get myself into. I keep falling into a deep, dark sleep and then waking up with a start not knowing where I am. I have no idea what time it is, but it's already dark out. I have such a sinking sensation in my stomach. I want to get up and make another go at a dignified exit, but this hideous dark sleep keeps pulling me under.

Later

I awaken to voices upstairs. It must be the guy with the speakers. It's pitch dark in this room. I feel like I've shrunken in size—like somehow the bed has gotten bigger and I've gotten smaller. Or maybe the bed has floated out to sea and the vast expanse I feel around me is the ocean. I should get up and leave. But I can't move.

"Heather? Heather, girl." It's Kieran. He's sitting on the edge of the bed. I can barely open my eyes to look at him. "Listen, girl, it's all going to be okay," he's saying. "Please don't leave. I'll sort everything. I want you to come tonight. I want you to be here. We'll work it out, I promise, girl."

"Okay, Kieran." My eyes are flickering. It's painful to keep them open.

"I'm going to my football match now," he says. "But please make yourself comfortable. Do anything you like. There's tons of food in the fridge. Will you eat something, girl? You've barely eaten since you got here. And then come out tonight. Okay, sweetheart? Will you come?"

"Yes, Kieran," I say, but I'm thinking, if everything is going to work out, why are you going to a soccer match instead of climbing under the covers with me? I'm pulled back into this dark, oceanic sleep before I even have time to get upset about it.

Later

A ringing sound pulls me awake. It takes me a while to figure out what's making the noise or where it's coming from. Finally I realize it's my phone and I scramble for it. It's Kieran. Behind him I hear people talking and glasses clinking. "I'm checking on you, girl!" he shouts through the noise. "Are you coming? Did you get my texts, sweetheart? Do you need directions?"

"I'm coming!" I shout back, even though it's just me alone in the dark house. It's past nine. I've been asleep all day. I scramble around in the cold, pulling on my skinny jeans from Topshop last year, a black tank top trimmed with lace, and my black platform shoes. I pull my hair back in a ponytail and apply red lipstick. I realize this is exactly what I wore the night I met Kieran, except now I have to belt the pants.

In the taxi back to the city center, I make a deal with myself. I say, if you don't have fun, you can leave. But you have to at least try. By the time we're getting near Grogans pub, where I'm to meet Kieran, I'm feeling quite good about myself. I think, fuck it. I am going to enjoy myself tonight. I'm on an adventure. You can't expect adventures to be smooth sailing. I'm not gonna let some guy run me boo-hooing out of town. If he wants to be with some other girl, fine, that's his problem. Plus, by the time I get there he has texted me like five times to make sure I'm not lost. So, okay then.

As I get out of the taxi, I see him standing by Grogans side door smoking a cigarette, surrounded by people. He's wearing a blue short-sleeve shirt over a black long-sleeve shirt and he's moving around in that liquid way I remember. I can't let myself think how attractive he is, because if I do, I'll hop back in the taxi and ride away. I saunter over, pretending to look at him but actually looking at a spot just over his head.

Kieran is like another person. He's got me by the arm and is introducing me all around. He's off to the bar to buy me a pint. He's saying, "This is Heather," to a plump woman up from Galway. And she's saying, "Heather, I've heard so much about you, what a pleasure! I've been dying to meet you." And I think, you have? You were? There's a French couple and a Dublin woman named Kathryn with papery white skin and gleaming red hair. I decide my best policy is to studiously avoid Kieran. Make him suffer. So I slide into the booth with his friends and jump into the conversation and pretend like he's not even there. You want cool, strong, and independent? I will show you cool, strong, and independent.

By the time we're at the club where the band is playing, Kieran is checking in with me every couple of minutes, asking if I'm good, do I need a drink, am I having fun. And I'm always like, yup, yup, fine. When people start dancing, I go out on the floor with them, leaving Kieran on the sidelines. When he tells me he has to head back to his house to get ready for the party, I say, "I think I'm going to stay awhile. I'll see you later." When he's gone, the girl from Galway puts her arm around me and says, "Kieran told me I'm to take very good care of you." So, okay then.

When we get back to Kieran's place, the party is just getting started even though it's already past one in the morning. There's a DJ in a tracksuit spinning in the living room, while people watch, waiting for that moment when suddenly it's time to dance. People are sitting around the kitchen table smoking hash, rooting through Kieran's fridge for beer. I'm sticking to my policy of total self-sufficiency, though I do keep one eye on Kieran's movements. And you know what, he's got an eye on me too. Every time he comes through, he gives me a big smile, an *all okay?* smile. And I cock an eyebrow Scarlett O'Hara style at him and he laughs.

I hang out for a while with Kathryn of the papery white skin, smoking spliffs and talking about Ireland in the Middle Ages and what "prosperity" is doing to modern-day Dublin. Then I go into the living room. Kieran is there. He gives me a big smile, but I continue the studious avoidance. Luckily for me, there are lots of men. This guy comes up to me and we start to dance, like partner dance. Like he's bringing me close and guiding me out, and twirling and dipping me backward. Soon people gather around to watch and they're clapping and cheering. The guy brings me in tight so our chests are pressed together and I can feel the stubble on his cheek against my own, and then with a flick of his wrist he indicates it's time for me to fly out; I turn, once, twice, three times, beneath the arc of our arms before he brings me back against his chest. He dips me; my head touches the floor. Everyone cheers. I think, oh my God, I love to dance. Kieran's face is a blur as I swing past him. I see that he's got two fingers up to his mouth and is whistling and cheering along with everyone else.

When, finally, this man and I collapse against each other, I am covered in sweat and panting. Laughing too. And then I find myself tumbling up against Kieran, who is suddenly right beside me. His eyes are glowing in that way men's eyes will glow, and I just go right on ignoring him, starting an eyelash-fluttering conversation with another man beside him until Kieran takes me by the arm and brings me close and leans his head down and says, "That girl isn't here tonight, you know."

I think, ha! I win!

"You know what, Kieran?" I say. "It's no concern of my mine. I support you in doing whatever you need to do in your life right now. Okay?"

Kieran looks shocked. And then he peers at me with the intense, intelligent curiosity I remember so well. And then his face breaks into a smile and he throws his head back and laughs, that wonderful, loose laugh I remember so well. And he pulls me to him, so that my face is pressed up against his chest. I can feel the laughter moving in him. Then he bends his knees, so his face is level with mine, and he looks right at me, as if he's trying to see into me. For the first time. For the first time since I arrived in this city, he *looks* at me. And it's that thing: his eyes are so familiar, and I have the feeling as if I were glimpsing infinity.

He whispers, "Heather, I'm so glad you're here. It feels so right that you're here. I don't even understand why it feels so right."

I think, that's what you said to me last year, you idiot. And then, it feels so right because you're in love with me, stupid. What a fool you were to keep me at arm's length. I feel a tremendous surge of victory in my chest. I think, maybe you *are* smarter and cooler than all those other single women. Maybe you are the smartest, coolest person in the world.

Then I decide to take a little ecstasy.

Tuesday, December 11, 2007

It's three days later. A kind of hazy mist is hanging over Dublin. I can't tell if it's actually raining. It's more like the air itself is wet. Although it's only about three thirty, the light is already beginning to wane in the sky. When I look up, it's all gray, beginning to fade not yet to black but to something close enough to it that I bring my head down and burrow deeper into my coat.

People passing me on the street seem vague. Not quite like actual humans. It doesn't bother me, though. I just notice it.

Later

It's dark in St Stephen's Green. Just past five. I sit on a bench. Something so odd I've seen. All over Dublin this winter, the cherry blossoms are in bloom.

Later

Sitting in Bewley's, looking out the big plate windows onto Grafton Street. Drinking hot tea.

Eleanor wants me to come home. She says she's scared for me. She sent me a list of flights for tomorrow morning and said she'll pay the cost of changing my ticket. My apartment is rented out until mid-January, but she says I should come live with her until then. I'm not wholly opposed to this. Just I can't really imagine getting myself from here to the airport. That seems beyond me.

I don't know what has happened. I will record as best I can.

I knocked back the ecstasy with a bottle of beer. And all the rest of the night until it began to grow light out, Kieran and I danced together. He wouldn't let go of me. He held me around the waist; he ran his hands over my hair and brushed his fingertips across my cheeks. He kissed the top of my head and my eyes. He didn't look at anything except me for the rest of the night, his eyes wide with what seemed liked love. I wanted to say, Kieran, is this real or is this the ecstasy, but I didn't want to be a spoilsport. As dawn broke, we sat together on his couch, his arm around my shoulder, our hands intertwined, our heads touching. When people were starting to leave, they came over to the couch to say good-bye, and Kieran didn't even let go of me then. He just extended his free arm to shake the hands offered him. "Okay, good-bye, thanks for coming. Okay. Bye. Bye."

He was whispering to me, "Stay the night with me, girl. Please. Sleep in my bed, where you belong. You will, won't you, sweetheart? Say you will."

Finally, I was too drowsy and happy to be cool, strong, and independent anymore. So I said, "Yes, Kieran." And I headed off to bed while he said good-bye to the last of the guests.

He said he'd be right behind me, but I'd hardly call it that. It seemed an eternity I waited for him, naked, in his bed. But finally he came down and I had him in my arms. He was kissing my neck and my throat and murmuring my name, and I just thought, I want to give him everything. I want to kiss him on every inch of his body until there is nowhere left to kiss. I want him to feel safe and protected and nourished. I want to take away the pain of his ex-wife and his mother and his poor, sick daughter. I want to infuse him with love.

I told him what a wonderful man he was. I told him he was brave and strong and that I could see he was suffering and that one day it would pass. I told him how beautiful he was and that he turned me on more than any man had in ten years. I kissed him everywhere.

It's hard to describe what happens in bed. What words do you even use? Making love? Blech. Sex? So clinical. Fucking? No way. But whatever you want to call it, that's what happened. I think, I have never really let myself be exposed sexually in front of anyone—only Josh at the very beginning. But here, now, in this moment, I can. I can be as open and ugly as an oyster cracked out of its shell and Kieran will love me and want me. And oh my God, I never knew how blissful it would be out of my shell.

There was late-afternoon sun coming in through the curtain above Kieran's bed when I fell asleep—on top of him, curled up against his chest, him holding me tight.

And then it was a little bit later. I'm not sure how much later. I was on my stomach and Kieran was behind me and putting himself inside me. I was confused because I'd fallen into a deep sleep. I said, "Kieran, hold on a second," because I wasn't quite ready. I said, "Kieran, wait." And I twisted around to see him, but he wasn't paying any attention to me. It didn't feel good. I was sore. "Kieran, hold on." His face was up to the ceiling, his back arched, and I didn't even recognize the expression on his face. But before I could even make sense of what was happening or figure out what to do, he was already pulling himself out and letting out a long cry and ejaculating across my back. He fell panting on top of me. I could feel his heart beating through his rib cage, through mine. It felt like he was crushing me. Then he pushed himself off against the small of my back with the flat of his hand.

"Now maybe I can fucking sleep," he said. And blackness descended on me.

"I come with you so hard—I don't understand," I heard him whisper. And then he was asleep. But I wasn't. I was back out in that dark ocean, drifting in this blackness. It stretched so far, just trying to imagine its boundaries made me dizzy. Even as I flailed my arms and kicked my feet, I was sinking. I thought, something terrible has happened and there's no going back from it. I felt Kieran's hand on the small of my back. I heard, now maybe I can fucking sleep.

I thought, there is something waiting for you at the bottom of this ocean and it is not a friendly thing. Kieran flung an arm over my stomach. I turned away, but he moved with me. I thought: What do you want from me? And even though he was there, I was completely alone, like I was the only other person on the planet, surrounded by this vast, black emptiness. I wanted to cry out, but I realized there was no point because there was nothing to be said, no words from Kieran or anyone else that would save me. I thought, that thing is coming. That thing I foretold to Eleanor in the waning light of autumn in New York—some slouching thing, creeping up from the bottom of this ocean to get me.

I clutched the comforter with both hands. I was waiting, praying, for sleep to take me away, but it never came.

In my tangerine room in Avalon House everything fell apart. On Sunday, the day after the party, Kieran and I didn't even get up until six p.m., when it was already black outside. And then we went to hear this Sudanese group Kieran had gotten us tickets for. But Kieran wouldn't even look at me. We ran into friends of his and he didn't introduce me. When we got back to his place, we sat in his kitchen and he started talking about his daughter. I tried to be sympathetic, but he was icily furious in his refusal to take my sympathy. And then he just sat with his head in his hands. I said, "Are you okay, Kieran? Is there anything I can do?" And he said, "I'm dead tired," and walked out of the room. Then when I crawled into bed beside him, he held on to me so tightly I could barely breathe, his arms wrapped around my stomach, his head buried in my neck. I wanted to weep in confusion until it occurred to me, I'm just a human teddy bear, being used to ward off fears of the dark. And the next morning, he gave me a big kiss on the lips like everything was normal—and then he left the country. Did I even mention that he had to go to Prague three days after my arrival?

I went back to Leah's, but you must understand, I couldn't stay there. I packed up all my stuff and headed back out. On my Black-Berry, shading it with my hand from the rain that had begun to pour, I looked up youth hostels. I had no money for a hotel. None for a hostel either, really, but I didn't know what else to do.

I found a place called Avalon House on Aungier Street, about half-way between Leah's and Kieran's. I lugged my stuff back across town, the wool of my tights and skirt giving off a faint steam as the rain came down on me. The lobby was filled with teenagers all talking at the top of their voices—German, French, Danish. The person at the desk gave me a key that said "409" on it. I climbed the four flights of stairs, banging my suitcase behind on each step, sticky with sweat, dripping with rain. My room was narrow—just a single bed and a sink. The walls were tangerine. The bed was hard—more like a cot than a bed. The sheets were stiff, rough to the touch. At the foot of the bed were two folded towels, scratchy and brittle. Overhead dangled a bare bulb.

I started to cry before I even had my coat off. Soon the entire front of my body all the way down to my waist was wet. Soon snot was running down my face and into the folds of my scarf. My tears turned into howls, and then I shoved my fist into my mouth to keep the howls from becoming screams. I sank to the floor. I put my face down on the bed and clasped my hands in front of me. Please, God, please. Don't let this be happening.

Then there was a break. Just like that, a break in my mind. I had been in one world, and then I was in another. Everything looked the same—same tangerine walls, same stingy towels at the foot of the bed, same glare from the lightbulb, but I had been whisked away somewhere else entirely. Ben Green ran through my mind. Before he swerved to the left. After. Two different universes traversed in the space of a single second.

Then it was fear. As familiar and old as anything I could remember. How could I have thought there was any escaping it? Pinpricks of heat spreading over my face and across my limbs. Laughter in my ears, mocking me, ridiculing me for being so pathetic, for thinking anything good could ever happen to me, for thinking there ever could have been any destiny other than to end up, alone, in some dismal room like this.

But then I was not alone in the room. Sitting here now, it's hard to believe what I experienced last night, but it was as real as anything that's ever happened to me.

I was at the gates of hell. A tunnel descended straight down. I felt like I'd been peeled, and now that I was soft and skinless I was going to be tortured. Down I fell, and I was surrounded by demons—all around me was sweat and tongues and eyes that glowed, toenails scratching across the floor, long fingers with long fingernails reaching out for me. Voices sneered, *Did you really think anyone would ever care about you? Did you really think you could escape?*

Even though in real life I was kneeling before the bed, my eyes squeezed shut, my hands over my head, in my mind I was falling downward, and there were naked bodies everywhere and something horrible going up between my legs. I was trapped in one of those Vietnam movies I told you about but more real than anything I'd ever had before. Finally I couldn't help it, and even though I was alone in the brightly lit tangerine room I began to cry out, "Please! Leave me alone! Let me be!"

And then I got up my nerve and opened my eyes and through my crying and with the mucus and tears running down my face, I groped my way to my bag and swallowed five Klonopins. But then I heard German in the hall outside. I froze on my hands and knees. The terror was not just in my mind—it was about to burst forth through my door. The German got louder, closer to my door. I squeezed my eyes shut, buried my head under my hands, and waited to be annihilated once and for all. I prayed. I thought of being a kid and the first time I'd climbed into my mother's bed after a nightmare and realized her presence couldn't protect me—lying awake, hot with fear, waiting to be put out like the end of a burning cigarette.

Then the voices outside my door began to recede and finally grow distant and I went limp with relief, torso and arms splayed across the bed. Then the Klonopin must have knocked me out, because the next thing I knew, it was two this afternoon and Eleanor was calling me, and when I picked up my phone she was shouting, "What happened to you? Why didn't you call? What is going on over there? You have to come home! I am booking you a ticket now!"

But I'm not going home, at least not today. I'm supposed to interview Colm McCullough's fiddle player, who I met in New York. I refuse to think of myself as mentally ill, a term Eleanor was throwing around quite liberally this afternoon. I suppose I did call her up screaming about demons. But now I feel like I must have been overdramatizing. I don't tell Eleanor about having gone off my meds. I don't know if it would reassure her or make things worse. And I'm back on them as of this morning. Believe me, I'm back on them. I also don't tell her about the ecstasy.

I just tell her I'm fine now. And she tells me no, you're not, you have to take care of yourself. You need to rest. And I keep thinking, I don't want to rest.

I don't know what to tell you, reader. I am as I am.

Later

After our interview, the fiddle player invites me to a poetry reading. A wild-haired man with bright blue eyes reads about the war in his garden between the thistle and the roses. Maybe I'm in a weakened state, but I find it incredibly moving and buy a copy.

After the reading, the fiddle player introduces me to a woman who seems to be in her early fifties with a huge head of graying hair. She's wearing jeans, Converses, and a black puffy coat with electrical tape on one of the elbows. She has a very confident, wide-legged stance, defiant really, like she could have been in the Clash. Her blue eyes are so pale, it's like you can see right through them. The fiddle player tells her about my article, and the woman tosses back her incredible mane and says, "You should come visit me. I've got a place out in Celbridge. What are you doing for Christmas?"

The fiddle player invites me to go hear some music with him, and before we leave, the lady from the Clash scribbles her number in my notebook.

We go to Vicar Street, which is where I saw the Flaming Lips with Kieran last year. I'm not entirely sure how I've made it this far—I have the feeling that my brain is bruised and tender. I find myself struggling to put sentences together. The words aren't just waiting for me in my mind the way words usually are. I have the feeling that I'm not really there, that some invisible film separates me from everyone else. I'm just flickering through this world other people actually inhabit. At Vicar Street, though, a feeling of such heaviness overcomes me that I think for a minute I must be dead and buried already, except I couldn't be, because if I were dead and buried already my heart wouldn't feel as if someone were digging into it with their fingers now.

Wednesday, December 12, 2007

I'm supposed to go to London the day after tomorrow and then plan a jaunt to Morocco with Phil for New Year's. How am I going to do this? The thought makes me feel ill. I can still feel Kieran pushing off against the curve of my lower back. *Now maybe I can fucking sleep.* Sitting here in this café, I feel infinitesimally small, like I can't find myself in space or remember how to hold my coffee cup. My heart feels like it's beating to some strange tempo of its own. It races so fast beads of sweat pop out all over my body. I haven't had this in a long time. It's like running into someone I'd forgotten existed.

Eleanor still wants me to go home. But I'm not. I can't. I don't want to.

Later

It's time to go meet Kathryn of the papery white skin. I was supposed to be working on my story for the BBC here at this café, but instead I've just been staring at the tabloids. It's all Katy French. She was like the Paris Hilton of Dublin. Dumb perfume endorsements; short, glittering dresses; snotty glowering at the camera. She was obviously a total nightmare. But I can't stop thinking, poor girl, poor girl. To be stupid is one thing, to die for your stupidity is another. My brain is not working. I want to be somewhere safe and quiet and warm. But I can't imagine where that place is.

Later

Kathryn of the papery white skin takes me to an art gallery where she has a show going up. We sit in the back room on folding chairs eating biscuits and tea with the two women who own the gallery, an American in an oversized sweater and an Irishwoman with an upturned nose, a big bosom, and a booming voice like an orator. I have the distinct impression that if she were running my life, my life would be much better.

The American woman gives me a tour of the gallery. She shows me photographs of a bunch of people fixing up a storefront in SoHo from the early 1970s. She's explaining how this group was trying to "reclaim" the role of food in American culture by opening an "eatery." I'm thinking, give me a break, it's a bunch of hippies in bell-bottoms outside a restaurant. When I find out the American's mother was part of this group but now lives in Greenwich and is an art collector, rage at this poor girl in her oversized sweater blossoms in my chest. Fucking rich girl, I think. It's strange, but the anger buoys me up, as if I'd been adrift at sea and finally have something to hold on to. It's like a shot of energy, so when they ask if I want to go to a party at another art gallery, I say, "Let's do it, man."

After the other art gallery, with equally ridiculous art on the walls, we go to a pub called Dice Bar, where we squeeze together into a red leather banquette.

I tell them about my story. The American says, "Who is it for?"

"It's with the *New Yorker*," I say. I don't say I'm doing it *for* the *New Yorker*, because that would be a lie. But I am aware that saying it's *with* the *New Yorker* creates the impression that it's *for* the *New Yorker*. Somehow at this moment, with these three women's faces turned to mine, I can't help myself.

I'm immediately filled with shame and dread. But it's too late. The American's eyes pop.

"I'm going home for Christmas," she says. "You should take my apartment while I'm gone and work on your story."

And then after a few more pints, she says, "Please use my apartment. It would be such an honor. I mean, the *New Yorker*, my God."

I don't correct her. I don't say, actually I haven't been able to get the editor to return my calls for two weeks. Instead, I give her a patronizing smile as if I deserve and accept her admiration. I have a nervous flicker in my stomach. I am crossing over into some new territory.

The American has her hand over her heart. She's saying to the other two: "The *New Yorker* is the absolute pinnacle of writing in America." She gestures to me. "This woman, sitting at this table with us, this woman is at the absolute pinnacle of her art. Cheers. I mean it. Cheers to you."

And they all raise their glasses to me.

"Well done! Cheers!"

"To the pinnacle!"

We clink glasses. And I think, oh God, she's *nice*. And then, oh God, what have I done? And then, what is this smugness I feel? As if I actually were the woman they think they're toasting. I adore the woman they think they're toasting. She is cool, strong, and independent. She didn't just have a nervous breakdown in a youth hostel. She is successful and beloved. This woman totally knows how to hold a coffee cup. I feel a tremendous sense of expansion, as if I actually take up more room in space. This woman has a place in the world. I feel myself as if clinging with all my might to the image of the woman I see reflected back to me in their eyes.

Friday, December 14, 2007

"Let me just ask you one thing."

It's Eleanor. I've told her I'm not going home but instead am taking the American woman's apartment for the month. "I like it better than you going to Morocco but I don't like it as much as you coming here," was her first response.

"Sure," I say. "Hit me."

"Are you staying in Dublin to *make* Kieran fall in love with you?"

"What?" I cry. "No!"

"I know you, Heather," she says. "I've known you a long time. And I have a hard time believing that's not what you're doing."

I'm outraged. "I don't ever want to see him again as long as I live. I'm not kidding. I can't even think about him without shuddering. The thought of him fills me with a kind of terror."

This is all true.

Eleanor says, "As you know, there isn't anyone I'd less like to meet at the end of a dark alley than Heather Chaplin." There's a pause. "And mostly I love you for this." There's another pause. "But right now I'm not sure it's going to serve you so well."

I don't say anything.

"I feel like Kieran holds a dangerous attraction for you," she says.

I don't say anything.

"I'm sorry," she says, "but I've known you since you were five and I've seen all of it. In high school . . . ?"

I know what she's talking about. My first boyfriend in high school. How he told me he loved me, and the next thing I knew I was hiding in a corner of my room, the air quivering around me, with my hands over my head because I thought there were footsteps outside the door even though I was alone.

"At the beginning with Josh . . ."

Those dreams. My father chasing me. Bluegrass music. Flying over that cavernous chasm in the earth. Waking up in terror.

"And now Kieran—I mean, it's a pattern, Heather. It's a pattern."

I see the pattern too, but I don't say anything. I'm starting to feel pissed, like she's rubbing my nose in something I can't help. It makes me feel defiant. And like I might scream.

Later

I'm flying to London tomorrow morning to see Phil and lay down my tracks at the BBC. I promised Eleanor I'd go to bed at eight every night, but when the ladies from the art gallery say they have invites to the Irish Film Board party and I should come with them, I can't resist.

On my way over, I keep imagining that I'm about to run into Kieran. In my mind, I'm looking superhot and in control with my new friends. When he wants to sweep me into his arms, I say, "Hi there," and walk away. I replay this fantasy over in my head so many times that my heart is pounding with the expectation that it's about to happen.

The first person I see when I get to the party is Andrew Dempsey, who I interviewed last week. The director of the movie in my story. I feel so pleased with myself for being taken to a fancy party and knowing not just somebody there but actually the star of the hour that I think, you know what, Kieran O'Shea should know about this. He should know that I *rule*. I give Andrew a blasé wave of my hand and get out my cell. As I pull it out of my pocket, it starts to vibrate. Motherfucker, but it's Kieran. How does he always know?

"How's London?" he writes. "Prague was fab."

"Not in London," I write. "At film board party."

"Still in Dublin, so," he writes.

I almost can't believe what's happening in my mind. I'm thinking, you totally overreacted. Nothing bad happened. He didn't use you and throw you off. *Now maybe I can fucking sleep?* You misunderstood. Not looking at you the next day—he was just down from the ecstasy. He didn't mean it. He wants you. In a minute he's going to invite you over to his house. Will you go? Should I play hard to get or just hop in a taxi?

I write: "Met some amazing artists who brought me to this party! What an incredible time I'm having! London in morning."

Cool, strong, and independent. Never let them see your pain.

I feel excitement like something being inflated in my chest. I start to craft my reply. When he invites me over, how do I both make him suffer and still get to go?

My phone vibrates. Here it comes.

"cool," Kieran writes. "njoy."

I stand there staring at my cell, waiting for the next message. Waiting for the invite to come over. I wait. I wait. I keep waiting. All around me people rush and music blares. I stare at my cell. I wait. But it's just my screen with the animated fish floating around.

It's like being dropped onto the ground from somewhere up high. No, it's like falling off a mountain ledge where you had no business being in the first place and where you certainly shouldn't have been standing on one leg and waving your arms around with your eyes closed.

I make a beeline for Andrew Dempsey.

Thank God for Andrew Dempsey. We end up huddling together in the back of a banquette talking for the next hour. I see people looking our way and I think, that's right, I rule, whether or not Kieran O'Shea will admit it. Somewhat to my surprise, though, it goes from being purely an ego trip to a real conversation. Andrew just broke up with his girlfriend and this is his first Christmas alone. I tell him about Josh and how I imagined walking into traffic last December. I tell him it sucks and there's nothing you can do about it, but that it beats being in a bad relationship. I say, "The most important thing is to have friends. You're going to need them. Do you have people you can really talk to?"

Andrew moves his head from side to side, like, well, maybe, no, not really. And I think, oh right, he's a man who's just lost his girlfriend, of course he doesn't have anyone he can actually talk to.

"Look, take my number," I say. "Text or call me every day, and I'll text or call you back. And that way you won't feel so alone. Half the battle is just having someone to check in with."

Andrew says, "What are you doing for Christmas? Come stay with me at my sister's. It would be brilliant to have you."

The ladies from the art gallery text. They have moved on. They're at a club called Spy across the street and want me to join them.

I say good-bye to Andrew with a big hug. I say, "I'll talk to you tomorrow, right?" Andrew holds on to my arm for a second. "Thank you," he says. And I think, the world isn't so bad. Connection is possible at any time in any place.

And then, as I run across the street, you are good.

Spy is packed and dark except for a strobe light going around illuminating the faux-wallpapered walls and everyone's faces in startling white light. The ladies are already hammered. They each insist on buying me a pint so soon I am too. It's a competition to say who's more awesome, me or them. I'm making eyes at every half-cute guy that crosses my path. At two, I stumble out and back to Avalon House, where I get into my tiny bed. I have to be at the airport in five hours. I close my eyes to go to sleep but then I open them again. I get out of bed. I pull my cell out of my coat pocket. I erase Kieran O'Shea's number. I don't ever want to feel the way I feel at the sight of his name again. Ever.

Saturday, December 15, 2007
London

Phil takes one look at me, tucks me up on his couch, covers me with three plaid wool blankets, and orders me Thai food. I find myself telling him about Kieran. Not the most humiliating bits, but the general story. He says the best thing in the world. He says that one thing almost every adult on the planet has in common is having been brought to their knees by heartbreak. He says it makes you feel like you're losing your mind. That it's happened to him and to the people I see walking down the street. I think, see, I'm not mentally ill. I was undone by passion. I find this so comforting that I immediately close my eyes and go to sleep until the next afternoon.

Sunday, December 16, 2007

London is dark and rainy and the wind whips against my skin. I'm meeting Ben Green's old friend Colin Landau, who is a columnist here at the *Guardian*. When I take a seat across from him, I have that feeling again that I am very, very small—that I'm not sure how much room I take up. I almost couldn't bring myself to leave Phil's kitchen, but then I was very firm with myself and said, no, you will not travel all the way to London and stay in Phil's kitchen. You will keep moving. Ben said I'd probably met Colin at Marie's and his wedding, but I have no recollection of this.

I meet him at a place called the Viaduct. The pub has a red tin ceiling and lots of men in dark blazers drinking pints. Colin has the most wonderful face. The word *merry* comes to mind when I think how to describe him. Not like ho-ho-ho, I'm a big fat Santa Claus, because actually he's wonderfully slim and tall. Rather it's his eyes—they seem open to the world, like they reflect a personality who is looking to be delighted. I think, these are not eyes to drown in. These are eyes that say, if you were drowning I'd help you out of the water.

After our pints, Colin takes me on a tour. I don't know if it's just that he's British and British people are polite, but Colin is, like, the most gracious person I've ever met. I feel completely at ease. There are construction cranes everywhere against the black sky. We walk past St Paul's, across a bridge, and to the Tate, which seems hideous and ridiculous to me, like something an Ayn Rand character would have built. Colin laughs when I say this with his head back and his knees bent and his whole face crinkling up in pleasure. I'm struck by what a wonderful sight it is. We walk past Shakespeare's Globe and narrow alleyways that I imagine Dickens rushing through in his nighttime walks.

I think, how can I simultaneously be having a nervous breakdown and such a good time?

Over Indian food on Brick Lane, Colin tells me he's thinking about writing a book on happiness. He has this idea that positive thinking and optimism are absolutely the wrong way to go about it. He says the minute you *try* to be happy, you can't be.

"You have to embrace the abyss," he says. But he says it in the most good-natured, cheery way possible. "My favorite saying ever," he says. "Abandon all hope." And he laughs delightedly. I must look confused, because he says, "You know, striving doesn't necessarily work."

I have a flash to myself swimming endlessly against the current in my indoor pool. To those five fleeting days of happiness and peace after I ceased to exist in my bathroom.

I tell him about the story I did on complexity and what Billy Santiago told me about subparticles only existing in relation to one another.

Colin says, "It's strange, isn't it, to realize there's no such thing as *you*."

But he doesn't seem bent out of shape about this at all.

I think, should I make out with Colin? But every time I look at him, and even as I'm thinking, this man is obviously one of the world's greats, I think of Kieran and I have an image of myself falling off my chair onto the floor and just playing dead until the waiters shut the place down.

I'm eating my matar paneer and thinking, well, I should still make out with Colin anyway, when suddenly I realize—I did meet Colin at Ben and Marie's wedding. *Colin is the guy I should have married.* I am sitting across the table from the man I should have married, and I'm nearly dying of longing for another man, a man who, when I think about him, I have images of a beast ripping my body to shreds.

There is no hope for you, Heather. None.

Wednesday, December 19, 2007

Kieran has been texting me. Or rather 011 353 86 870 9822 has been texting me. "How's London, girl. Hope you're njoying. XXXX"

Why is he texting me? What does he want from me? I am *not* texting him back.

Monday, December 24, 2007
Dublin

After much agonizing, I came back to Dublin last night. I thought about staying in London with Phil for Christmas, but I was feeling so lost I took another assignment just to help relocate myself in space. I'd seen that the Pogues were playing and pitched my editor at the *New York Times* on a story about Christmas in Dublin with Shane MacGowan. Colm's fiddle player had given me the phone number of MacGowan's girlfriend, who apparently I'd met at that poetry reading only I didn't know it, and she and I hashed it out over text. I got a press pass to the show, and we'd been all set to go and then the girlfriend changed her mind at the very last minute. I was crushed, but I flew back to Dublin last night anyway because I figured if you have a chance to see Shane MacGowan playing a Christmas show in Dublin, you should, even if you're not going to be allowed backstage and even if you're sort of having a nervous breakdown. But my flight was delayed *five* hours and I arrived just in time for the doors of the auditorium to open and all the crowd to come pouring back out into the night. I almost started crying when I realized I'd missed the whole thing. And I was missing Kieran like a hole in my stomach even as simultaneously the thought of him was making those beads of sweat pop out—so I said to myself, you can make friends anywhere, you will make new friends *now*.

I walked back into the city center with some people I met and decided this cute guy with dark hair in a soccer zip-up would be my next Kieran. Then, just as he was buying me a Guinness at a pub on the edge of Temple Bar, he launched into series of racist jokes involving Mexicans, African-Americans, Jews, and the Polish. I didn't even finish my beer. I just crawled on back to my apartment.

This morning I went to Brown Thomas, the department store I was in with Seth last year, and circled a pair of high gray boots. I watched a six-foot-tall woman in a white fur hat, long ironed black hair, and a diamond ring bigger than my head buy six Yves Saint Laurent lip glosses without trying them on. I got up close and listened to her thick Russian accent and imagined she was the imported trophy wife of some newly wealthy Irish developer. I thought, man, what a life. Why wasn't I born beautiful and alluring enough to be a kept woman?

Now I'm sitting in that open-air market where I had breakfast with Kieran last year. Been talking with a guy whose Croatian girlfriend ran off back home with their kid and another "bloke." He was amazingly sanguine about the whole thing. He kept saying, "What do you think, that life is here to serve you?"

Later

Thank God for Andrew Dempsey! Just as I was wandering around South Dublin, watching the blue sky fade to black and thinking, here you are, it's Christmas Eve; you're all alone in a strange city with no one to buy presents for and nowhere to go, he called to see how I was doing. I told him about the invitation I had from the woman I'd met at the poetry reading, and he said, "Heather, that's Marina Guinness! You know, of the Guinnesses? She's the most interesting woman in Ireland. Colm McCullough is living out there with her. Every artistic venture that's ever happened in Ireland in the last thirty years has her fingerprints on it. You'll have the time of your life. Go!"

It was already 5:30 p.m., but I thought, what the hell else am I going to do, and I thought, this is what I get: I get adventures. So I called her. To my amazement, she said, fantastic, I'll pick you up at the bus stop.

So I bought an armful of the red Christmas berries mixed together with white lilies, and now I'm on the bus to Celbridge.

Later

Marina picks me up in a tiny car that looks to be from 1987, with trash in the backseat and a terrible grating sound whenever she shifts gears. She's got on the same puffy coat with electrical tape on the elbow and her gray hair stands up so that it grazes the roof of the car.

We drive out of the village and through fields dark as pools of water in the night. Marina keeps turning to look at me.

"You're brave," she says finally. "I've been thinking about this ever since you called. I don't know that I could be traveling alone in a foreign country at this time of year. I don't know that I'd have the nerve to get a bus on Christmas Eve to visit someone I didn't know."

I don't even answer her because I can't think of anything to say. Brave? Am I brave? Is this possible?

We drive past more fields. It's totally dark, illuminated only by moonlight and hazily covered stars. Then Marina makes a sharp turn into a road I didn't even see, and a gray stone house looms up in front of me. It's enormous and seems to go off in many different directions at once. It's got a peaked entranceway, and wings stick out on either side. There seem to be a dozen chimneys. Marina hops out of the car and waves for me to follow. We go around the side of the house and in through a mudroom. There's a pile of dogs shivering in a corner and a big stack of Wellington boots against the far wall. Marina pushes open a door and we're in a kitchen that is about the size of my apartment back in Brooklyn. There's an iron stove that looks to be a hundred years old at one end, and antlers with a span of at least five feet on the wall at the other. There's a long wooden table in front of me, heaped with magazines, piles of mail, jams, Marmite, honey, Nutella, candlesticks, a mortar and pestle, and a stack at least a foot high of blue-and-white china plates.

"Tea?" Marina says.

There are more Wellingtons piled in a corner and a poster of Sinn Féin's Gerry Adams with 1970s glasses and a big bushy beard on the wall. Shelves hold dainty teacups hanging from little curved hooks. I can hear the dogs whining from behind the closed door.

A swinging door on the other side of the kitchen flies open and an enormous young man comes in. I can't tell if he's twelve or twenty-five. He's got a huge head of massively curly blond hair, and Bob Marley is smoking an enormous blunt on his chest, his face distended by the size of the enormous belly beneath him.

"Have you seen this?" the young man says, dropping a magazine onto the kitchen table.

"This is my son Finbar," Marina says. "Finbar, say hi to Heather. She's from America."

"Hullo, dear," Finbar says.

They both peer into the magazine. It's *Vanity Fair*. One of their high-concept spreads of a million people grouped together. It's all young people in ball gowns and crumpled tuxedos, sitting around on couches and gazing out French windows in some gorgeous hotel room styled to look as if they've all been having a marvelous time for at least twenty-four hours.

Marina points to one of the girls, sitting on the floor in a pink dress spread around her like a blossoming rose. "That's my daughter, Violet," Marina says. "Oh, God bless her, isn't she lovely."

"Todd's in there too," Finbar says. "And Dexter. All the cousins."

"Oh yes," Marina says. "Look at that. How funny. How gorgeous they all are."

I peer over their shoulders and see the spread is titled "The New Aristocracy." I think, what am I doing here?

"So, do you ever go to the cockfights in Queens?" Marina asks me.

I think, what? But before I can even cover for the fact that I don't have an answer, Marina has launched into a story about living in New York in the early 1980s and becoming friends with a Haitian cabdriver who picked her up every Tuesday night at eleven fifteen to go see midnight cockfights in outer Queens.

"I should put you two in touch," she says. "He's the loveliest man. His name is Jorges." And then the outside door slams open and an elderly man with stooped shoulders and glasses, blinking rapidly, steps into the kitchen.

"Hullo, Mick," drawls Finbar. The more I look, the more I think he can't be over eighteen.

"Hullo, Mick," says Marina. "This is Heather. She's from America. Heather, this is Mick the Sheep Farmer."

Mick the Sheep Farmer is blinking rapidly at me and twitching his nose. "I've never understood the Americans," he says. "They think they have the right to be happy. It makes no sense."

And then the door flies open again and Colm McCullough steps into the kitchen.

"Hullo, Heather," he says. As if it were the most natural thing in the world for me to be there.

"Oh, do you two already know each other?" Marina says. "How lovely."

At dinner, I sit between Colm and Mick the Sheep Farmer. The dining room table could easily sit fifty people. I would say there are twenty of us there. It's set with ancient silverware, paper-thin wineglasses, and warmed blue-and-white china. A huge vase of lilies and eucalyptus leaves sits at the table's center. By the fireplace, which is so big I could easily go and stand in it, I see Violet, who in real life has skin that seems never to have been blemished by a pore, pale yellow hair and is as slight as a sheet of paper. The phrase *English rose* comes to mind, except she's wearing a zip-up hoodie with dollar signs in primary colors and big gold bamboo earrings.

The dining room ceilings are at least twenty feet high, with windows in the front covered in chintz curtains that cascade onto the floor. There's a grand piano that somehow fits into a corner. There's a stuffed alligator on top of it. Paintings of greyhounds cover the walls, and the biggest Persian rug I've ever seen covers the floor. The carpet is threadbare and has a layer of thick dust on it. In fact, everything in the room is covered in dust. I have never seen anywhere so simultaneously magnificent and filthy.

I learn that Mick the Sheep Farmer was, indeed, a sheep farmer. He lived on the farm next door to the castle—yes, castle—where Marina grew up. When his father died and left the farm to a distant cousin out of spite, he moved in with Marina. Colm is filling me in on everything. He says they call him Mick the Sheep Farmer to distinguish him from Marina's other good friend Mick Jagger. Colm tells me he first met Marina when he was a sixteen-year-old busker. She stood there listening to him sing on Grafton Street for a while, then swooped him into her car and brought him back here to where Van Morrison was staying. He mentions that Marina has another son from back when she was with Stewart Copeland. I think, Stewart Copeland of the Police?

I'm thinking, why has she brought *me* into her circle? What do I have to offer? Answer: nothing. Then I think, maybe her standards are very low—because there are some travelers on the other side of Colm who live in tents at the back of the property raising chickens, and though I know it's probably an unacceptable thing to say about people who are already marginalized, they really don't seem too bright. I wonder which I am, a young Colm, destined for future fame, or a traveler, destined to sell chicken eggs and bear too many children?

"The Irish are disgusting," Mick the Sheep Farmer is saying to me. "That's what you should put in your story. Gorging themselves on newfound riches." He snorts. "Look at Katy French, a lot of good prosperity did her. It won't last, you know. It will all come crashing down. And then what happens to all of these people in their fancy new apartments with their big mortgages?"

I look over at Colm. He raises an eyebrow at me.

"The Irish are not meant to be rich," Mick the Sheep Farmer says. "It's not real. It's a big scheme and the Irish are falling for it. It's like a pig trying to be a horse. The pig may have wanted all its life to be a horse and think its day in the sun has come. But it hasn't—and it won't. If you're a horse, you're a horse. And if you're a pig, you're a pig."

"That's not true," I say. "People can change. Circumstances can change. Why can't a city, or a people, be transformed?"

Mick the Sheep Farmer squints at me. "I'll tell you exactly why," he says. "Because that's not how the world works."

After dinner, one of the travelers plays his accordion by the fireplace. It's the loneliest sound I've ever heard. I find tears coming into my eyes. Every time I think I'm okay, that I must have imagined the horror of the tangerine room, I just as suddenly find myself with a sense of being so frail and skinless that I really ought not be let out of doors. I get the feeling that there is so much sadness in me, and such a desperate sadness, that I could cry for the rest of my life and it wouldn't be enough.

Colm leans his head closer to me. "You all right there?" he says. And I see that there are tears in his eyes too. I imagine throwing myself into his arms and sobbing while he holds me. Then I think, okay, Heather, keep your shit together. You can't just go around throwing yourself into people's arms. And I just smile back at him and say, yes, yes, I'm fine. And when he drives me back to Dublin later, through the pouring rain, and tells me that the real reason his girlfriend didn't want me coming backstage this summer was because she was "threatened" by how "intelligent and attractive" I am, I only fantasize for a minute about how satisfying it would be to wreck that girl's fairy tale. Then I think, if he's bad-mouthing her now to a *reporter*, he's probably wrecked her fairy tale seventy-five times already. Fuck that, I think, I'm not sleeping with some second-tier rock star.

How's that for sensible?

Thursday, December 27, 2007

Coffee with Andrew Dempsey at the Steps of Rome café on Chatham Street, off Grafton. I have to say, Andrew Dempsey is awesome. We drink espresso and roll cigarettes. We talk about the Marx Brothers, *Deadwood*, and *The Wire*, which on my recommendation Andrew has finally started watching. We talk about whether there's a God—or a Universe or whatever. We talk about the fact that Andrew didn't kill himself on Christmas. I say this is a great accomplishment, which Andrew thinks is funny, although I wasn't trying to be funny. A man with an armful of lilies stops at our table and congratulates Andrew on a piece he had in the *Irish Times* this morning. Andrew says, "I'm glad you liked it. I thought I sounded melancholy and up my own arse."

Andrew's movie has been nominated for an Independent Spirit Award, but he says he can't be bothered to go to LA. Says he can't stand all the sunshine. I say, "What is your problem? Go to LA and let everyone make a fuss over you." He says, "We're not all as self-sufficient as you are, Heather." I think, what? Eleanor has been writing me every day to tell me that I'm mentally ill and have to come home and address this. But maybe I'm just self-sufficient and brave. Can you be both?

Friday, December 28, 2007

The castle Marina grew up in is from the eleventh century. I have never seen anything like it in my life. She shows me around the whole place, sauntering ahead of me in her slouchy jeans, Converses, and black puffy jacket with the electrical tape, gesturing at medieval tapestries and marble staircases and balconies. She takes me into a room to show me a picture of her grandmother, and it turns out her grandmother was Diana Mitford! The woman who ran off with England's most famous fascist, Oswald Mosley, right before World War II. It was Marina's grandfather she ran away from. I'm in a room full of portraits of the famous Mitford sisters! There's Unity, who fell in love with Hitler, and Decca, who ran off to America and became a communist. And Nancy, the novelist, resplendent in a floor-length evening gown, gazing imperiously down her nose at me from her life-sized portrait on the wall. I think, how did a little scrub like me from Baltimore end up in this room? Marina is telling me some story about her grandmother and Wallis Simpson having a squabble over a dressmaker in the fifties. And when I say, "Your grandma knew Wallis Simpson?" She says, "Oh dear, yes, all those fascists were great friends after the war." And as we're leaving the room, "Oh, poor Granny, God bless her, she never would have approved of the Final Solution."

In the kitchen, which is the only warm room in the house, her father, Desmond, makes us tea. He's got pale blue eyes like Marina's and snow-white hair. He's the most polite man I've ever met in my life. He says, "Oh, how *are* you?" when we meet. And everything I say, he responds, "Oh, that *is* the most charming story."

Man, oh man, the Guinnesses. How did I land here?

Saturday, December 29, 2007

Tonight, Marina put me in a spare bedroom on the third floor with a nineteenth-century opium-den bed in it. It's all carved wood with blue silk paneling hanging over the side and a blue silk bedspread with golden chrysanthemums embroidered on it. The walls of the room are navy blue and covered with Victorian prints of botanical drawings. I feel I have landed where I was always meant to be— this is my childhood fantasy room. I wish I could stay here, right now, in this moment, in this bed, in this house, with this woman taking care of me, forever.

Sunday, December 30, 2007

Finbar and I have taken to smoking large quantities of marijuana and listening to reggae music in his room. He's a really nice kid. Seventeen. Just moved back to Celbridge after being at boarding school for the last ten years. I ask him why he left. He takes the joint from his mouth, blows smoke into the air. "My mum said I was becoming a fucking cunt," he says.

Later, Marina takes me in her car to see the ruins of a hut where a famous ninth-century monk lived. There's nothing but stone walls and ferns and bramble and gorse growing everywhere. I walk inside and around. It's so quiet out here in this green countryside. There's a tiny bit of a doorway left and I have to stoop to get under it. It's like being taken back in time, or dropped onto another planet. Marina leaves and I hike across fields, past cows and horses, up steep inclines, and then running down long hills. Sheep. Sheep. Sheep. Everywhere sheep. I climb until I'm panting to the top of a hill where the whole country in its electrifying greenery is laid out before me. It's not raining. But it's not dry either. The air feels incredibly clean. I have that expansion in my chest like maybe life is a beautiful thing. And I think, I have to tell Kieran. I have to tell him how beautiful his country is. I am flooded with forgiveness. I must share this moment with him.

He writes back right away. "You're in Ireland????" And I'd be lying if I said I didn't take great pleasure in writing back, "yup, been back for a week." I haven't responded to a single one of his texts since I erased his name from my phone, not even the one he sent on Christmas saying he was thinking about me.

Later, I ride the bus back to Dublin with Marina's daughter, Violet. She's going to hear a dance hall DJ at Temple Bar Music Centre. She's only twenty but is so lovely and confident and obviously doesn't even wear blush although she has a pink stain on her cheeks at all times, that I feel hideous and awkward around her. I can't think of anything to say, which is fine, because she's on her cell phone to her boyfriend in Trinidad the whole bus ride anyway. ("Oh, Mum, you're going to love him," I heard her say to Marina. "He's got *two* gold teeth.") I figure, what the hell, adventure! and go with her to the club. Inside everybody is talking in thick West Indian accents and patois so thick I can't make heads or tails of what anyone is saying. I don't want to cramp Violet's style, so when I see an older Rasta dude dancing by himself off to one side I go to him and ask if he minds if I dance alongside him. He's like, ja, man. And so I dance. And dance. And dance. God, I love to dance.

I end up dancing with a guy who turns out to be a professional soccer player from Ghana. He's been playing on professional teams around the world since he was fifteen. What interesting lives people have! Whatever you want to say about this trip, I have met some extraordinary people. When the club is closing, this Ghanaian soccer player asks if he can walk me home. I say, "Yes, sir." I'm thinking, how ya like me now, Kieran O'Shea? I got me a rock star, a movie director, and a professional soccer player. I can find a new Kieran O'Shea every day of the week. When we get to my door, the soccer player bends down to kiss me, and I get ready to have my molecules scrambled. I'm thinking, finally, finally. But when his lips touch mine, he shoves his entire tongue in my mouth and seems to be trying to get it down my throat all the way into my large intestines. Immediately, there is saliva dribbling down my chin. I'm gagging as I pull away. I have to wipe away the slobber that's dripping from my lips. Okay, I think, maybe we got off to a bad start. I let him kiss me again, and it's the same thing. It's like there's a squid in my mouth and it's still alive.

When I climb into my cold bed, I feel like a sheet of ice has wrapped itself around my heart. I drop into blackness. I think, you will not meet a new Kieran every day because there is only one Kieran. You will never feel about anyone else the way you feel about him, and yet he does not want to be with you. You are fucked.

Monday, December 31, 2007

"Please just come home."

"Jesus Christ. I don't want to come home. I'm fine. If it's news to you that I go up and down in my life, I don't know what to tell you."

"I don't think I ever realized the severity of it. I should have. I should have. But I didn't. I'm sorry."

"Yeah, well, now you do."

Eleanor tries again. "You're out there all on your own. You don't have any money. This Ghanaian banquet you're going to to-night—do you even know who these people are?"

"Yes! They're friends of the guy I met last night. I've never been to a Ghanaian New Year's celebration. Have you?"

"I feel like you need to come home and, like, start going to bed every night at seven. I feel like you need to come home and, like, find a good psychiatrist."

"I've hit my lifetime limit on psychiatrists," I say.

"But if you were honest with one—"

"Did it ever occur to you that maybe I'm brave and self-sufficient?"

It's all I can do not to hang up on her.

"You're an interventionist," I say. "Don't you understand? There's no skipping the rough parts. Whatever I'm going through, I have to go through."

"What, like you have no free will?"

"I can't explain," I say. "I just know I'm at point A, and I have this sense like there's no detour on the way to point B."

"I just want you to be safe, Heather."

"As if there's any such thing," I say.

I no longer believe we have as much control over our lives as other people seem to think. Or I don't know. Maybe that's just what self-destructive losers always say.

Thursday, January 3, 2008

I talked to Josh on the phone for a long time tonight. I told him I had a break. I don't tell him about Kieran or any of the details. I just say I had "problems," but Josh knows what that means. Josh took care of me when I had problems. He really did. I miss him. I think, maybe I will go back to him when I get home.

Friday, January 4, 2008

Topshop. Two new dresses and *a pair of size 25 jeans*!!! I think, there is nothing in life left for me to accomplish. I am a size 25.

Brown Thomas. Got the high gray boots to replace my platform shoes, which have broken beyond repair. The boots make me at least five three if not five four. I simply must be tall when I'm abroad.

Sunday, January 6, 2008
Last night

There's a pink strobe in the courtyard outside my apartment that goes on every night, flashing a hazy, rose-colored light through my living room windows. It's like living next door to a fairy lighthouse. The room falls into darkness and then a minute passes, and then around comes the light, casting pink shadows on the walls, one and then the other and then the other. How many afternoons have I sat here, having woken up after it's already dark, or come home just before it's gotten light, and basked in this man-made rosy dawn and imagined Kieran sitting beside me. Now he is, and I think he's more beautiful than I even remembered.

"I'm sorry, girl," he's saying. "I was horrible. It was bollocks. Total bollocks. I abandoned you. I don't blame you if you never forgive me."

Our heads are nearly touching. We're sitting on the floor, our backs against the sofa. The pink light washes over us. It's all I can do not to put my hand in his beautiful black curls and say, take me, please take me away from all this and put me somewhere safe.

But I don't. I am cool, strong, and independent, and I know that that is what it will take to snare Kieran O'Shea. That's what has brought him to this point, isn't it? I helped him pick out a suit today at Arnotts in north Dublin. And I was very sassy the whole time—this works on you, that doesn't. Try this. Give me that. And then I was burbling about the Guinnesses and Andrew Dempsey and Colm McCullough and my new best friends from the art gallery and my story for the *New Yorker*. And he kept saying, "My God, girl, you have more friends in Dublin now than I do. Look at you." And I kept thinking, that's right, motherfucker, look at me.

Then we came back here and I modeled my new clothes for him. When he started groaning and came up and wrapped his arms around my waist and started kissing my neck, I pulled away and said, "No, it's not like that anymore."

He backed away and rubbed his hands across his face. "I'm sorry, girl," he said. "I swear I didn't come here meaning to do that."

I could have screamed at him. What is your problem, I thought. Weren't those kisses an acknowledgment of what you've wanted all along? Why won't you just admit you're in love with me?

Now he's looking at me slavishly, and I try to stay firm and not melt into a little pool of butter. The look in his eyes fills me up. The admiration feels like oxygen in my lungs after having been trapped underwater.

"You didn't abandon me," I say.

"Yes, I did," he says.

"Okay, you did. You were a first-class asshole."

He closes his eyes. "I'm sorry, girl."

"I was so vulnerable with you and you were so rough with me."

"I know, girl. I'm sorry. You seemed needy and I just had a terrible reaction to it. I couldn't handle it."

"Bad timing," I say.

"The worst."

He takes my hand. "But look at all you've done since then. None of that would have happened if I'd been here for you to lean on. Maybe it was for the best."

I think about that night in my tangerine room, and I think, speak for yourself, asshole.

The hours go by in the hazy pink light. Kieran tells me how they thought his daughter was making progress in a new school but now she's slid backward, that his other daughter isn't getting the attention she needs, that every conversation with his ex-wife becomes a screaming battle. He says the guy his ex-wife was seeing is now her new partner, and even though he knows it shouldn't, it's killing him. He says he's felt at times as if he were going out of his mind.

"I have nothing left, girl," he says. "Nothing left inside me to give."

He's looking as if he were pleading with me.

I squeeze his hand, let myself run my fingers through his hair. I tell him I understand. I'm thinking, why couldn't we have just started here three weeks ago and saved all the suffering? I'm thinking, he's not *totally* still in love with his ex-wife, is he?

Somehow we start talking about Kieran's school days. He tells me how the priests used to beat the boys silly—that once one of the priests found him where he wasn't supposed to be and grabbed him by the collar, threw him up against the wall, and threatened to throw him out the window. He tells me how every year the upperclassmen would chase the weakest freshmen through the grounds of the school until they were cornered against the side of a building and then beat the shit out of them. Kieran says this never happened to him but that if it had, he wouldn't have told. He says if it had happened to him and he had told, his own father would have beat the shit out of him all over again for being a tattletale.

"You're hard," I say. "I didn't know that about you last year. But I see it now."

Kieran looks at me sharply. "It's different here," he says.

And he tells me about his father, and how he always told him he was too "soft," too "feminine."

Then he says, "Jaysus, I don't know why I'm telling you all this. I've never really talked about this stuff with anyone. Not my ex, not my best friends." And I think, if I had a dollar . . .

He wants to take me out for dinner, but I have no intention of leaving the intimacy of the apartment. I serve him a bowl of boiled potatoes and cauliflower with a dollop of curry paste on it. He says, "Are you kidding, girl? This isn't a dinner. Why don't you eat, Heather? Hmm, why don't you eat?"

I wave him away with my hands.

Later he says, "Come out with me tonight, girl. Will you? I'm meeting some friends at a pub right around the corner from here."

I say, "Well, I'm supposed to go dancing with the ladies from the art gallery. And I told Andrew Dempsey I'd meet him for a drink. So I'm kind of already double booked."

Kieran closes his eyes and nods his head, looking solemn. "Okay," he says. "I understand." And I think, ha-ha-ha-ha-ha.

He asks me three more times and finally I say, "Look, I'll try to come by your thing. No promises, though." I pause, let him nod, with his eyes closed, a little boy accepting his punishment. I think, what do you want from this situation, Heather? And I say, "But I tell you what, Kieran. Whether I do or not, let's meet back here at the end of the night."

Kieran's eyes fly open. His eyes are bright. He peers at me so intently and with such warmth that I think, you fool, you do love me even if you won't admit it. And then he takes my hands and kisses me on the cheek and says in a near whisper, "Yes, girl. Yes. Let's do that."

When he leaves, after the sweetest, gentlest kiss on the lips, I wait until I hear the elevator doors in the hallway close and then I jump into the air and let out a whoop. I skip around the apartment, my arms raised in the air, fingers in a V, Richard Nixon–style, shouting "Victoire! Victoire! Victoire!"

Do I need to tell you that I go to Kieran's thing? Of course. I never had any other intention. I just wanted to see him sweat. When I get there in my new size 25 jeans and the high gray boots, all five three, maybe five four, of me towering along the Dublin streets, I feel as if there are electric currents coursing through my veins instead of blood. My hands are shaking, I'm so excited. I am *juiced*. I can't stop talking. Talking, laughing, smiling as if my face would split in two. And Kieran is positively glowing at me. And I think, this time it's not ecstasy because no one has been doing any ecstasy. I have finally, by being cool, strong, and independent, *finally* made him love me. It is all over his face. Any jury in the world would convict him of being in love. He introduces me to all of his friends, and even when I'm somewhere else in the pub, I see him watching me and I feel like the force of his gaze is a line drawn through the room between us.

When the ladies from the art gallery come to pick me up, I say, "Okay, bye, see you later." All casual, even though my knees are already trembling with the thought that soon I will be in bed with him.

And do I need to tell you what happens later, when he comes over? It's around 3 a.m., and yeah, I'm a little offended that it's taken him so long to get here, but the minute I open the door, he is kissing me and has scooped me up and is pulling off my pajamas and calling me "beautiful girl" in my ear, and we're having sex— making love, fucking, whatever you want to call it. Once. Twice. Three times. I cannot get enough of the man. And he cannot get enough of me. In the morning we have more sex. And then we lie together while I read to him from the poetry book I bought, stroking his hair, his head on my chest. He marvels at my intelligence, my beauty. I think, it has all been worth it. It has all been worth it.

Later

The pink light is rolling through my apartment. It's just like last night except tonight I'm alone. Kieran waltzed off back to his real life. No, that's not fair. He had to pick up his kids. But right before he left, we were walking together, along the river, and he said, "I'm so glad you realized this trip wasn't about me, girl. You're like a different person now. So strong. I can't tell you how relieved I am. I wouldn't have been able to stand it if you were here for me." You are so full of shit, I thought. And then, *strong?* I have pulled myself back from the brink of madness and forced myself to walk along these streets, head held high, with a stamina that has nearly killed me—and *that's* what you're happy about? Fuck you, Kieran O'Shea. Fuck you.

Except the fury didn't last more than a second. It was replaced instantly by the feeling that all the energy coursing through my veins for the last twenty-four hours was flooding away.

He texts: "Goodnight, sweetheart. What an amazing weekend. So cool to be with you, talking, learning, making love. I miss you. Sleep well darling. X"

It doesn't matter. I'm still sitting here alone. That is the reality. And next week I go home. And I'm seeing him Thursday because that's the one day he doesn't have his kids this whole week and he won't ask his ex-wife, who, let's face it, he's still in love with, to take them even one extra night. And then I won't see him again. And right now that feels like a relief. I tried. No one can say I didn't try. I can't make the man love me. He said it himself, only I didn't want to hear it. He has nothing to give.

Saturday, January 12, 2008

Today, hiking in Glendalough. I think this might have been the highlight of the whole trip. Tenth-century monastery. Through a forest, up a mountain. Hours of trekking across fields of heather up to my knees. The sun beating down, even as a light rain fell. Rainbows on both sides of me. Deer everywhere. Then back down through the forest, under a canopy of trees where even the light seemed green. I walked all day, only stopping to eat an apple I'd brought. Everything under the trees was covered with moss. I had the most wonderful feeling in my chest the whole time as if I could have stretched out my arms and they would have been wide enough to scoop up the whole mountain. Met an elderly lesbian couple who gave me some homemade granola. They said Irish drinking was like American optimism—the national pastime and ultimately self-defeating. They recommended a good sweat lodge nearby.

Sunday, January 13, 2008

Out to Celbridge to say good-bye to Marina. Finbar and I sat beside Mick the Sheep Farmer and her as they played chess on an outdoor picnic table. Then I headed back into the city. No big good-byes from Marina. She said, "Oh, you'll be back." Finbar gave me an enormous hug against his big belly and said that of all the people his mother insisted on bringing home every minute, I was his favorite so far of 2008. I'm thinking, that's a pretty small sample size, but I take it as a compliment.

Colm is on the road. But I don't care. I haven't even been pretending to work on my "story" anymore.

Kieran and I text all day. It's lovely. It makes my heart sing. But it doesn't matter. I understand this now. I can't be who he needs me to be. I just don't have what it takes to be that cool, strong, and independent. I feel so tired. I will see him again on Thursday and I have no doubt it will be fantastic. And that will be the last bit of juice I will ever attempt to squeeze out of him.

It's time to go home. I want to go home. I miss Josh. I feel as if I could wail aloud. I wonder if he will have me back. I don't know where else to go.

Monday, January 14, 2008

Dreamed I was asleep. In the dream, I was lying in the bed I was actually lying in, but someone was in the room with me. I thought, is this a dream? Everything was in scratchy black and white, like an old, wrecked VCR tape. I thought, can I escape by waking up? I clawed at the bedclothes, trying to get up and run away, but it turns out I wasn't moving at all. I was screaming but it turns out no sound was being emitted. Total terror.

Woke up with a shout, drenched in sweat. Had to change the bedclothes because they were soaked through to the mattress.

Spent the afternoon at a coffee shop reading the tabloids. Katy French's funeral was yesterday. Did she really have to pay such a high price for wanting a life different from the one she'd been born into—for believing that times had changed, that this was her moment to shine? Did she have to die for it?

Tried to go to bed early but now can't sleep. The pink lights come in and out of the apartment. I don't think I've seen more than a few hours of sunlight in a day for weeks. I stay up until three or four every morning, wake up at twelve or one, and then the sun goes down at three thirty or four. I feel like I'm getting sick. I want to go home.

A voice in my head says, *You don't have any home.*

Thursday, January 17, 2008
Last night

I go to a dinner party with the Irishwoman from the art gallery. It's in the basement of a fancy restaurant called the Mermaid Inn. It's Dublin trying to be New York. Polished concrete floors, exposed brick, and minimally designed tables and chairs. I'm talking to some guy about Katy French and how I never got to Krystle, where Dublin's nouveau riche dance the night away. This guy says, "You don't need to see that fancy-schmancy place. Fancy-schmancy places are the same all over the world." By the end of the night, he was so drunk, I couldn't even understand what he was saying.

Sitting next to me is a woman about my age, an investment banker, quite tipsy herself. She says, "I hate to break it to you, but your story is too late. You watch, all these mortgage companies, they're all going to come crashing down. The party is over."

The art gallery owner makes her way around the table at the end of the night, drinking any last drops of wine from all the glasses. Walking home, there are people pissing and puking in corners, wandering, drunkenly, down the middle of the street. I think, I hate it here. It's too much. I have the sudden sense that things have spun out of control.

Friday, January 18, 2008
Last night

It turned out Kieran's sister was in town so he couldn't even see me until 9 p.m. I said, fine, I accidentally doubled booked and had dinner plans anyway. I'll meet you afterward. Then I sat drinking whiskey at a pub and checking my appearance in the mirror every five minutes until he called and said he was ready for me. I said, great, we're just finishing dinner, I'll grab a cab.

Kieran and I had been on the phone and texting every day, all day long, since I saw him last weekend. When I arrived at his house we sat on his couch with our arms wrapped around each other. "We've moved to the next level, haven't we, sweetheart," he said. "Last weekend was so special. I missed you so much this week." Instead of thinking, finally, finally, I thought, it's too late, it's too late. Why now?

So I changed the subject. I told him about a church I visited yesterday. "It was really weird," I said. "There was this Hebrew dude hanging on a cross. I gotta say, I didn't like it. I feel really uncomfortable being somewhere that's got one of my guys nailed to the wall."

Kieran could not stop laughing. It's Josh's line, but Kieran will never know. I watched him laughing, and I saw the light pouring out of his eyes, and I thought, this man does like me. Whatever happens, he likes me.

And then I had the best sex I ever had in my life—and that includes all the good sex with Kieran I've already told you about. I don't even know what to say. I was like one of those people you see in a movie and think, no one acts like that. I was screaming. Literally screaming. Somewhere in the back of my mind, I thought, where are those sounds coming from? And then I realized they were coming from me. You know how I said I didn't like the word *fucking*? Well, I get it now. Because I was fucking him. I mean really, I fucked him. I've never done that before to anyone. I was on top and moving myself all around for maximum pleasure, like I couldn't help it, like pleasure was a magnet and I was a penny. He was dying and touching me everywhere and crying, "You beautiful, beautiful, beautiful, gorgeous woman." And although technically it was not an orgasm I had—whatever, I'll take it.

We were both pouring sweat and panting for like ten minutes after we finished. Kieran looked exhausted. I wondered if I did too. He held me tight. He said, "That's the kind of sex only people who really know each other can have." I thought, maybe. But I didn't say anything back. I fell asleep curled up on his chest. When we woke in the morning, he whispered in my ear, "It's a dream to open my eyes and have you here." It occurred to me to panic. But then I thought, what's the point? I could pepper him with questions—What's going to happen? Why did this take so long? Will I see you again? What happens after Saturday when I leave? But then I thought, why would I ask those questions when I know the answer? The answer is, nothing. Nothing is what's going to happen after I leave. Kieran said, "I'm going to be seeing you in New York very soon. I promise you that, girl." And I thought, no, you're not. You're lying. Not that you know you're lying. I'm sure you mean it entirely—just like you've meant every other lovely thing you've ever said to me that was a lie.

Saturday, January 19, 2008

Last day in Dublin. I leave tomorrow morning.

I take the DART out to Sandycove to see Joyce's beach where what's her name had her famous orgasm. When the train gets to Sandycove, though, I feel so tired, I say, oh fuck Joyce, and keep on going.

The train rides so close to the water's edge, it's like I could just tumble into it. I get off at Dalkey. Walk through a little town with a Dalkey News and the ubiquitous Paddy Power. I stick to the twists and turns of the road as it follows along the ocean. There's a tiny island offshore with a roofless stone building that I'm sure is from the seventh century or some such. Through the clouds and the rain, it looks like the most lonely, desolate place on earth. I walk and walk and walk until I am pouring sweat and find myself suddenly too exhausted to go any further. I take the DART back to Dublin and sleep all the way, as if I were passed out rather than just sleeping.

My sinuses hurt. I really feel like I'm getting sick, though whenever I think that, a little voice pops into my head and says, *Shut up. You're such a weakling.*

I think, please, not these voices. I survived the tangerine room. Isn't that enough?

Went back to Dice Bar with the Irishwoman from the art gallery. The bartender was wearing a T-shirt that said, "Do I look like a People Person?"

We got very drunk. I told her for the first time about Kieran. She said, "Oh, those boys from Galway. Everybody knows. You have to be very careful."

I said, "Why did I come to this country anyway? I was supposed to be working on a story, but I feel like it ended up being all about sex."

The art gallery woman said, "Well, that would be very Irish of you—to ignore your work in favor of cavorting."

"Trust me," I said. "If you ever get the chance to have sex with Kieran O'Shea, you should."

"Thanks," she said. "I'll keep that in mind."

Then I kept drinking pints until she practically had to carry me home. Before this whole separation business, I didn't even like drinking.

Sunday, January 20, 2008
American Airlines

Who will I call when I get home? Who cares about my geographical location? *Nobody. Nobody cares*, says a voice in my head. I feel like I'm coming down with some kind of epic cold. *You're such a weakling*, says a voice in my head. Kieran and I were going to have lunch before my flight, but when my phone rang this morning, I knew. There'd been a flood in the building where he was shooting, and he had to take care of it. I barely even responded to his "sweethearts" and "I'm sorry, girl, I'm sorry." I just thought, of course there was a flood where you're shooting. "Good-bye, Kieran," I said. "Good luck with the movie." And I called a cab. Again, I felt a sense of relief. I want Sakura. Sakura loves me even if no one else does.

The pilot says we're almost in Manhattan. I can't believe how much I have to do when I get home. I haven't heard from the guy at the *New Yorker* this whole time. My finances are in even worse tatters than when I left. My house is filled with the furniture of a life that is over. What am I going to do? *You're not going to do anything*, says a voice in my head. *You're going to die.* I squeeze my eyes shut to the voice and think, no, no, no.

There's Manhattan coming into view in all its glittery, golden glory. It's like a fairy dream emerging out of the blackness of the sky. I'm home, whatever that means.

BOOK SIX

THE GARDEN

Sunday, January 20, 2008
New York

Has there ever been anything more depressing than arriving in JFK after a long time away? That looping video of happy multicultural Americans welcoming you to the US as you spend an hour inching forward to get your passport stamped. Waiting half an hour in a cavernous room with fluorescent lights for your luggage. Airplane smell coating your skin and clothes.

Then you realize JFK was nothing compared to what's outside. You wait half an hour for a cab; it's dark and bitterly cold; there are plastic bags hanging off the bare tree limbs and a wind that burns your skin. Then you get into a taxi and it's foul-smelling and that fucking TV screen is singing you songs about what a great place New York City is. You find yourself on the BQE stuck in traffic because it's rush hour even though it's the middle of the night. The driver curses and swings over to Atlantic Avenue, and you stutter, bumper to bumper, horns blaring, past shuttered-up row houses and fried chicken chains and auto shops. Blackened heaps of what once was snow at every corner. And you think the world is an ugly place and you will never feel good again as long as you live.

Sunday, January 27, 2008

Been home seven days. I haven't been writing much. Working desperately. So many things due. So many bills. My chest hurts. My throat hurts. I keep breaking out in sweats, not only at night but during the day. I cannot, however, be sick. The minute I walked into my apartment from the airport, I knew I had two choices: (a) burn the place down, or (b) pack up Josh's things. I cannot live another day in this horrible apartment surrounded by the remnants of a past life. I choose the latter, narrowly. I have to do this.

Kieran emailed three days after I got back. He says he'd been waiting to hear from me and is confused. He's afraid I'm mad at him. He says when I left he took a long look in the mirror and he didn't like what he saw. He says he's filled with regret for not making more time for me. He says it hit him the first day I was gone that he's a wreck and he has to change. He writes, "Please tell me if you still want me to come to New York and I will sort immediately. xxxxxxxxxxxxxxx."

No. The minute I write back, you will only disappear.

No.

I have things to do.

Am I over you? No. Not even close. You are like a bruise that has left me black-and-blue. But am I done with you? Yes. I have to be.

Wednesday, February 6, 2008

For the last two weeks, I've been inventorying everything in the house. Josh says he's too busy to come get his stuff, so I'm packing it up for him and sending it to LA.

Faith says, "I'd put it out for the trash collectors."

Summer says the same thing: "If he can't come get it himself, dump it on the street."

But for all my spite and venom, I would never do that.

Seth drives me to U-Haul to buy boxes and tape and rolls of Bubble Wrap.

I try to act very calm. I don't want to push Seth away by being overly emotional. I'm still sort of amazed not only that he came to help me but also that I got up the nerve to ask.

He says, "How you feeling, Heath? It sounds like you have a cold or something?"

"There is sandpaper in my lungs, and it's hard to breathe."

Seth says, "Heather. Go to the fucking doctor."

It's true that since I've come home I've been having the strangest sensations—like when I'm walking, I feel like I'm not moving but that the street is rolling by as if it were the backdrop in an old-fashioned movie. This morning, I was going up Ninth Street and I felt like it was getting longer and longer with every step. It's as if everything is shape-shifting around me. But when I think to myself that I'm sick and maybe I should rest, there's a voice saying, *Shut up. You're not sick.*

I turn my eyes away from my brother's.

"I'm fine," I say.

Saturday, February 9, 2008

Katy and I go into the basement. Dust hangs in the air as if it's another planet with another atmosphere. We have to break down half a dozen empty boxes with X-Acto knives just so we can get to Josh's stuff. It's like we're hacking our way through some monstrous jungle. We stop even talking. We're covered in sweat. Soon we're covered in dust that settles on the sweat. We trek up and down the stairs. At some point, we just start dumping all the trash bags labeled "Stuff" I put here last year into boxes labeled "Stuff" and not even making decisions anymore. My breathing has become so labored that Katy suggests we stop. But I can't. I need this to be over.

On the way back upstairs, I notice hives popping out on my skin—enormous white welts the size of small countries. First they're on my arms and legs, then in my ears, then around my eyes and inside my lips. Katy runs to the store and gets me Benadryl and Epsom salts to bathe in.

When I burst into hysterical sobbing, Katy says, "It'll pass, H. This whole thing will be over, and one day we'll laugh about it. I promise."

I don't believe a word of it but I'm too polite to say so. Instead

I just continue to cry hysterically. At least I cleaned out the basement? I think tentatively.

When Katy leaves, I take the Benadryl, lie down on the floor exactly where I am, and go to sleep.

Tuesday, February 12, 2008

The sloping bookshelves—now perilously drooping on the end where Josh never put brackets—freeze me every time I go near.

"I can't do it," I say, or gasp, because since being in the basement, I seem to have lost my voice.

When I try to talk, it feels like there are giant sores in my throat restricting any sounds from coming out.

Peter is kneeling in Josh's office area, wrapping cords around his elbow and the V shape between his thumb and the rest of his fingers. He's laying each coil in a box, much more carefully than I would have.

"You can," he says.

I go the first three steps up the ladder. This is the furthest I've gotten in my attempts to deal with the bookshelves. I've gotten the ladder out many times. But this is the first time the sight of all our books together hasn't sent me slinking away.

I keep climbing. Even on the highest rung I can barely reach the top shelf. I don't know what else to do so I start at the far left, as if I were reading a book. I'm trying to be systematic about this. But then, as I pull Josh's books out, as holes begin to widen in the shelves, as books that were standing straight fall over onto their sides, I have a growing sense of horror. I realize that somehow over the years I'd come to think of everything in the house as representing *me*. That Josh was just some awful void, a leech sucking my blood. But as I'm searching for his books, I realize how unfair this is, that proof of its falseness is in my hands.

I think, all these pieces that I thought were part of me are actually part of Josh—and, at some point, of us together. It gives me the sense suddenly that I'm fracturing into a million disparate slivers. I'm not the person I thought I was. I thought I was so multifaceted, so interesting. But it was Josh and me together who were. I didn't buy those physics books, those philosophy books. I can feel myself becoming more one-dimensional. People will no longer come into my living room and think, wow, how interesting she is, how marvelous. It hadn't occurred to me before that perhaps alone, I'm not.

Then, I don't know what changes, but suddenly I'm so angry, I feel as if I could rip the books out with my teeth. Peter goes off to get a slice of pizza and I start throwing the books on the floor. I pull out handfuls of philosophy books and then start reaching for the science books with both hands and dashing them onto the floor with enormous crashes. When I get to Josh's fiction, I lose it entirely. I yank out the Burrows and I yell, "You third-rate piece of shit!" Bam! I grab the Dostoyevsky and the Faulkner and yell, "Only pretentious asshole men read you!" Bam! At Bukowski I nearly have an epileptic seizure. "Bukowski?" I cry. "Bukowski? Are you fucking kidding me?" Bam!

Peter comes back. He walks around the corner into the living room, one of his earbuds in, the other hanging down his chest. "Um, what are you doing?" he says.

I've got a novel by Carlos Fuentes held up over my head. I pause for about five seconds before going ahead and throwing it with all my might onto the floor. Bam! Peter jumps back a little.

"Who the hell likes Carlos Fuentes?" I shout.

Peter takes the earbud out of his ear, pulls his iPod out of his rear pocket, turns it off, puts it back in his rear pocket, coils the ear plugs, puts them in his front pocket.

"Who's Carlos Fuentes?" he says.

"He's a hack!" I cry. "But his days on my bookshelf are over!"

"Maybe you should come down from there," Peter says.

I stomp down the stairs. I can feel the ladder shaking, and I think, I don't care, just let this thing fall and knock me off. Let it try.

I stand amid the pile of books I've created. I punt a copy of *Philosophy of Mind: Classical and Contemporary Readings* across the floor, and then a fat volume of Wittgenstein I know for a fact Josh never read.

But when I look back up at the shelves, with their gaping holes and books collapsing on one another, I feel faint. Why is my breath so bitterly painful? Josh and I together were more than just the sum of either of our parts. In the best version of us, in the version we should have been but somehow weren't able to be, we were a wonderful, tremendous whole. I thought it was all just me. But it's not true. The bookshelf is more than half empty. I think, I will never in a million years have enough books of my own to fill those shelves.

Wednesday, February 13, 2008

Seth made me go to the doctor, even though the movers are coming tomorrow.

The doctor says, "You have to rest. You're very sick. You have serious bronchitis. It's on the way to becoming pneumonia."

I'm stunned. I thought I was faking. Does this explain the shape-shifting?

"I can't rest right now," I croak through sandpaper lungs. "I have too much work and I'm in the middle of a move."

I'm thinking of the two stories I have due. I'm thinking about my credit card bills. I'm thinking of my house torn apart as I pluck out the bits that are Josh's.

"I can't make you rest," she says. "But if you don't, you will end up in the hospital. There's part of me that thinks I should put you in the hospital now."

I don't have health insurance, and I feel a wave of pure fear pass over me.

"I'll rest," I say. "I promise."

Also, I weigh 104 pounds.

Thursday, February 14, 2008

By 11:30 a.m. the movers are gone and there is no furniture left in my living room. What was Josh's office is now just empty space. Behind where his record shelves leaned are black lines of grime. There's a similar black line behind where his desk was. They're like etchings in a cave wall, a faint reminder of a whole other existence before you happened to stumble by.

I sleep all afternoon. I have permission to rest now because the doctor said she wanted to put me in the hospital. When I wake up, it's dark. Why is it always so dark?

I cannot face going into my empty living room, so I sit in bed with my computer and open Facebook. The first thing I see is that a picture of Josh Reed has been tagged. It's posted by someone I don't know. When I click on it, there's Josh standing by the Louvre. I think, huh? As I scroll down, more pictures pop up. There's Josh in the Tuileries. I'm thinking this is maybe something akin to the shape-shifting? But no, there's Josh buying a fish in an open market with a baguette under his arm. There he is under one of those art nouveau subway signs. And there he fucking is beside the Seine, a woman with blond hair and a shy smile on the other side of him.

I think, holy shit. I'm lying here on my deathbed, alone, after a week of packing up his stuff because he was too busy to come get it. And he's off for a jaunt in the City of Lights with his new girlfriend.

And you know what? Thank God I'm Jewish, because all I can think to do is laugh.

I call Summer because she's the only other person I know who will find this funny. I'm howling. I say, "Summer, can you even believe it? You cannot make this shit up!"

After she's done being outraged, Summer howls along with me. Then she says, "Oh my God, Heath, it's even better."

"How can it be better?" I say.

"Heath," she says. "It's February fourteenth. It's Valentine's Day."

And Summer and me, we laugh until we have tears running down our faces.

Friday, February 15, 2008

Still in bed. I'm not good at being sick. I'm crying a lot. I sleep during the day and am up all night. I haven't even gone to the front of the house. I can't bear to see it. I'm living off water from the bathroom sink.

Peter wants to move in with me because Katy and Mac need their spare room back. This would be major help financially. Sure, I tell him. If you don't mind that your roommate is having a nervous breakdown. Well, I don't say that, but that's what I think.

And oh Lord: voices, voices, voices.

Sunday, February 17, 2008

I get up my nerve and write Colm McCullough's manager and tell him that I have pneumonia and can't follow through on the story. I can't bear to tell him the *New Yorker* has simply stopped returning my calls. Every time I think about it myself, I start to cry and then I can't stop. Have I even mentioned that Colm got nominated for an Academy Award and that now probably every magazine in America is going to write a story on him—*now*, now that it's too late for my story?

I'm lying in bed with my laptop. An email comes in telling me a book-editing gig I'd lined up has been canceled. There goes my income for the next two months.

Then a friend emails asking for an introduction to the main character in Josh and my book. The editor at the *New Yorker* who won't return my calls has commissioned him to write a profile.

Then, because I wasn't already crying enough, Josh emails that he was in Paris. Did he forget to tell me? He says he went to the Montparnasse Cemetery to see Simone de Beauvoir's and Sartre's graves and he missed me so much he wanted to die. He wants to know if we're still considering reconciliation. This makes me get up from bed and throw my pillows on the floor and stamp my feet and shout. I cannot stop crying.

"Why didn't I tell Kieran to come visit?" I wail to Faith on the phone. "Why didn't I say yes when finally he was ready?"

"Try to let it go, Heath," Faith says. "Can you try?"

But I can't. I would cut off one of my hands to have him sitting beside me. I think, if he were here everything would be okay.

Sakura watches me from the foot of my bed with baleful eyes.

They're here all the time now, the voices. They're not voices like people who shoot up movie theaters talk about. I know they're *in* my head. It's just they're so mean and so loud that I find myself cowering before them. All day long—*you're so stupid. You're nothing. You're nothing. You should die. Why don't you just die.*

And images. You know those images I mentioned? The ones I had when I was a kid? I'm starting to have them again.

Monday, February 18, 2008

I've been in bed four days now. I sleep here and there in the afternoons, but at night I'm wide-awake. I cannot sleep. I think it's been several days since I had a night's sleep. This is not good.

I work on my stories by the glow of my computer. I don't have the energy to get up and turn on the light. I'm so tired, but sleep will not come. I'm repurposing my Dublin story for every magazine I can think of. I will *make* someone take it. I can't stop crying. All the voices are laughing at me. And I cannot control the images. They're as bad as when I was a kid. Worse than in Dublin. Someone is sawing at my flesh with a serrated edge.

I call Eleanor and she freaks out entirely.

I hang up on her and I scream at my phone to shut up when it keeps ringing.

In the front of my house there is nothing. Just Styrofoam peanuts and wrappers from packing tape. Tumbleweeds of Sakura's hair blow through the open space. A cardboard box, half-assembled. A bookshelf half-full. What was Josh's office is a void. My footsteps echo. I get down on my hands and knees and crawl down the hallway back to my bedroom.

I try on my size 25 jeans. I think, they're getting tight. The voices say, *You should kill yourself.* There's no way out of this.

Sunday, February 24, 2008

I fucking knew it! Colm McCullough just won an Academy Award. He and Miss Fairy Tale get a standing ovation. Online everyone is all, who are these people? Aren't they just the most fascinating people on the planet? "A new Dublin?" ponders a TV anchorwoman in a ridiculous sparkling evening gown. "Fuck you!" I shout at the TV screen. "That's my story!"

"Dublin, the new coolest place on the planet?" muses E!

"You motherfuckers!" I shout. "I'm going to blow up Condé Nast. I swear to God! Just like Guy Fawkes! I'm going to be a cultural hero to freelancers everywhere!"

Then I'm facedown in my pillow, sobbing.

Monday, February 25, 2008

I was awake again all night after the Oscars, tearing at my covers. I wrote a pitch to Talk of the Town about Colm and Dublin. I'm so tired, and it's hard to breathe. Eleanor doesn't understand why I can't let this story go. But I can't. I *won't.* This was supposed to be my big break. There's such shrieking in my head.

I fall asleep around six in the morning. When I wake up there's an email for me from the Talk of the Town lady. She writes, "Thanks for writing. This story has already been assigned."

I call her up on the phone to force her to change her mind, but her voice mail picks up. I start to say there's been some misunderstanding because *I* was assigned this story. But halfway through I realize how totally untrue this is. I start to panic and I find myself instead saying how much more qualified I am to write the story, and then the voices in my head are laughing and saying, *Loser, loser, loser*, and I lose all track of what I'm even trying to say and finally hang up on myself, barely making it to the end of a sentence. So now, even if there ever had been a chance, I can pretty much say for sure that I will never work for the *New Yorker*.

I scream, "Shut up, shut up, shut up," to the voices and bury my head under my pillows and pound the walls with my fists.

Wednesday, February 27, 2008

I can't take the images. They're becoming increasingly severe. I hung in there for a long time, didn't I? Almost thirty-seven years. I left Josh. I didn't die in Dublin. But it doesn't matter. The images are winning.

Imagine they're on a caboose and just let them run right by you, I can hear my mother saying. Go to hell, I think. You have no idea.

Thursday, February 28, 2008

"I just *love* your writing," Tyler Patterson says. "It's fantastic. It's such a good pitch. The best I've gotten in a long time."

Tyler is an editor at *Esquire*, and I'm sitting in his office, trying to act like I haven't been in bed for ten days curled up in a ball fending off images of my body being violated in every way imaginable. He's very well dressed, in a bright checkered shirt and horn-rimmed glasses, like someone cast to play a magazine editor in a movie. I sent him the pitch about Colm and Dublin and he wrote back right away asking me to come in. I think, finally. I will not be foreclosed on. I will survive this.

"The thing is"—Tyler taps his hands on his desk—"the story isn't right for *us*. It's a great idea, but not for us." I'm thinking, you made me come to Midtown to tell me this? I unfurled myself from the fetal position, left my house, got on the subway, and sat there like the crazy lady in the corner with my coat up to my chin giving people the evil eye for this? I don't know who I want to kill, him or myself.

I try to keep the smile—I think it's a smile—on my face.

"But God, you have a great voice. I *really* want you to pitch me some other story ideas."

Please, I think, is it so hard to give me an assignment? I have no other ideas. Don't you see? This is my last stand.

Tyler stands up. "I *really* enjoyed meeting you," he says.

Go fuck yourself, I think. And then there are the voices, *Ha-ha-ha*, they're saying. *Told you so. What a fool you are. Crawl on home, loser.*

Saturday, March 1, 2008

It's like a siren song in my head. *Go into the kitchen*, those beauties croon. *Right foot. Left foot. It's just down the hallway. Open the drawer to the right of the dishwasher. Go on, you can do it.* I see the knife rip into my flesh—globules of fat just like on a raw chicken, veins bursting open, muscle tissue torn apart. I see serrated edges carving through my skin.

Do it, the voices say. Should I? I think. All I'd have to do is walk into the kitchen, right foot, left foot. Just down the hallway. It's starting not to seem that unreasonable. It would be so easy. Like

Sartre's man standing on the edge of a cliff and realizing the only difference between life and death is his own decision not to jump. The terror of freedom, Sartre said. All it takes is making the choice. There's no brick wall or iron door between you and it.

Hang in there, Heather, another little voice whispers. *Hang in there.*

Sunday, March 2, 2008

Seth insisted on coming over today. At first I thought he must be mad about something, but when he got here, he said he was checking in on me. He left almost immediately upon arriving and went to the corner bodega and came back with a can of soup. He said, "This not-eating business is bullshit. What are you trying to do?"

"I'm not hungry," I said.

"I don't care if you're hungry or not."

"It doesn't matter," I said. "My life is over."

"It will be if you don't eat."

It's funny to think he cares. Does he? Could he? Seth doesn't know about the images, and I will never, ever tell him. To please him I eat a little soup.

Eleanor calls me like every five minutes. I don't answer. I text her, "LEAVE ME ALONE." My claws are out. I have no control.

Tuesday, March 4, 2008

"We think this is an untapped market. A lot of unrealized potential and easily monetized," says Ari Goldstein.

"Totally," I say. "That's why I'm here."

"Awesome!" says Ari Goldstein.

It's my first job interview since I was twenty-four. This idiotic Goldstein and his brother have left investment banking to start a website about luxury travel, and they want someone to edit the "content." Somehow I manage not to scream in their faces.

"As soon as I heard about what you guys were doing, I knew I wanted to be a part of it," I say.

"Awesome!" says Ari Goldstein.

I had to spend about forty minutes in my hallway with my head against the front door psyching myself up to leave the house. But I have negative $437.16 in my bank account and the mortgage is due in two weeks. You can do this; the voices aren't real; it's just a trick of your mind, I say to the howling demons. And then, oh God, what do you want from me, as another voice says, *Why bother? You won't get the job anyway.*

The Goldstein brothers ask me to come back next week for a second interview. Score one for me, I say to the voices. *Don't kid yourself*, the voices say back. *They just felt sorry for you.*

Thursday, March 6, 2008

Peter shows up with all his possessions—two duffel bags and a box of books.

"You okay, dude?" he says when I greet him at the door.

"Yeah, I'm fine."

And then I crumple onto the floor sobbing.

"Oh, dude!" Peter says. He helps me up. I have my hands over my head. "The images, Peter! The images! They're killing me!"

Peter helps me back into bed. He's saying, "What? What? What do you mean?" Then he puts a hand over my forehead.

"You're burning up," he says.

"I'm not feeling so well," I sob.

Peter comes with me on the subway to the doctor. I have my head on my knees the whole time and my arms wrapped over my head. I don't want anyone to look at me. The voices in my mind are shrieking. It's hard to believe no one else hears them.

"Ms. Chaplin," the doctor says. "Have you been taking care of yourself? I can hear that your lungs are filled with fluid. This is not a joke. I'm going to put you into the hospital."

"I don't have health insurance!" I cry. "I don't even have any money in my bank account!"

She gives me a long look and then administers a procedure that involves dropping a tube down my throat and suctioning out some of the crud that is apparently lodged in my lungs. I cry and sputter and gag the whole time. The voices say, *Just let her die.*

I weigh a hundred pounds. I am, at last, as small as a ballerina. The voices shriek.

Friday, March 7, 2008

From my bed, I see Peter going by pushing the couch from my sitting room in the back of the house down the hallway to the front. Sakura is lying at the foot of the bed. He watches too.

"You can't have no furniture in your living room," Peter says. I watch the couch go by. Sakura watches the couch go by. I think, he can do whatever he wants. I have no intention of ever getting up again.

Monday, March 10, 2008

For some reason, since Peter has been in the house, I've been sleeping better. Two full nights. No dreams. No sweats. No up all night watching the dawn creep in. I even answered Eleanor's call today. She's pregnant again. She was calling to me tell me she's bringing a new life into this world, and I was not answering because I have voices in my head threatening to kill me if I did.

Why is her life moving forward and mine has halted?

There is a world outside of my apartment and the images in my head. I know I should care about other people's lives, but somehow I can't. I've become like Josh—so consumed by my own pain that everything else just fades away.

Friday, March 14, 2008

Dr. Chester is, I think, a dwarf. He sits in a big leather chair with brass studs around the edges, but he only half fills it up, like some child king on a man-sized throne. He's got a big, square-shaped head and big, sinewy hands but a tiny body. His hands don't reach the edges of his armrests and his feet don't touch the floor. His neck is torqued so that he has to sit slightly sideways to see me straight. It looks painful.

I tell him about the images. He opens his eyes wide.

"That sounds horrible," he says. He has a strange, high voice.

I tell him how I was awake for about a week and a half.

He says, "You have to sleep. Not sleeping often precedes a psychotic break."

"Are you calling me psychotic?"

Dr. Chester pauses. "I'm not calling you anything," he says finally.

"When I was in high school, a psychiatrist told me I had a personality disorder and I was like, fuck you, I have a great personality."

Dr. Chester smiles the tiniest smile and keeps watching me.

"Have you had a lot of diagnoses?"

"I have."

"Have you had these images before?" he asks.

"All my life," I say. "They just usually don't come so close to winning. Usually I win."

"That's terrible," Dr. Chester says.

Now it's my turn to squint at him. Is this psycho making fun of me?

"I'm sympathizing with you," he says. "I can only imagine how hard life would be with those kinds of thoughts."

"You know, I'm not a specimen," I say. "I'm a perfectly fine, high-functioning, responsible adult who just happens to be having a little bit of a hard time right now."

Dr. Chester raises his enormous hands in the air and now he does actually laugh.

"I believe you!" he says.

I start to cry. "Oh Christ," I say, and drop my head into my hands. There's a voice in my head saying, *Don't tell him another thing*. And like a shadow passing over me there is breathing in the room and someone is just outside the door. The skin is being grated off my knuckles. My nipples are being sawed off.

Dr. Chester leans forward in his chair. "Heather," he says. "What just happened?"

"Nothing."

"Heather, what's going on? Where are you?"

You will be punished, say the voices. I feel like the room is getting bigger and I'm getting smaller.

I hear Dr. Chester's voice as if from somewhere far away. "Listen to me, Heather," he's saying. "Your mind is playing a trick on you. Can you look at me?"

I pry open my eyes, but I'm too scared to meet his gaze. I'm not at all sure it's going to be Dr. Chester sitting there. I'm not at all sure there isn't something waiting outside the door for me. But I tell myself, just a trick, just a trick, just a trick. It's not real. You don't have to pay attention. I cover my breasts with an arm to try and stop the feeling that someone is sawing off my nipples.

He writes me a prescription. "You need to start taking this right away," he says. "It'll help."

It's an antipsychotic.

"I'm not psychotic," I say.

"I didn't say you were," Dr. Chester says. Then, "Just do me a favor and take the medicine, will you? You don't need to suffer like this."

I snatch the prescription out of his hand and make a dash for the door.

Monday, March 17, 2008

The medicine has made the left side of my face go numb. The images, however, remain.

Wednesday, March 19, 2008

Peter says, "Come on, let's go check on your garden."

"My face is numb," I say.

"No, it'll be good," Peter says.

Scowling, I follow him down the stairs to the garden. Everything is covered in leaves, several inches thick over the flower beds and across the flagstone. I never raked last fall or pruned or did any of the things you're supposed to do in the fall.

"I've killed everything," I say. "It's ruined. Do you think anything is alive under all this? Anything at all?"

"I'm sure it all is," Peter says. "Leaves aren't going to kill your plants. We just have to rake."

"Let's do it right now."

"Didn't the doctor say you needed to rest?" Peter says.

"We'll just check," I say, and I scoot past Peter and get on my knees and start pulling leaves away with my hands.

"This is where my bleeding hearts should be," I say. "Please don't let them be dead."

The first layer of leaves is dry and flies away easily. The second layer is wet and the leaves are stuck together into a single sodden covering. I peel it off and toss handfuls behind me. I'm trying to be careful, because if anything is alive under there, I don't want to accidentally rip it out along with its leaf covering. I scrape and scrape with my fingers and then I scream aloud.

"Peter!"

I leap to my feet, staggering backward. Peter is right behind me, peering over my shoulder.

"Oh my God, what is that?" I cry. I'm pointing at something

that looks like it belongs underwater, a nearly translucent green thing rising out of the dirt with strange, ragged, underwater wings unfurling along its edges. Peter gets on his knees. I get back down beside him. We both have our noses almost in the dirt, peering at the thing. Peter pokes at it gently with one finger. He sits back up on his heels.

"I'll tell you what that is," he says. "That's your bleeding heart."

"No," I breathe. "It couldn't be."

"I think so."

I touch it gingerly with my fingertips. "That thing is not human," I say.

"No, dude, it's a plant."

"It's so creepy. It looks like it's alive."

"Well, it is alive."

"No, I mean *really* alive."

"It is really alive."

"Peter, look at my arm." I show him how all the hairs are standing up on end. I start laughing. I slap my thigh with my hand, then cover my face, then laugh some more, then bring my face level with the little green stalk. I can't stop laughing.

"You need to rest," Peter says. "Let's get some lunch."

Sunday, March 23, 2008

New meds. No images for twenty-four hours. Is it possible who I *am* is determined by a few milligrams of some drug?

I am very, very weak, but I am alive.

Tuesday, March 25, 2008

Peter and I don't talk much as we walk back from the hardware store. He's carrying our bags because I'm too weak to carry a glass of water more than a block.

When we get home, we spread out garbage bags on the floor under the windows and put the plastic trays we've just bought on top. In each tray, we put the little biodegradable cones the guy at the hardware sold us, and then Peter looks at me and raises his eyebrows and I raise my eyebrows back and he knows to go ahead and cut open the bag of soil.

We're surrounded by little paper packets. Lavender, rosemary, thyme, sage, and cilantro. Lupines, Lilliput zinnias, cornflowers, peonies, sunflowers, and snap peas.

I open the pack of lavender and peer in.

"Dude," I say, "this is never going to work." I've already said this about six times, and Peter answers as he always does.

"Dude, it will."

I tilt the pack of lavender into my hand. What looks like a bunch of extracted blackheads falls out.

"No way," I say. "I'm not stupid. You cannot tell me that one of these dots"—I wave my hand under Peter's nose—"is going to turn into a flower."

"They will," Peter says.

I'm highly skeptical, but I plunge my hand into the bag of soil anyway. I forgot how much I like the feeling of running my fingers through dirt. I bring out a handful and let it fall into one of the little cones. I pat it down gently with the tips of my fingers.

Sakura comes along and sniffs in the bag of soil. Then he stares at us like we're a couple of idiots.

"He doesn't believe it," I say.

"Yeah, well, that dog is a cynic," Peter says. "Borderline nihilist."

"I've decided to become a nihilist," I say.

"You can't," Peter says. "You're too into flowers."

I grab the pack of lavender from him. "Let me read these instructions," I say. "If we're going to do this thing we need to do it right."

We have thirty-six cones in our trays and we fill each one

three-quarters of the way up with soft black soil. Then, with our fingertips, we poke a hole in the middle of each one and drop in a few seeds. We brush the soil back over the indents, and when we've finished we gently pick up all the trays and put them in the window ledges.

"Water," Peter says.

"Water," I affirm, and go to the sink, where I fill up two watering cans. Peter starts on the left and I start on the right and we water our way into the center, so that all our little cones are damp and a thin layer of liquid covers the bottom of each tray.

Sakura puts a paw up on what was his window ledge.

"He's pissed," I say.

"He'll get over it," Peter says.

It's just noon and the sun is pouring in those big back windows as if it were midsummer. We're both squinting.

"So now what?" I say.

Peter wipes the soil off his palms onto the front of his jeans. He looks over at me.

"Now we wait," he says.

Sunday, March 30, 2008

I've interacted with Kieran three times since I got back. The first time I wrote to apologize for not responding to his email apologizing to me, and he was like, oh, I'm fine, I just wanted to make sure *you* were fine. And I'd thought, wow, Kieran is a pussy just like the rest of them. Then we talked on the phone and I told him I was having a hard time. He said I had more friends than anyone he knows and I should reach out to them. He said he would always be there for me because of how much I'd given him, which was sweet, but, based on past experiences, I take as more symbolic than literal. This morning he called and we talked for a long time. He was talking about his ex-wife and how tormented he is that she's settling down with someone. Finally I just said, "Of course you are, you're still in love with her."

There was a pause and then he said, "How long have you known that?"

"Always," I lied.

"Jaysus, girl," he said. "I'm sorry."

Friday, April 18, 2008
San Francisco

Billy Santiago holds the sprig of lavender up to his nose. He sniffs it. He looks at it. He tosses it onto the ground.

"It's not that I don't have a sense of smell," he says, striding on. "I've checked with other people. I've done experiments. I seem to experience the same thing other people are experiencing when I hold something to my nose. It's more that I don't have any internal reaction to it, not the way it seems other people do. It's like, I don't care that there's a smell."

I'm trotting to keep up with him. At least I'm not trying to record as we walk. I'm in San Francisco, in the Mission, breaking from our interview to get a burrito. I'm sweating and shaking and my teeth feel like they're rattling in my head, but if I'm appearing outlandish in any way, it doesn't seem to be affecting Billy. But then, Billy isn't affected by the smell of lavender so who really knows. This morning when I was taping him, I could see the mike in my hand perceptibly shaking, but he didn't seem to notice anything.

I don't know why exactly I'm sweating and shaking, but I have a feeling it's because of some other changes Dr. Chester made to my meds. Or maybe traveling again was a bad idea. I was so psyched to have beaten the images that I threw a party, stayed up all night making out with an editor from Knopf, did two stories back-to-back, and then got an ear infection and had to do the last one in bed. I am so broke, though, I cannot afford to turn down the work. And my friend who went through a horrible divorce is getting married tomorrow in Sonoma and I wanted to show my support. Now I think maybe I was being stupid. It's like I don't learn. I must be the most exasperating person in the world. Is this why Eleanor has stopped returning my calls? I've never heard her so upset as when I told her I was coming out here.

I run to keep up with Billy. He is without a doubt one of the most interesting people I've ever met. He told me earlier, in passing, that he thinks in multidimensional visualizations. He's supposed to be one of the best programmers in the world. When I asked him about this, he said, "Yes." Then he resumed staring at me.

Billy says his game is a model of what enlightenment might look like. He says it's about what happens when you realize science is so much weirder than the mind can fathom and that reason will not lead you to the answers.

Later
Sonoma

I didn't last long at the reception the night before the wedding. I didn't know anyone there except my friend, but he's the groom, so what was he going to do, stand around talking to me all night? I tried to insert myself into a circle of laughing people by standing near them and laughing too, but they didn't expand the circle to include me. I went and stood by myself at the edge of the bar with a glass of champagne, trying to look beautiful and alluring and waiting for some man to come and start talking to me—but no one came. I went and stood by the buffet eating Sonoma nuts and dried cranberries and tried to look alluring there, but still no one came. I realized, I am the only single person here. It was all couples. Men with their arms draped around women. Women with their hands tucked through men's elbows. You are alone, I thought. You are entirely alone.

It was an open-air reception in the redwoods, so I couldn't just leave without everyone seeing. Finally, I tiptoed away through the woods and found a little bridge to the hotel where I'm staying. The bridge had a sign saying "Danger: Do Not Pass." There was a picture of a guy falling backward with a red "no" symbol through him. There was only a tiny bit of water under the bridge, but it was about ten feet down. I tiptoed across it as lightly as I could, holding my breath and trying not to imagine a jump cut to me lying in the creek below with a broken back while everyone came running to see why I was sneaking out of the party across a bridge with a big sign saying "Danger: Do Not Pass."

When I get back to my room, I stand with my eyes closed against the cool tile of the bathroom wall. Trying not to vomit. Then leaning over the toilet. Trying to vomit. After a lot of dry heaving, I splash cold water on my face. I look in the mirror to see who'll be looking back at me.

My skin is very, very, very white. Not as white as a dead person's, but not quite as rosy as a living person's either.

You're the ugliest person I've ever seen in my life.

My mouth turns down at the corners like a kid about to cry. No, I'm not.

Yes, you are.

Later

Peter writes, "A guy came into my class today, and he said that when he looks around all he sees is data flowing. I was thinking, if you had a mind that saw data, and you thought in three-dimensional space, you might not be interested in smelling flowers either. You'd want to see the connections, not the beauty. Or maybe the connections are the beauty. I don't know."

Then, later: "Actually smell is important. Smell brings up memories and memories are connections. My girlfriend in high school loved lavender, so I gave her a pillow stuffed with it. Then it turned out I was allergic to lavender. Lavender + puberty = allergies and glasses."

I write, "Heather + puberty = acne and fat."

Peter writes, "Yeah, but I still have glasses and allergies."

Later

I sneak back across the bridge to the party and say good-bye to my friend and his bride-to-be, as if I'd been there the whole time. I tell them what a great night it's been. What I really want to say is, you're making a terrible mistake. In fact, I want to scream it. I imagine myself grabbing those bottles of Sonoma microbrews and smashing them on the floor one by one and then collapsing in a writhing, sweating heap onto the broken glass. Would that bring us any closer? I think again how very, very slim the line is between doing something and not doing something. At this moment, it feels like it's just a breath of air between me staying in control of myself and a complete loss of all bodily functions.

Back in my room

I think, the beauty is in the connections. How did Peter get so smart? Right now the only connective tissue I feel is to the past. Like Peter and his lavender pillow, only so much uglier. What are these things in my mind? Am I really connected to them? I don't want to be. I want to be connected to the people at the party, to this room, to the stars outside me. To what's happening *now*. But nothing. Nothing.

I thought I was better. I thought I was overdramatizing the voices. The minute the images left, I told myself they'd never been there. I shouldn't have thrown that party. I shouldn't have stayed up all night with the editor from Knopf. I shouldn't have come out here. Eleanor was right. I should have stayed home. I should have stayed home a long time ago. It's happening again. I've been ejected from this world. I'm sliding away. The thing that waits outside my door will get me soon.

Saturday, April 19, 2008

It is time to get your shit together. You have come for this wedding. You will attend this wedding. You will enjoy this wedding.

Okay. Okay. I'll go, I say to the voices.

I have a beautiful dress from that same Barneys Warehouse sale in that other lifetime. It's lightly form-fitting silk with a soft, low V-neck, spaghetti straps, and the tiniest train—just maybe six inches of extra fabric—in the back. It's got green and pink flowers on it that are edged in matching beads. I wear it with little silver slippers and, since they were giving them out, a parasol over one shoulder. The ceremony is outdoors among the redwoods, with a raised platform and rows of white folding chairs placed before it. I plant myself behind all the seats next to a tree with wide, low, spreading branches and try to take solace in thinking how beautiful I must look framed by my parasol and the green leaves, even if no one wants to talk to me.

I'm approached by my friend's business partner. Turns out he runs something at the University of San Francisco called the Center for the Future of the Internet and he's very interested in my work. I can't tell if he's an actual geek or an ironic geek, but his wife is very pretty, which makes me think the latter.

So things are going well. I have a little posse to hang out with, and I keep seeing men staring at me, even with ladies on their arms. By the time dinner is over, I'm loving my friend's business partner and he's loving me, and he keeps saying, "I have a project I want to talk to you about. Are you looking for work?" And I'm like, "oh, I don't know, it depends"—not at all like, yes, God, please pay me to do something, because I'm about to be foreclosed on.

Then I start to get sick again. Except this time it isn't just the sweating and the shaking, which I've kind of gotten the hang of. This time it's as if there's some growth on my brain that is swelling at an inordinate rate and pushing against my skull and at my eyeballs from the inside out. I start seeing little silver dots swimming around in front of me, and, from one second to the next, half the room goes out of focus. My friend's business partner says, "Are you okay? Did you still want to hit the dance floor?" Because we'd been just about to go dance. I flee. By the time I get to my room that thing has happened to me that happened in Dublin in my tangerine room. A break. Not a vague sense of slipping away—but a total break from one reality into another.

I take off my dress. I'm sweating in a serious way, and not just on my face but all over my body. I'm shivering. I wrap myself in towels and climb under the blankets. I can't find any words in my brain to correlate with anything I'm seeing or doing or wanting. Kieran is there, hovering, but every time I think, it's okay, he's here, I'm safe, he's gone, and it's just me and the shrieking. I want to say to him, please save me, but I can't find words. And by the time I find the words, I don't know to whom I'm talking anymore. Then, fear. It's not the mopey feeling of being alone. And it's not the fear of devils like in Dublin. It's fear like I imagine you'd feel if someone were pointing a gun at your face or you've lost control of your car on a four-lane highway. I have my eyes closed, but I know there's a man's face above me. Heavy breathing—I can hear it; I can just almost feel it. I open my eyes. It's gone, but I know it's just outside the door. Then it's right up against me again; it's breath on my face. I squeeze my eyes shut. My heart is pounding.

I think, here it comes. I think, no, not these connections. Please, Kieran, Josh, someone, anyone, where are you? Aren't you going to save me?

Suddenly, I'm leaning over the edge of the bed and retching onto the floor, except there's nothing in my stomach to throw up, so it's just enormous dry heaves, like my intestines are trying to come out through my mouth. And the owner of the face is right there in the room with me, crouching in the corner, biding his time, waiting for me.

Total fear.

Total clarity. I know exactly what is going on. Oh God, I think, please don't let this be the end of my story—because it's here, at last. It didn't go away when I got rid of Josh. Kieran can't save me. This thing, it owns me. That's what I keep thinking. He owns me. No matter how far I go, it'll always be there to drag me back. There is no now. There is only then. Don't you see, it's my father.

Tuesday, April 29, 2008
New York

What can I tell you about my father? That he wore his dark hair long and wild down to his shoulders. That he had brilliant blue eyes with long black eyelashes and a black beard. That when people found out I was his daughter, they said, you must be a very smart little girl, because your father is the smartest man in Baltimore. That when he came into my school every year to play the banjo, I clung onto his arm as we walked through the hallways so everyone would know he was my dad.

Should I tell you that I loved him? That he broke my heart into so many pieces, no man in the world will ever be able to put it back together again? Should I tell you that I still love him? Even as the thought of him brings hands to my breasts and up between my legs? I look at my friends' kids, at their tiny, beautiful bodies, and I'm afraid to touch them, afraid I'll accidentally damage them in some way. I have to look away when I see my male friends hold their daughters. I think, don't touch her, don't touch her. Fear has been a man's face looming over me for as long as I can remember. Shame is the oldest feeling I've ever had.

I've told you enough. I'm going back to sleep.

Saturday, May 3, 2008

I'm heavily sedated. This is because of the shouting. I don't know how I made it back from San Francisco to New York. But when I walked in the door of my apartment, I started shouting and I couldn't stop. I called Seth. He came over and sat with me that first night because I was so scared someone was outside the back door that the air around me was growing quivery and time was skipping around to some strange rhythm. Seth kept saying, "You know it's not real, Heath. Right?" And I was thinking, no, it is real. That's the whole point, although I will never in a million years tell him what is real. He doesn't know about my father, and I won't ever tell him. I don't want him to know what I know.

Peter always seemed to be about five feet away from me, his hands folded across his chest, looking like he was about to cry. Faith took the bus up from Baltimore. Eleanor came from DC. Summer called every day.

Dr. Chester quadrupled the antipsychotic, tripled the antidepressant, and started me on sedatives every two hours. Then I stopped screaming. Instead, I cried. All day long, and at night too, as if that's what I'd been put on the planet to do. I got sick again. The bronchitis came back and another ear infection just for extra measure. Then I stopped crying. I slept. For about a week, I just slept. It's impossible to stay awake on all these meds. When I'm awake, I lie in bed and wait to die. I'm still waiting. There's no craziness around it. No violent images, nothing frenetic at all. I just know I can't stay alive knowing what I know.

Tuesday, May 6, 2008

There was a rumor about me in the sixth grade, a rumor that I'd been molested. Stacy Klien started it. I imagined pushing her in the chest and knocking her to the ground and watching her bleed, but instead I crept away and refused to speak to my mother on the way home and then hid in bed burning up as if I had a fever.

I used to say to my mom, "There's a man's face looming over me. He's got long hair and a beard and his eyes are blazing." And she said, "How awful. How strange." Once, when I was fourteen, I said to my father, just to see what he'd say, "There's a man's face looming over me. He's got long hair and a beard and his eyes are blazing." I described him to him. I said, "Do you think anyone who looks like that ever did something terrible to me?" And he said, "Heather, how awful. Let me think about it."

Wednesday, May 7, 2008

This morning I went over and peered into the tray of seedlings and almost fell over backward. There were tiny green shoots, the breadth of a hair from my head, emerging from the dirt.

"Peter! What is happening here?"

Peter was like, "They're growing."

"Are you insane?" I said. "It's a fucking miracle."

"Yeah, it's called the miracle of life, dude."

All the hairs on my arm were standing up. "I never in a million years thought it would work," I said.

And then Peter helped me back to bed.

Friday, May 9, 2008

What can I tell you about my father? Should I tell you about the time I was eight and he put Faith and me in the backseat of his car and talked to us about the joys of child-adult sex? He used to talk to me about this fairly regularly, actually—these "other cultures" where people went off to eat in private but made love all together in one joyous group, grown-ups and kids together. He said these cultures were far more advanced. He quoted Plato. Did other fathers not have similar conversations with their daughters? Faith and I had huddled together, silent and shivering in the back of the car, and in my mind I'd shouted, No! No! No!

Saturday, May 10, 2008

Soon, Peter and I will start putting the seedlings out on the back steps. It turns out that you can't introduce plants to the outdoors all at once. It has to be in stages. One hour for the first few days. Two after that, and so on, until, eventually, when they're hardy enough, you leave them out over night. Only after that do you plant them.

"How will we know?" I say to Peter. "Let's just kill them now instead of waiting and watching them die."

Peter says we should hold off.

Sunday, May 11, 2008

At night I lie in bed and listen to the little sounds that Peter makes on the other side of the house. I want to call out to him to come sit with me in bed. I know this would be highly inappropriate so I refrain, but I find it very difficult when he's not near me. He's so kind. All day long, he cooks little bits of vegetables and soup and lentils to try and tempt me. Sometimes I eat a bit. Sometimes I don't.

Peter doesn't want to have sex with me. Or if he does, he would never show it. He's only twenty-six and he's so shy. His eyes never glow at me. This is why I can trust him. It's just like how I made my marriage a nonsexual one. That was the only way I could trust Josh. Although a fat lot of good that did me.

It's been two years and a month just about exactly since I started keeping this whole thing. I don't want this to be the end of my story.

Wednesday, May 14, 2008

What can I tell you about my father? Should I tell you that I called him up when I was graduating college and had fallen in love with Josh and had my last breakdown? "I know what you did," I said. "I know what you are. And I will never speak to you again." And he'd said, "I know I was a terrible father. You have every right to hate me, but what are you talking about specifically?"

I'd sputtered and cried and said, "You know what I'm talking about!" And then he'd gotten really mad, madder than I've ever heard him, and he screamed, "That is not reality, Heath!" And the way he said "Heath" had deflated me entirely.

The voices had said, *You little shit. Why are you always making things up? Why are you trying to make your father's life difficult with your lies?* And I'd gone to my room and taken a serrated knife and cut three long gashes across my midriff, just to punish myself, to get myself to shut up. The next day he sent me two dozen long-stemmed red roses with a card saying, "I love you." And I'd screamed and screamed until my dorm mates had pounded on the door and the mental health department had called my mother.

Thursday, May 15, 2008

I went out into the garden tonight, after it had gotten dark. The whole place was swarming with slugs. I don't know if that's right. Do slugs swarm? Whatever they do, they were doing it. Slithering. They were slithering. Peter said, "Dude, it's just part of having a garden." But I gritted my teeth. "No," I said. "There will be no slugs in my garden. I will eradicate those fuckers. I will triumph."

Friday, May 16, 2008

Seth and Cecilia are lending me ten thousand dollars. Do I need to tell you I didn't get the job monetizing content for the Goldsteins? I can't tell you how I cried when Seth and Cecilia did this, all day. I could not stop. I felt so confused—like it was shattering my world-view. Do people actually care? And then Eleanor lent me five thousand dollars. They want me to rest for a while. This generosity fills me with rage and shame and wonder.

I talk to Seth almost every day. He comes over all the time. But it's hard because I can never tell him what the problem is.

Peter says I should tell him. But I don't think Seth would ever forgive me.

Please don't let this be the end of my story.

Saturday, May 17, 2008

Brought the seedlings out into the garden with me this afternoon for their first hour outside. My rosebush is almost four feet high this year and looks like it's about to bloom. I think, that'll be nice. I wonder, vaguely, who will take care of my flowers when I'm dead. Surely I will be dead soon?

Monday, May 19, 2008

I'm sick of telling you about my father. I have a chafing sensation between my legs when I think of him, is that not enough? I have phantom hands on my breasts. You'd probably like something more specific, wouldn't you? Maybe, secretly, you want something graphic, even. Well, sorry to disappoint. All I have are shards of memory. What a stupid phrase. My shrink after college used to say that. He'd say, "Survivors often don't remember abuse. They are left only with"—and here he'd raise his hand in the air and close his eyes—"shards of memory." He was such a pretentious fuck. Me, I'm not a poet. I'm a facts-based person. I told you that at the beginning. I've spent my whole life feeling ashamed of this knowledge I have about my father, but no, I told myself, no way, shards of memory are not enough. You got facts or you got nothing. But then the shards got so bad when I was leaving college, pointed and spiked, like glass breaking in my hands. Then after I told my father off, I spent more hours than I care to recall sitting in the closet crying while voices called me a sniveling liar and images of a leather strap ripped my back to shreds and a machete went up between my legs.

So now, at this point, I give up. I'd say *shards of memory* is pretty fucking apropos. My hands are bloodied with them.

Tuesday, May 20, 2008

"Peter . . ."

"Yes, dude?"

"Once he picked me up from school when I was sick. And he was so nice to me. He brought me soup. He said he wouldn't be mad if I accidentally threw up and didn't make it to the bathroom on time."

I've been crying all day.

"I know, dude."

"And Peter. He taught me how to use chopsticks."

"I know, dude. I know."

And then I just lay in my bed, the tears running down the sides of my face and into my ears. My father is with me all the time. He owns me. There's just no way to stay alive, this being the state of things. It is too oppressive. Eventually, all the lifeblood will simply drain out of me. There's nothing dramatic about it. It's just that the struggle is over, and soon, I imagine, I'll be dead.

There are aphids on my foxgloves.

Wednesday, May 21, 2008

I've come up with a better term than *shards of memory*. You know how dancers develop muscle memory—your body learns what to do so your mind doesn't have to think about it? That's what it's been like for me. I would call what I have *physical memories*. Between my legs knows. My chest knows. My neck knows. My brain remembers nothing, but my body knows it all.

It's funny, isn't it. At the end of the day, there really is nothing that will save you—no man, no medicine. Just the moments as they tick by.

Saturday, May 24, 2008

After I took the seedlings into the garden for their outdoor time, I lay on the couch and watched six hours of BBC's *Edward the King*. The scenery is made of cardboard but I don't care. It's good stuff.

"That's my girl," Eleanor says. "A little European royal history to get you up and running."

Sprayed the aphids with soap and water. Didn't help at all.

Peter went on online and found out you need ladybugs to deal with aphids. I ordered some.

Monday, May 26, 2008

Seedlings continue to grow.

On couch. Finished *Edward the King*. Started a book about Louis XIV. What filth they lived in at Versailles. Was it worth it for the jewels?

The ladybugs arrived. Peter and I went out back and released them, spooning them out of their container onto plants all around the garden. We shall see. I doubt they'll help. I'm feeling a bit of my old homicidal self return. Am very angry at aphids. Also at the lilies my mother gave me because they're growing sideways instead of straight.

Tuesday, May 27, 2008

Walked a small circle around the block with Sakura and Peter. That was a step. Watched first four hours of *Fall of Eagles* about the Hohenzollern, Hapsburg, and Romanov empires. Wilhelm II. What a maniac. He was in *Edward the King* too, always driving his English cousins crazy. Amazing how history turns upon such things as a person in the wrong place at the wrong time being out of his mind.

Wednesday, May 28, 2008

Didn't take seedlings out today because it was raining. Peter thought they'd be fine, but I don't think they're ready for that yet. Finished *Fall of Eagles*. World War I not actually Wilhelm's fault. Franz Joseph of Austria gives order to go into Balkans. Why does he do it?

Thursday, May 29, 2008

Sitting in the garden. Sakura is sniffing the miniature English daisies.

"Peter," I say. "Why do you think Franz Joseph invaded the Balkans? I mean, he started World War One."

Peter takes his laptop off his lap, puts it down on the bench beside him, and crosses his arms high up on his chest.

"It was an act of nihilism," he says.

"You think everyone is a nihilist."

"No, I'm serious. I've thought about this."

"Okay," I say. "You're the student. You tell me."

"Everything he knew was over. His era was up. He'd been raised from the day he was born to be emperor of all this territory that didn't even make sense anymore by the time he was an adult. He married the most beautiful princess in the world, who then spent all her time traveling instead of staying in Austria and being empress. She fucking supported Hungarian independence."

"I always wanted to be the most beautiful princess in the world,"
I say.

"His son and heir was an opium addict who killed his seventeen-
year-old girlfriend and then himself in a suicide pact. His wife who
wouldn't stay home got murdered by an Italian anarchist on one
of her trips. And then his next heir, Franz Ferdinand, marries a
commoner, which no one in their family has ever done in like six
hundred years. I mean, shit is falling apart."

"The center cannot hold," I say.

"Franz Ferdinand only goes to Sarajevo in the first place because the officials there promise not to snub his wife."

Peter raises his arms in the air. "And then *he* gets assassinated
by anarchists." He recrosses his arms. "So it's like an honor thing,
but also, it's just kind of saying, fuck it, I give up, I don't understand
what's going on anymore, I can't make sense of this world—and
jumping into the abyss, you know?"

"Damn," I say. And then, "I thought you were studying reli-
gion."

Peter opens his laptop. "They make you take history too."

Saturday, May 31, 2008

All the ladybugs flew away, while the aphids remain. I am losing
control of my garden. It is the one thing in the world that gives me
any pleasure, and I am losing it to a bunch of pests.

Kieran calls me. He's met someone. Someone he really likes.
He says he has me to thank for the relationship. I assume he means
because I forced him to look into himself. I'm thinking, okay, I was
his training wheels; there are worse roles you could play than helping someone learn to love again. I say, "How so?" because I want to
hear him say these things. But no. Apparently his new girl is friends
with the Irish art gallery owner. At first this girl didn't want to go
out with Kieran but the art gallery owner said she had an American

friend (me) who'd had the best sex of her life with Kieran O'Shea, and that convinced her to give him a try.

"Thanks for the recommendation, girl," Kieran says.

So I guess that was the point of my connection with Dublin. To help Kieran O'Shea find his real love. Christ, why me? I think. And then, this cannot be the end of my story.

Tuesday, June 3, 2008

Something in the night took Cookie Monster–sized bites out of my lupines. It's slugs, I know it. I put a border of pennies around every flower out there. Copper is supposed to be like kryptonite to slugs. I might be dead soon, but first I will kill all the slugs in my garden.

Summer is coming to visit next month.

Friday, June 13, 2008

Left the seedlings out for eight hours. And there they were, looking green and hearty. Some of the Lilliput zinnias are even beginning to flower. This is good because I had to remove two foxgloves yesterday—I haven't been able to get rid of the aphids and I didn't want the whole garden to become infested. Then, the lilies my mother gave me are essentially lying down. Also, my pansies have grown long and stringy and they cause me a great deal of distress to look at them.

Saturday, June 21, 2008

Colin Landau came over today. He's in the US now covering Obama's campaign for the *Guardian* and when he asked if he could visit, I said, "Well, I'm housebound, but if you want to come sit in my garden, you can." And apparently he did. We sat under the Christmas lights, beside the pink blooms of my rosebush. I made him look at the slugs slithering along between my flowers. Colin did not agree with me that this is necessarily a disaster. "I think they're quite common," he said. "You need to do something about them, sure. But is your garden wrecked? No."

He's very reasonable, that Colin Landau.

He said, "So, how you doing since I saw you in London?"

"I've been a little lonely," I said.

He tilted his head to one side. "That's funny," he said. "By your own philosophy, there's no such thing as alone."

"What?" I said.

"Well, all that business about complex systems, right? Isn't the point that everything is interconnected? Like you said, subparticles only exist in relation to one another."

Then his eyes grew very kind. "But I'm just being a twat and intellectualizing everything. Of course sometimes a person just feels lonely. That's okay too."

We sat out there for a long time. Colin is so elegant. He's long and slim and, just like in London, he was wearing a neat charcoal blazer. He looks so straight, but his mind seems so unusual. I find him disarming. He said I should come visit him in DC. If I don't die first, I think I will.

Sunday, June 22, 2008

Ben and Marie and my brother and Cecilia come over with Alex and the new baby, whose name is Owen. He's a beautiful baby. A perfect oval face with a tuft of blond hair on top. Totally alert, watching us all through blue baby eyes. Ben and Marie sit together on the iron love seat I have out there. Ben's got his arm around her shoulders. His other hand is on Alex's head, who leans between his knees. They seem so well. I can't believe anyone could ever seem so well after what they've been through.

"The garden's looking good," my brother says. He's eating a burger that Peter just handed him. Peter is manning the grill.

"No, it's not," I say. "It's all fucked-up." I start pointing around. "See that bare spot? Those were my foxgloves. And there, look at those pansies—look how they're growing sideways. And the same over there with the rosebush—it's nearly horizontal. And my lilies too—look at that. It's like they want to lie down on the ground."

"Oh, shut up," my brother says.

"Yeah, enough," Cecilia says. "It's amazing back here."

"And I can't get rid of the slugs."

"Slugs are part of a garden," Peter says.

Alex is two and a half now. I don't think he remembers me at all. I find myself staring at him, looking into his eyes, trying to see if there's some connection between us. He has a startled look about him. It makes me feel tremendously sad. Even as I'm oohing and aahing over Owen, the new baby, I'm thinking, poor little guy. Does he know? Does he remember? Even if he doesn't, will he ever escape it? Surely you can't just step around something like that. I'm afraid almost to look at Marie. If it were me, I'd hate the world so much that I would never, ever feel safe enough to have another child. Then I think, there's no such thing as safety anyway.

I watch her, with her head bent over Owen, giving him kisses on his eyes that make him gurgle with pleasure, and scrunching her face into funny positions to make him coo. Then I wonder if there's a kind of freedom to having had the worst thing that can happen to you happen. Franz Joseph started World War I when he didn't know what to make of the world anymore. But maybe the Greens have found another way to deal with the abyss.

Monday, June 23, 2008

I went out to water the garden this evening. It was so beautiful I dropped to my knees. The whole space was illuminated in a ghostly pale way by the Christmas lights that run along the fence. The bottom branches of the dogwood tree were drooping, languidly, almost all the way to the ground, borne down by the weight of their blossoms. I don't know why it's still blooming this late in the year, but it is. I lifted up my arms and took one of those branches and put my face into the petals of the pale yellow flower and thought, they are the texture and color of moonbeams.

Tuesday, June 24, 2008

The guy I met at the wedding in Sonoma wants me to work with him on a grant about the future of the Internet and universal broadband policy. He said, "What's your day rate?" I said, "One thousand a day, but for you, I'll make it seven hundred and fifty." He said, "Deal."

I will be able to pay my mortgage. The relief is so great, I have to sit down.

Thursday, June 26, 2008

Summer rents a car and we drive to Jones Beach. In the ocean I feel better than I have in as long as I can remember. I lie on my back in the gray-blue waves and let the sun bake into my skin. I can feel the nutrients sink in. Oh God, I love the sun.

When we get back, Summer is walking around in these little short shorts that are nothing more than underwear and a cut-up tee, and I can't stop laughing because really the woman is an exhibitionist. Then she will only talk in a Baltimore accent, which has me doubled up laughing with tears rolling down my face. I don't think I've ever had a visit with Summer that doesn't involve me pissing myself I'm laughing so hard.

And then I start to cry because suddenly I'm overcome with

sadness. She lies in bed with me stroking my hair and telling me it will be all right in the end. She's wrong of course. We all die in the end. But it's very comforting nonetheless.

Friday, June 27, 2006

The day Summer leaves, I get an email from Eleanor. She is cutting off contact with me. She said she was waiting until I was "back on my feet." She said all she does is give and all I do is take. That I'm a terrible friend. Only, she's vicious about it. It's the most vicious email I've ever received. As if anger has been eating her up for years and years and it just came spewing out. I didn't know she could be so vicious.

My best friend since I was five doesn't want to talk to me anymore.

How can I survive this? Did I let my venom and spite leak out? I've been so busy thinking I was nothing that it never even occurred to me I could have an effect on anyone else.

Saturday, June 28, 2008

"I feel like it will never end, Josh. This time he's really got me."

"It'll end, Heath. It always does. You always get back up. But this was inevitable. You couldn't go your whole life pushing it away."

"Do you think it's true? Do you think I'm making it up?"

"Are you really asking me that? Remember, I know your father."

"Why me, Josh?"

"Trust me, that line of thought is not going to get you anywhere."

"I'm really struggling, Josh."

"I know you are."

"Josh, are you happy?"

"Happier," he says. "I'm happier."

Tuesday, July 1, 2008

Warning. I am about to tell you a story you may not believe. As you already know, strange things happen sometimes in my mind. This might seem like the strangest of all. The night before last, I fought an epic battle in my mind, and I lost. Yet somehow I seem to have won. I am just going to record it exactly as it happened, and you'll have to trust me that these are the facts and judge as you will.

I was lying on my bed with my feet dangling off the edge and my arms extended out by my sides, and I was letting my mind go where it would and just kind of watching. Do you ever get the feeling that you're watching what's happening in your mind—as if it were an enormous stage and you were in the audience, not controlling the action but just saying, oh my, look at that? That's how it was last night.

In my mind, I was dancing with my father. I watched us waltz across a vast open space with no ground beneath us. Every time we turned, his long hair blew across my face, taking away my vision. I could feel pressure against my chest. And though we were dancing, I felt as if I couldn't move, as if I were being held in place. It was the same as in all those dreams I have where I'm straining every muscle to get away but no movement will come. I was trapped under a heavy beam of wood in a house that had caught fire. I could see the flames. I could feel the heat as if it were inside me. I was sick with fear.

The demons were there. Like from Dublin. My father was pressed against me. I was holding myself so rigid, I imagined I might fracture into a million pieces. I was struggling to get away. There was such a great weight on me that no amount of thrashing brought even an inch of freedom. In my mind, I cried out, as I always do, No! No! No! I was struggling as hard as a human can struggle. And the voices were saying, *You're nothing, you're nothing, you're nothing.*

And then it was as if the edges of what I could see were

expanding, and soon there were no edges at all. A little thought ran across the theater of my mind, so quiet it was barely audible, and it said, *Okay. You win. I'm nothing.*

And then, for a second, there was total silence in my mind. Then the demons were doubly furious, and the screeching got louder, and their faces were right up against my face. But at the same time, my mind just kept expanding—expanding out beyond the demons, beyond where there was any end of anything at all. And I thought—or rather it wasn't me thinking but instead simply a thought wafting through this great expanse—*Go to town. Do your worst. I can't fight you anymore. You win.*

Now, I don't believe in revelations. I don't believe in one-stop shopping, potions that cure all, or single grand theories that explain the meaning of life. Eating fat won't make you fat, and cutting out carbs won't make you thin. There is no single answer to everything. But I have to tell you, it was as if I'd pushed a magic button. In my mind, whiteness began to unfurl. And suddenly I had the most extraordinary clarity and a simple series of thoughts presented themselves. *These are not my demons. Why should I have demons? I didn't do anything wrong.*

It was like I'd made some terrible faux pas at a dinner party. The devils were frozen and silent. The whiteness was spreading—not a dazzling light you hear about in near-death experiences. Rather a steady, calm white, the white of a good piece of paper—it unfolded itself out of my chest, through my belly, down my legs, into my arms, and up through my head. I was completely in my body, yet the boundaries between my body and the vastness with no end were blurred because all was spread with this whiteness. And it was like I was breathing, only I wasn't making myself breathe, and it was the most relaxed feeling I ever remember having in my life. The thoughts kept drifting through, so calm as if they were reciting what was for dinner: *I've been walking around with someone else's demons my whole life. These are my father's demons. He has demons because he's done terrible things and he hates himself for it. I didn't do anything wrong. Why should I have demons?*

And then very simply, something that had never occurred to me before: *It's not my fault.*

And again, *It's not my fault. It's not my fault. IT'S NOT MY FAULT.*

Maybe you're thinking, well, the meds obviously haven't kicked in, or maybe you're thinking they finally have. I don't know. All I know is a battle ensued. The demons began to howl and shake and then they descended, but not on me—on my father. And then they were gone, taking him with them. My mind was completely empty. And I was left with the sense of being suspended, weightless, in the vast white nothingness. It was as if all the buzzing of the universe had ceased. And laughter was bubbling up out of the whiteness, out between my lips, and into the world.

Wednesday, July 2, 2008

Today I left the seedlings out overnight.

Thursday, July 3, 2008

"Peter, do you think I'm crazy?"

"Dude, I'd wish you'd stop asking me that. It's a really hard question to answer."

I sigh. "I suppose.

"Peter?"

"Yes?"

"Can I have some lentils?"

Friday, July 4, 2008

The hydrangeas are blooming spectacularly. They're enormous pink things, each flower made up of dozens of tiny blooms that in turn are made up of a multitude of little petals, each with their own networks of veins and creases. I stare into this flower, and no matter how long I stare, I always see more.

Saturday, July 5, 2008

Outside, the sun has just set and there's a cool breeze.

"It's weird," I say to Peter. "I'm sad. But it doesn't hurt."

We sit in silence.

"Peter?"

"Yes?"

"Why do you think all my flowers are lying down?"

"I wouldn't really say they're lying down, dude."

"I hope my garden isn't wrecked."

"I promise your garden isn't wrecked."

"Peter?"

"Yes?"

"Will you live here with me forever, just exactly like it is now?"

Peter blows out a plume of smoke.

"I kinda doubt it," he says.

I sigh. "Yeah, you're probably right. But it's good now, isn't it?"

"Totally," he says.

Sunday, July 6, 2008

Today I sat in the sunshine of my garden talking to my friends and family. I have to say, there are a lot of them. It took me nearly all day. I called Katy and Mac, Summer, Faith, Ben and Marie. I spoke with my brother for a long time—just shooting the shit. Shooting the shit with my brother! I emailed Kieran and told him how glad I was that he was suffering less. I emailed Colin Landau and he wrote me right back. I even emailed my mother and asked how she was liking Florida. I didn't talk to Eleanor. That is a black hole in my chest. But we will come back together. I don't know when but I know we will.

Tuesday, July 8, 2008

It's time to plant the seedlings. They've been out several times overnight now.

I take the trays down the stairs into the garden. And suddenly I get nervous. Maybe I should just throw them all away, I think. Then, it's total chaos out here. Nothing has gone according to plan. My flowers are not growing straight and tall like they're supposed to. They're all twisted and climbing wildly, in different directions. My mother's lilies are growing on the diagonal. My pansies are long and stringy. I don't know what's going on with the delphiniums.

I put the trays down in the center of the garden and go for a closer examination of those lilies. I get down on my knees. I look up and I see how much the dogwood has grown since I planted it last year. I notice that it's growing slightly slanted, as if to get away from the trees next door, which have also grown. I look back at the lilies, and I realize that the dogwood, growing slanted, is casting a big swath of shade over them, and that they in turn are growing slanted as if to get out from under that shade. Something dawns on me. I take hold of one of these lilies from my mother, growing in that strange diagonal away, and bring it toward my face to see if it's alive or not. The green stalk breaks away in three directions at the top, each with a bud that's made of several tightly overlapping petals that just almost but not quite close together at the top. I think, this fucker is about to bloom.

I turn around and scan the rest of the garden. I see that my redbud is also beginning to grow at a slant, out from under the branches of a tree growing in my neighbor's garden. In turn, the rosebush beneath the redbud is growing out from under its shade, and so on across the whole garden. I think, how did I not see this before—me, with all my big talk? It's not chaos. I'm sitting here, on my heels, in the midst of an infinitely complex system, in which the roses and lupines and cornflowers and alliums, the billy buttons, the blazing stars and the bluebells, the dahlias and delphiniums, gardenias and gladioli, grape hyacinths and sweet williams, and even the miniature English daisies at the border—they're all doing exactly what they need in order to bloom. They and me, we're all part of the same thing and we're all doing the same thing. My flowers are stretching this way and that, and never in the way I intended, but all so that they can get themselves out of the shadows and into the sun. It's very simple. My flowers are growing toward the light.

EPILOGUE

July 17, 2016

I'd love to tell you everything was just fantastic after that moment in my garden, but I can't. No, it took me another year to shake off what turned into a nice, long, low-level depression. It wasn't a bad year—I started dating Colin. I became a professor at a university. But a sense of sorrow and futility clung to me.

It was the next summer that I realized it had passed. I had a sensation I can only describe as an absence of suffering. Have you ever had a terrible migraine or toothache? And the doctor prescribes you a Percocet. And as you lie there, you feel the pain ease out of your body. There's release, then a sense of near weightlessness. Or that's how it felt to me. I realized over the summer that I was not in pain—and I realized there is no greater pleasure, nothing more blissful, than its absence.

Over the next few years, incredible things happened. Colin and I fell in love. I became increasingly close to my brother and Cecilia and to their daughter when she was born. I founded a journalism program at my university. I started a new relationship with my mother, in which I forgave her, and (I hope) she has forgiven me. For the first time in my life, I stopped having insomnia.

On more than one occasion I found myself marveling over the lack of pain—as if I'd washed up onshore after a shipwreck and, instead of being reduced to a heap of broken bones, found all my limbs intact and fully functioning. Can you imagine the leaping and running and shouting for joy along the coastline? That was me.

I still travel. I go somewhere warm by myself every January— Spain, Greece, Sardinia, Costa Rica—and Colin and I go somewhere cool together every August. We write in the mornings and hike in the afternoons. We've been to Ireland together several times. Back in New York, we have two apartments down the street from each other.

I take ballet at least three times a week—and modern and West African and hip-hop sometimes. I dance almost every day.

The images are gone. Sometimes I get them when I'm very tired or stressed—I catch a shadow out of the corner of my eye. But that's it, really. They came back when my father died two years ago. Then there was a screaming inside me again. Except it wasn't the shrieking I told you about before. It was more of a roaring in my chest, as if there were a little lion trapped in there. I still have it sometimes. But it's not shrieks of fear, and I don't care if it sounds crazy. In my chest, there is a little lion who roars.

ACKNOWLEDGMENTS

In rough chronological order, I want to acknowledge Paul Artz, who spent a frightening amount of time talking with me about how to organize and structure the book. My aunt Alison Chaplin was my first reader, and without her unflagging enthusiasm for the project I would have dropped it years ago. Her excellent editing on every single version kept me on my toes, and I probably never would have become a writer in the first place without her. Delia Ephron has been amazingly helpful in every way—from emotional support over countless lunches to incredible dramatic and structural advice. Delia's late husband, Jerome Kass, showed me what good dialogue looks like. Lisa Dierback, Lila Cecil, Marian Fontana, and Corena Chase read early bits and thought it was worth continuing. Jane Fransson served a crucial role as editor, champion, and friend.

Thank you Autumn Lucas, Alix Spiegel, Connie Phelps, Catherine Crawford, Mac Montandon, Joanna Ebenstein, and Ardith Ibanez-Nishi for your generosity and years of friendship. And a special thank-you to my mother, June Chaplin, for always, no matter what, encouraging my creativity and telling me to follow my bliss. Also, for tolerating this book.

My agent, Kimberly Witherspoon, and editor, Karyn Marcus, deserve a huge amount of credit, as does everyone at Inkwell and Simon & Schuster—Lena Yarbrough, Sydney Morris, Elisa Rivlin, Jessica Chin, Alison Forner, and Lewelin Polanco. I can't thank you enough for your time and care. Also, thank you to Quinn Heraty of Heraty Law.

And without Oliver Burkeman, who knows what would have happened.

ABOUT THE AUTHOR

Heather Chaplin is a writer living in Brooklyn. She's written about all kinds of things in her journalism career and is the founder of the Journalism + Design program at The New School. In the evenings, she can be found taking ballet classes she has no business attending but does anyway.

ALICE PAUL

AND THE FIGHT FOR WOMEN'S RIGHTS